ALL THE TROUBLES

Jessie,

Its been great getting to know you this semester. Safe travels home.

Fred
2004

Through no fault of his own Simon Adams was born in Auckland in 1968. Following a peripatetic childhood in New Zealand, Canada and the United States, his family moved to Australia, where he has lived for the majority of his life. After working as an apprentice carpenter and building the nation's new parliament house (for which he was not singularly responsible), he travelled the world. He has worked in South Africa, Ireland, East Timor and Cuba. He has published two previous books, *Comrade Minister* (2001), about the transition to democracy in South Africa, and *Exit Wounds: Murder, Diaspora and the Irish Troubles* (2000), about the murder of a relative in Northern Ireland. Simon Adams is Dean of Arts and Associate Professor of Politics and History at the University of Notre Dame Australia and is a regular political commentator in the West Australian media. He lives in Fremantle with his wife Amanda and their daughter Aislinn.

ALL THE

TERRORISM, WAR AND THE WORLD AFTER 9/11

TROUBLES

SIMON ADAMS

Fremantle Arts Centre Press

Australia's finest small publisher

FREMANTLE ARTS CENTRE PRESS
25 Quarry Street, Fremantle
(PO Box 158, North Fremantle 6159)
Western Australia
www.facp.iinet.net.au

Consultant Editor Janet Blagg
Cover Designer Adrienne Zuvela
Printed by Griffin Press

National Library of Australia
Cataloguing-in-publication data

Adams, Simon, 1968-.
All the troubles : terrorism, war and the world after 9/11.

Bibliography.
Includes index.

ISBN 1 920731 10 5.

1. Terrorism. 2. Political violence. 3. World politics. I. Title.

327.117

For Amanda, my comrade in arms. Mo cushla.
And for Aislinn Ungurrbin, our little turtle girl, who was born
during the writing of this book.

Rage for the world as it is
But for what it may be
More love now than last year
And always less self-pity

Muriel Rukeyser

Preface

Since the 9/11 terrorist attacks three years ago the Taliban have been overthrown in Afghanistan but are now regrouping; Iraq was quickly invaded and occupied but the fighting there is far from over; war has been narrowly averted on the Korean peninsula; the situation in Israel/Palestine has gone from bad to worse, and so on. Other parts of the world, with their own unique histories and troubles of their own, have generally faded from the attention of the world's media. These days, the ongoing war and US-led occupation of Iraq dominates the western media and continues to polarise global opinion.

The war in Iraq is becoming, propagandist flourishes aside, this generation's Vietnam. I had thought that, if nothing else, the US military had learnt one powerful lesson from the Vietnam War: never let reporters capture the image that could potentially galvanise world opinion, or shake the faith of a nation. There could be no pictures this time round of My Lai, no little girl running down the road naked with her skin burnt off by napalm, no television footage of the execution of a Vietcong prisoner on the grubby streets of Saigon. CENTCOM and the Pentagon press-pool would see to that. This would be a sanitised, globalised, 'spin-doctored' war. This is the twenty-first century and the 'war on terror' has no room for the moral ambiguities of the Vietnam era.

However, every month of the US-led occupation of Iraq just seems to bring some awful new twist. I thought April 2004 — with the Fallujah uprising and the worst US combat losses in Iraq since the war began — was a new low. Then came May and the release of photos of US soldiers torturing Iraqi detainees. The truth is — although Bush, Blair and Howard will not admit it — the war in Iraq is already lost. Even those in the western world who fervently believed in the war have had their faith corroded by images of US soldiers tormenting, brutalising and humiliating Iraqi detainees. In the Arab world, across Africa and Asia, the response has been much, much worse. The prisoner abuse scandal has also presented the 'war on terror' with its most powerful and indelible images since the shaky video of airliners smashing into the glittering Twin Towers on the morning of 11 September 2001.

This book is not just about Iraq, although the shadow of that conflict invariably looms over any analysis of contemporary international politics. This book is about global politics after 9/11 — about our world of terrorism and war. I wrote it with the idea that a reader might rethink some previously held assumptions. By exposing some of the connections between our fractured 'civilisations' and challenging the historical amnesia that seems endemic in our society, I hoped thereby that readers would feel more 'informed' about global politics and maybe, just maybe, feel provoked to action. Because we are all just one person. And in these troubled times, every word counts.

Contents

Maps and Tables

Maps

Tables

Acknowledgements

I would like to thank the following people who, while not necessarily agreeing with the politics of this book, were supportive during the writing of it. They include all my colleagues in the College of Arts at Notre Dame; Celia Hammond and Simon King for their encouragement, friendship and leftover nappies; Kevin and Úna Murphy; Joe O'Sullivan and the Australian Irish Heritage Association; Greg Craven, who helped make my last research trip to Ireland possible; the indomitable Peter Moore of Crossing Press; as well as everyone who wrote to me about *Exit Wounds*. My family, as always, were very supportive, although I suspect my brother Marty felt I should have written more about the politics of sport and Muhammad Ali. I would particularly like to acknowledge the entire ET5 group from Notre Dame University whom I had the pleasure to live with in East Timor, especially Carmel 'Pondy' and those hardened veterans of Letefoho — Val, James, Barry, Zoe and Grace; and of course all the members of the ET3 Letefoho group — Carita, Sofia, Chanel, Tim and Andy.

I should also give special thanks to all my students at Notre Dame, whom I continue to learn from and who never forgave me for leaving them off the acknowledgements page of my last book.

Some of the ideas (and diatribes) presented here were first tried out in lectures upon captive audiences of Notre Dame students. They thoroughly deserve my thanks and your sympathy. A special mention should also be made of my editor, Janet Blagg, who helped transform my scribbled thoughts on the state of the world into something coherent. Her sense of vision created this book.

In the United States of America I need to acknowledge and thank Fr Bill Miscamble at the University of Notre Dame; everyone at the Keough Institute of Irish Studies; and Dan McGinty for being a tower of friendship and support ('Look kids, I brought you a giant to play with').

There are many others in Australia, Ireland, South Africa, Cuba and East Timor who contributed in one way or another to this book. I hope they will forgive me my rudeness in running out of space. It should also be noted that any mistakes in these pages are entirely my own responsibility and I apologise in advance for them.

Introduction

Flying into Chicago at night during September 2001, it was hard not to be impressed. I could see sparkling lights laid out in grids and the faint outlines of ghostly skyscrapers. The whole horizon was lit up like glowing embers. The yellow arteries of the freeway pulsed with tiny luminous specks of cars. And above it all, a bloated full moon. Strangely, the impressive scene got me thinking about Letefoho in East Timor, where I had been working a few months previously. No such displays of wealth and power there. The entire village only had two petrol-fuelled electric generators and two small illuminated islands of night-time light — the church area and the United Nations compound.

It was only two weeks after '9/11' when I arrived in America and on the bus driving out of Chicago I noticed that the electric freeway warning signs were all switched to 'United We Stand'. Eventually we drove into Indiana, or as a sign told me, 'the crossroads of America'. There was less glitter and more factories off the side of the freeway. Billboards invited me to 'change my luck' at the local casino. Mostly I just looked out the window at the ripened full moon. For some reason it started me thinking about the layers of history, the global connections, and the terrible traces of our past which 9/11 had revealed.

In 1991 New York construction workers building a government office in Lower Manhattan accidentally discovered old wooden coffins and the remains of four hundred African slaves. As the *New York Times* later explained, the 'accidental discovery of the African Burial Ground, which originally contained 10,000 to 20,000 bodies, came as a shock to people who grew up believing that New York had always been a free state and that slavery had been confined to the downy white cotton fields of the South.'[1] In fact, the first black slaves arrived on Manhattan Island in 1625 and the original Dutch rulers of New York imported slaves in large numbers during the seventeenth century. African slaves built many of the houses, streets and walls of the emerging colony. One of those slave-built walls was designed to repel attacks by Indians and to keep 'hostile savages' out of the colony. The wall eventually disappeared as colonists settled beyond its protective frontier. Today it is remembered only in the name of the street which ran alongside it — 'Wall Street', now the richest street in America and the centre of global capitalism. It was on Wall Street in 1711 that New York's most impressive and lucrative slave market was also established.

The African Burial Ground was just outside the city limits — beyond Wall Street and the market — because the colonial authorities of New York prohibited African slaves from being buried in settler graveyards. Even those slaves who had converted to Christianity were denied access. The African Burial Ground was also used in 1712 and 1741 as a final resting place for those Africans hanged, burnt to death, or 'broken on the wheel' for their involvement in slave rebellions. The Burial Ground was closed in 1794 and eventually the modern city was built over it. Its existence and location, like its banished African dead, were forgotten.

Over four hundred skeletons of African slaves were eventually recovered from the Lower Manhattan building site and taken to Howard University in Washington where they were studied. The results were extraordinary. About 40 per cent of the skeletons were of children under the age of fifteen. Scientists also determined that many of the slaves had died of malnutrition or hunger-related diseases. As the *New York Times* commented, the 'grim data have dispelled the commonly held belief that slavery in the North was less harsh than its Southern counterpart.'

In October 2003 the last of the 427 skeletons were finally reburied in a solemn ceremony in New York City. Four coffins were brought ashore on Manhattan Island at Wall Street, not far from where the old slave market had been. They were buried in dignified circumstances far different from those which they had endured when they first arrived in America several centuries earlier: brought ashore in chains and mustered along to be sold into human bondage.

The discovery and reburial of the African slaves of New York City got me thinking about the role of history in our society. It's a simple point, but when you dig in the dirt, what you discover may change your perspective on the past forever.

Famous Czech author Milan Kundera once wrote that the struggle of human existence is the struggle of memory against forgetting. In this context it is also worth noting that any serious dictatorship undertakes the rewriting of history. The Nazis organised the public burning of books that did not accord with their world view, and dissident intellectuals were sent to concentration camps. In the former Soviet Union, Stalin not only had his rivals in the Communist Party shot, he also had them written out of history. Texts were altered, statements changed, photographs airbrushed. The campaign to erase Leon Trotsky from the history of the Russian Revolution was only the most notorious case of this campaign to purify public memory.

Which brings me, in a roundabout way, to the nature of the world that we live in post-9/11. As westerners we generally accept that nasty regimes in the world today, like Syria or North Korea, distort their history to suit the interests of those in power. We are less inclined to believe that the same is true of our own societies. Back in 1945 the US Air Force dropped an atomic bomb on the Japanese city of Hiroshima. Around the same time Robert Menzies, who would become Australia's longest serving prime minister, wrote something quite profound regarding the intellectual frontiers of the world he inhabited. Menzies commented that 'the greatest failure in the world in my lifetime has not been the failure in technical capacity half as much as the failure of the human spirit.'[2] I'd like to think that the ghost of Menzies would support the idea that any person who doesn't understand our past, or doesn't bother to analyse our political present, is truly shrouded in the darkness of convenient mythology.

Although Nazi Germany ended with the fall of Berlin in May 1945, the Second World War did not really come to a close until after American atomic bombs were dropped on the Japanese cities of Hiroshima and Nagasaki that August. It was a horrifyingly innovative way to end the war, with over 100,000 civilians killed immediately and tens of thousands more dying of the after-effects of atomic radiation by the end of the year. Speaking to the American public on the day his air force incinerated Nagasaki, US President Harry Truman commented that the attack was only 'a warning of things to come.' He told the American people that an 'awful responsibility' had befallen them, that of being the world's only possessor of such a weapon of mass destruction. A bomb that could melt cities. He thanked God that this responsibility 'has come to us, instead of to our enemies' and prayed that God 'may guide us to use it in His ways and for His purpose.'[3]

Truman's speech revealed the key elements of American thinking at the end of the Second World War. Truman invoked God, as American presidents always have and continue to do, to bless and guide United States foreign policy. But the 'awful responsibility' Truman mentioned was something new. There was a growing belief in American circles in 1945 that given that the United States' military had been decisive in the victory over Nazi Germany and Japan, and that the US was now unquestionably the richest and most powerful capitalist nation on earth, the burden of global leadership had shifted onto its shoulders. The Americans realised that the French and British empires were finished, even if the French and British governments didn't. Of all the major nations who waged war from 1939 to 1945 only the Soviet Union and the United States emerged with increased military and economic strength. The United States was acutely self-conscious of its unique opportunity to politically, militarily and economically shape the post-war world.

In the forty-four years between the end of the Second World War and the fall of the Berlin Wall in November 1989 global politics was dominated by the efforts of the two post-war superpowers, the United States and the Soviet Union, to achieve supremacy over one another. During that period both hegemons constructed informal empires, called 'spheres of influence' in diplomatic parlance, in a 'Cold War'. As historian Chalmers Johnson has explained, both superpowers also relied upon 'extensive alignments based on ideology, economic interactions, technology transfers, mutual benefit, and military cooperation.'[4]

However, in the 'Third World', as the emerging underdeveloped ex-colonial countries were called, the Cold War was often distinctly hot. Both the Soviet Union and United States supported all manner of ruthless dictatorships and exacerbated internecine civil wars in an effort to gain geopolitical advantage. Although the Soviet Union and United States barely succeeded in avoiding an all-out nuclear confrontation with one another over the five decades of the Cold War, millions of people died in Third World proxy conflicts.

With the end of the Cold War and the disintegration of the Soviet Union at the start of the 1990s, outright global dominance passed to the world's sole remaining superpower — the United States of America. In comments reminiscent of Truman's atomic bomb speech in 1945, American politicians again invoked God and spoke of the United States' divine mission to bring peace, democracy and economic prosperity to the world. America had emerged triumphant over what President Reagan described in 1983 as the 'evil empire'. Communism was dead, liberty reigned supreme.

Except that it didn't. The legacy of the twentieth century (the bloodiest in history) and the Cold War was a divided world. The 'West' (including Australia) emerged from the Cold War with its economies dominating global trade and its freedoms protected within its constitutional democracies. In the former Soviet bloc, however, the situation was one of growing impoverishment, political instability, economic strain and social despair. Where these factors were able to be exploited by desperate demagogues the results could be deadly. The bitter civil wars in the former Yugoslavia, which continued through most of the 1990s, were a reflection of this.

Meanwhile in the Third World there was a fundamental reconstruction of alliances. Dictators who relied on Soviet arms and aid for sustaining their regimes suddenly found themselves out in the cold. Some regimes collapsed while others, facing popular unrest and economic bankruptcy, negotiated transfers of power and the introduction of some semblance of democracy. Cold War dictators who relied on the United States for support were similarly concerned about their futures. Some were judiciously abandoned as their regimes disintegrated around them (Mobutu in Zaire and Suharto in Indonesia for example). Others found that the ongoing strategic or economic importance of their country meant that authoritarian rule and human rights abuses would continue to be discreetly ignored (Saudi Arabia). What was clear, however, was that America's renewed confidence in its global mission meant it was prepared to act more forcefully to project its world view in the absence of a rival superpower.

Iraq's Saddam Hussein was only the most notorious Third World dictator to fail to appreciate the new rules and the dynamics of what US President George Bush publicly proclaimed to be a 'New World Order'. Although the 1991 Gulf War failed to topple Saddam's regime, it revealed a greater willingness on behalf of the United States, with its overwhelming military superiority (as dramatically illustrated during the war with the use of 'smart bombs'), to punish those who challenged US interests. In this sense the Gulf War was never solely about oil. It was fundamentally about global power.

Australia's role in all of this has been as a staunch ally and regional 'deputy' to the United States. During the Cold War Australian soldiers fought alongside US troops in Korea and Vietnam and the 'domino theory' — which suggested that unchecked 'communist aggression' would cause the countries of Southeast Asia to fall one by one — was perceived as having grave national security implications for Australia. The frontlines of the

Cold War in Asia were in Malaya, Korea, Vietnam and Indonesia, and it was not difficult for Australians to imagine a day when 'the communists' might threaten their northern shores. While slowly relinquishing attachments to the British Empire and notions of a 'White Australia' during the 1950s, Australians embraced their protective alliance with the United States. After all, many Australians argued, it was the Americans who had helped save Australia from Japanese invasion during the Second World War.

The end of the Cold War and the declaration of a 'New World Order' did not substantially alter Australia's relationship with the world's sole remaining superpower. Australia sent a small military contingent to join the US-led force during the 1991 Gulf War and continued to see itself (rightly or wrongly) as the most significant and trusted US ally in the Asia–Pacific region. The 9/11 terrorist attacks have enhanced the current Australian government's notion of itself as a crucial regional player in America's global 'War on Terror'.

However, contrary to popular opinion the events of 11 September 2001 have not fundamentally changed the world. On 9/11 America suffered what Chalmers Johnson (borrowing terminology from the CIA) described as 'blowback' — the unintended negative consequences of half a century of interventionist foreign policy in the Third World.[5] In response the United States, capitalising on the international political sympathy generated by the horror of the terrorist attacks, has simply become more vigorous and determinedly unapologetic in pursuing and defending its 'national interest' by means of diplomacy, economic coercion and war. 9/11 changed the form of the debate about US leadership of the 'free world', but not the substance. US rhetoric justifying its foreign policy by reference to 'humanitarian intervention' (Somalia and Kosovo during the

1990s) and a 'New World Order' (1991 Gulf War) has been dropped in favour of an all-encompassing and endless 'War on Terror'. The Islamic terrorist bogeyman has replaced the old communist one.

Underlying the post-9/11 speeches of President George W Bush, like those of Harry S Truman nearly sixty years earlier, was the same invocation of divine mission, the same consciousness of America's ability to obliterate its enemies by overwhelming superiority of firepower, and the same overriding objective — protecting American global hegemony. All that has changed is the language of power. In 1945 Truman spoke of defeating Nazism and defending democracy from the scourge of communism. In 2004 Bush speaks of defeating 'terrorism' and 'evil' in the world. He wants to protect western democracy from people he calls 'the enemies of civilisation'.

The 'war on terror' is about reducing US foreign policy in the world today to palpable simplicities to be easily digested by passive spectators — meaning us, the public of the western democracies. But in presenting its global imperatives in this way it becomes necessary for the United States government (along with its allies in Australia, Britain and elsewhere) to take history out of the equation. Political amnesia is encouraged. We are supposed to forget that Saddam Hussein was once a western ally. That Osama bin Laden cut his terrorist teeth in the CIA-funded war against the Soviets in Afghanistan. And that the West (including Australia) supported a military coup in Indonesia in 1965 in which Muslim extremists were encouraged to hack to death communists and any other progressive secular threat to 'Western interests' in Southeast Asia.

History and politics are tools to understand what is happening in our world today. This book is composed of four sections within which are a series of essays. Section one looks at the 'War on Terror', 9/11, Afghanistan and the US-led invasion of Iraq. It attempts to examine the history beyond the speeches of prime ministers and presidents, seeking the connections between peoples and places that the so-called 'Coalition of the Willing' (including Australia) have recently invaded. In doing so I have also taken a peek at the dark underbelly of American society — understanding what sort of country the United States has become is essential to understanding why it acts the way it does in the world today. Finally, several of the essays in this section touch on the issue of Israel and the Palestinians. It is my contention that comprehending why Jews and Arabs are killing each other on land which is holy to Judaism, Christianity and Islam is central to understanding the Middle East, 9/11 and our world of war.

Section two gazes into 'our own backyard', focusing on Australia's entanglement with our most powerful neighbour, Indonesia. The country is the fifth most populous in the world and contains more Muslims than any other nation on earth. Historically Indonesia has both frightened and awed Australians in equal measure. In the early 1960s Australian politicians feared the growth of the Indonesian Communist Party, the third largest communist organisation in the world. The Australian government supported General Suharto's 1965 military seizure of power, over the corpses of half a million dead communists, precisely because they saw him as a bulwark of stability in a region of poverty and uncertainty. Ironically, forty years later the Australian government is now nervously supporting Indonesia's fledgling democracy as its government seeks to confront the legacy of Suharto's rule — poverty, corruption, violent secessionist struggles — and the growth of Islamic terrorism. This section also examines one of the most vexed issues in

Indonesian–Australian foreign relations over the last three decades — East Timor. More than any other foreign policy issue in our recent past, Australia's attempt to deal with Indonesia's illegal invasion, occupation and eventual relinquishment of East Timor reveals the sort of country Australia aspires to be, for better or worse.

The third section focuses on countries the United States government has designated as constituting an 'axis of evil'. History provides some interesting insights into how and why certain countries have ended up on the United States' list of nations in need of 'regime change.' History also provides us with earlier examples of popular revolution, coup d'état and civil war in Iran, Cuba and on the Korean peninsula. The implications of these largely forgotten moments in history are hugely significant for contemporary world politics. This section looks at past western intervention in these countries and offers some alternative perspectives on regime change.

The final section of this book examines some other parts of the globe and issues which appear regularly on our nightly news but about which most of us are largely ignorant (the United Nations, the AIDS pandemic in the Third World, etc). This section also looks at the resilience of 'ethnic violence' in the world today. 'Ancient tribalism' and 'political backwardness' have become convenient western rationalisations for explaining (and dismissing) the seemingly relentless civil war and 'ethnic cleansing' that plagues parts of Africa, the Balkans and Northern Ireland. But what created the hate, and why do these conflicts seem to defy the logic of history? Rather than viewing such issues and places as isolated trouble spots, I wanted to uncover and sift through the remains of the past in order to see if there were any grounds for hope and/or resolution. Above all else this section is about the secret history that gets left in the margins of memory.

Finally a quick word regarding you, me and this book. On 5 April 1968 a Chinese worker called Wu Bingyuan was sentenced to death for writing a political pamphlet. The pamphlet was called 'Looking North' and was considered to be critical of Mao Zedong's foreign policy towards the Soviet Union. In 1968 Communist China's 'Cultural Revolution' was reaching its feverish climax, with Red Guards attacking 'revisionists' and 'counter revolutionaries' and people being forced out of work or into prison because of ideological deviations, both real and imagined. Any criticism of Communist Party Chairman Mao was considered to be tantamount to denouncing God — he was, after all, supposed to be the 'Red Sun' that shone in every Chinese heart. Wu, who was a technician at the Harbin Electric Motor Factory, would have been just one of the countless forgotten and insignificant victims of the Cultural Revolution if not for one remarkable act of defiance which captured the imagination of a young Red Guard, Li Zhensheng, who photographed it. When Wu's death sentence was read out he stared at the sky and proclaimed, 'This world is too dark.' Heroically, he then shut his eyes and refused to open them again even as he was dragged from the 'People's Court', placed on a truck with a placard around his neck, driven to the cemetery, forced to his knees and shot in the back of the head.[6]

I invite you to think of Wu Bingyuan, open your eyes and keep reading.

Simon Adams
Fremantle, Western Australia
May 2004

1

THE 'WAR ON TERROR':
9/11, AFGHANISTAN AND IRAQ

Remembering 9/11

We're angry, but we're not stupid.

George W Bush, September 2001[1]

Indeed, that was an apt and true reply which was given to Alexander the Great by a pirate who had been seized. For when that king had asked the man what he meant by keeping hostile possession of the sea, he answered with bold pride. 'What thou meanest by seizing the whole earth; but because I do it with a petty ship, I am called a robber, whilst thou who dost it with a great fleet art styled emperor.'

St Augustine, Book IV, The City of God

Like everyone else I remember 11 September 2001 well. News that the first plane had hit the World Trade Center reached Perth at around 9 pm West Australian time and I sat up, like millions of others, watching the horror unfold live on television. I was woken early the next morning by ABC Radio who wanted me to comment on what had happened. I remember the interviewer asking me who I thought was responsible, a simple question admirable in its disguised complexity. At the time I had Timothy McVeigh in mind. Not because I suspected his ghostly presence as being responsible for 9/11 (he had been executed in June 2001), but because the lesson of the 1995 Oklahoma Bombing (the previous 'worst ever' terrorist attack in the US) was that after the bomb went off the police immediately started searching for Arabs on the freeways out of Oklahoma. They caught Timothy McVeigh almost by accident — a white, angry, Gulf War veteran who had declared war on his own government. I later sat thinking how bizarre it was that Islamic fundamentalists (like most 'specialists' I assumed Osama bin Laden was probably responsible) who rejected the modern secular world chose to strike a blow against America in such a 'media friendly' extravaganza of violence, drama and death.

Two weeks later I was in the United States of America to give some guest lectures. It was only seventeen days after September 11 and already people were talking about it being the defining event of our age — planes slamming into glittering glass and skyscrapers collapsing like folding broken arms. Dust clouds of Biblical proportions. It was also two weeks since President Bush had said that, 'Those who make war against the United States have chosen their own destruction,' and the whole world was waiting for a war that we all knew was now inevitable.[2]

There was definitely a heightened sense of both security and patriotism at Los Angeles airport when I arrived. Outside, American flags were everywhere — in the windows of offices, on top of buildings and flying from every second car. Not just small flags attached to car radio aerials either, but large full-size flags whipping in the wind, tied to broom handles sticking out of windows, or otherwise affixed to vehicles. While on the shuttle to my hotel we passed a man at the traffic lights selling 9/11 patriotic paraphernalia to passing motorists. There were t-shirts with 'Wanted: Osama bin Laden — Dead or Alive!' 'USA will exterminate terrorism', 'Osama — Yo Mama!' and multiple variations on the 'God Bless America' theme with eagles, flags and fighter jets superimposed over images of the World Trade Center. To be in America just after that fateful September morning (made perfect for television with a New York backdrop and bright morning light glinting off shattered skyscrapers) seemed somehow disturbing. I already realised that 9/11, not Y2K, would now forever define our fin de siècle.

In my hotel room I checked the TV and seven stations were doing lengthy 'America Under Attack' live updates. These reports varied from mildly informative and intensely jingoistic, to downright corny. In the latter category was a news story regarding a Los Angeles doctor who had reported 'an alarming increase in the number of people grinding their teeth since September 11.' The doctor's diagnosis, which can only be described as a stroke of medical genius, was that mass stress was the cause and he recommended people take muscle relaxants if the problem persisted. Even the beer commercials had gone all patriotic and downbeat with one company urging all its customers to give a donation to the Red Cross appeal for the families of the victims of September 11. Beer drinkers against terrorism.

Outside, the lights of LA were twinkling awake for another night. Darkness descended and I was in magic America. A dream land where everyone was suddenly wide awake.

If nothing else the terrible attacks of September 11 should have revealed the lunacy of America's current plan to build a multi-billion dollar 'missile defence shield' in space in order to protect itself from harm. The enraged killers who hijacked four American passenger airplanes and crashed them into buildings (or into the ground) did not need intercontinental ballistic missiles to wreak their vengeance on America. They simply took box cutters (or Stanley knives as we call them in Australia) and turned domestic planes into missiles. To retaliate, America bombarded Afghanistan with millions of dollars of high-tech lethal machinery and overthrew the Taliban in the first stage of its war on terror.

War costs money. In February 2002 a new budget was sent to the United States Congress for approval. It was wrapped in a US flag and projected annual increases in military expenditure rising to US$379 billion for 2003, and reaching US$451 billion a year by 2007. Even for a country whose military budget was already bigger than those of Britain, Germany, France, Russia and China all combined — such increases seemed excessive.[3]

By comparison, with a valid credit card you can order a dozen box cutters on the internet for US$35. If, like Al-Qaida on 11 September 2001, you have a dozen or so hijackers willing to die to make a point, you can arm each of them at a per unit cost of less than three US dollars. Islamic fundamentalists dedicated to martyrdom didn't need 'smart bombs' and billion dollar technology to strike back at those whom they blamed for the problems of the Middle East, or whose secular 'decadent' society they despised. All they needed was the raw unforgiving courage of the suicide bomber and a little bit of flight training. There is a lasting and important lesson here, one which all too many western leaders have chosen to ignore. Weapons and technology may help win wars, but it is only ideas that have the power to truly change the world.

In total, 3016 people died cruel and unnecessary deaths in the September 11 terrorist attacks. Of those, 2645 died within or beneath the Twin Towers, as well as 147 passengers and crew on the planes (ten hijackers also perished). At the Pentagon, 125 people were killed on the ground, plus 59 passengers and crew (and five hijackers). Forty passengers and crew as well as four hijackers died on Flight 93 in Pennsylvania. Most, but not all, of those who died on 9/11 were American. Since then a far greater number of innocent civilians have died in Afghanistan and Iraq during the US-led invasion and occupation of those countries. On top of this were the 290 US soldiers killed in Iraq between the initial invasion and the second anniversary of 9/11, and almost 40 in Afghanistan where elusive Taliban 'remnants' are still able to mount significant assaults on US troops. Does anyone truly believe the killing might actually stop before the next anniversary of 9/11?

George W Bush certainly doesn't. He requested an extra US$87 billion funding from the US Congress in order to support the ongoing US military occupation of Iraq and Afghanistan. This puts the current bill for the invasion and occupation of Iraq at US$150 billion, making the extravagant US$9 billion cost to the United States for the 1991 Gulf War now look like a bargain basement deal. The extra expenditure will also push the current US budget deficit out to half a trillion dollars. Even the extra $87 billion that Bush requested for Iraq is, as one US Senator pointed out, 'more than the federal government will spend on education this year.'[4]

Osama bin Laden, who remains at large despite one of the biggest manhunts in world history, doesn't believe the killing is going to stop either. Nor do his friends and supporters. Even in mountainous ruined Afghanistan, under partial US occupation for almost two years now, the remnants of the Taliban appear to be regrouping and growing in confidence. A journalist from French newspaper *Le Monde* interviewed Gul Rahman Faruqi, a former Taliban military commander in the city of Gardez, who is leading resistance to the United States forces and their Afghan supporters in the southeast region. Notwithstanding the false bravado of all military figures, Faruqi told the journalist that, 'The situation is now going very good for us, and it's getting better every day. You're going to see more and more clashes.'[5] Previously such comments could have been disregarded as wishful thinking. However, Faruqi was speaking after a nine-day battle in the mountains of the Dai Chupan district, possibly the largest confrontation between Taliban and the Americans since late 2001.

When the same French journalist asked locals what they thought of the deposed Taliban, he got a surprisingly mixed response. A local car dealer commented that, 'The Americans' great mistake was to get murderers and gangsters to bring peace here,' a reference to the Northern Alliance forces and the government of the new Afghan president Hamid Karzai.[6] Despite all efforts by the United States and its allies to construct a stable pro-western state in Kabul, Afghanistan remains broken.

Another reporter from the *New York Times* interviewed an American soldier standing guard outside a US military base in Gardez. Eyeing off passing Afghans, he told the journalist that, 'I know they hate my guts, but they can't say so because I've got a gun. Kind of funny, isn't it?' Not for the Afghans, nor for the Iraqis and not even for the American soldiers who continue to die in occupied Afghanistan and Iraq. Even America's salaried allies in the region, like the new Iraqi Highway Patrol, are turning against their paymasters. Patrolman Muhammad Khobaeir Waeel told a western reporter that, 'I hate the Americans. They don't respect us. They throw us to the ground and put their boots on the backs of our heads.'[7] The United States appears to have forgotten one of the principal lessons of the Vietnam War — obedience and loyalty are not the same thing.

What is remarkable is how far the world — and especially Americans — have already come from that fateful Tuesday morning in New York. On the second anniversary of 9/11 both the *New York Times* and the *Washington Post* ran articles pointing out that President Bush's 'exploitation' of 9/11 had become 'crushingly obvious'. In the lead up to the second anniversary of the terrorist attacks Bush had invoked 9/11 as a magic wand to protect against questions about his policy in Iraq, about Arctic oil exploration, and 'in response to questions about tax cuts, unemployment, budget deficits and even campaign finance.' In particular, Paul Krugman of the *New York Times* criticised the 'crudity of the administration's recent propaganda efforts, from dressing the president up in a flight suit to orchestrating the ludicrously glamorised TV movie about Mr Bush on 9/11.' Although 9/11 initially lifted Bush's popularity ratings through the roof, the 'deficit is about to go above half a trillion dollars, the economy is still losing jobs, the triumph in Iraq has turned to dust and ashes, and Mr Bush's poll numbers are at or below their pre-9/11 levels.'[8]

Certainly 'Team Bush' has utilised 9/11 in fairly mercenary ways. For example, when US Secretary of Defence Donald Rumsfeld was questioned by the Senate Armed Services Committee on his suggestion that there was a pressing and immediate need to invade Iraq and destroy its alleged 'weapons of mass destruction', he was asked by Senator Dayton why the United States needed to take such 'a precipitous decision'? In short, why now? Rumsfeld's simple reply was that, 'What's different? What's different is three thousand people were killed,' wilfully linking Iraq to 9/11 even though there was no evidence of Iraqi involvement and despite the fact that fanatically religious Osama and secular despot Saddam were mortal enemies.

Although the Bush administration now claims that it never directly alleged that Saddam Hussein was responsible for 9/11, prior to the US invasion of Iraq they certainly encouraged people to think that Hussein's regime and bin Laden's terrorist network were allied. It is therefore not surprising that a poll by the *Washington Post* revealed that 69 per cent of Americans believed Saddam was somehow involved in the September 11 terrorist attacks. The Bush regime had encouraged such a belief just as they would repeat again and again to whomever would listen their basic post-9/11 mantra — everything is different now, and you are either with us or against us.[9]

Two years later, people were already getting tired of the script. Not least of all because the weapons of mass destruction (WMD), which justified the invasion of Iraq, failed to materialise. The September 2003 official report to the US Congress by the Iraq Survey Group, whose hunt for WMDs cost American taxpayers $300 million, explained that Saddam had no nuclear weapons, was not building any, and the only evidence of chemical weapons their extensive search found was a single vial of botulinum, a substance which can be used for weapons but also to vaccinate cattle or in cosmetic surgery. A single scientist had been storing the botulinum in his refrigerator for the last ten years. As one 'weapons expert' told the press, 'we don't know if this scientist was going to get rid of Saddam's wrinkles or kill people.' The *Guardian Weekly*'s report on the search for WMDs opened with three striking photos; one of US soldiers massing on the Iraq border, one of an Iraqi man mourning over a coffin, and a final shot of the single tiny vial of dangerous material. Above the photos was a simple caption — '200,000 troops, 10,000 killed, 1 (old) vial of botulinum.'[10] Hardly a convincing case for war.

Even Bush stalwarts and veteran Cold Warriors, Wolfowitz and

Rumsfeld, who seemed to be most closely connected to an American populist desire for revenge in the aftermath of 9/11, now seem hopelessly out of touch. For example one 'military analyst' described Wolfowitz and Rumsfeld — the two members of the Bush administration who most wanted to hit Saddam for 9/11 despite all evidence that he was not involved — as being like people in Plato's cave. 'They've been staring at the shadows on the wall so long, they think they're forms.'[11] Related to all of this is the fact that opinion polls, including one by the *Washington Post/ABC News* published only days after the second 9/11 anniversary, revealed that 46 per cent of Americans now disapproved of Bush's policy in Iraq. Possibly representative of this growing sentiment among ordinary Americans were the views of Frank Jessoe, a sixty year old former US Marine who served in Vietnam. Asked what he thought about the US occupation of Iraq he replied that, 'It's a disaster — it will get worse and worse and we will leave the same way we left Vietnam: with our tail between our legs.'[12]

His prediction seemed correct when, during the two months after the second 9/11 anniversary, guerilla attacks on US soldiers in Iraq increased. As the *New York Times* worryingly reported at the start of November 2003:

> President Bush declared an end to major combat hostilities in Iraq on May 1. But in the six months since then, 222 American soldiers have died, more than one a day. In October, at least 33 American soldiers were killed by hostile fire, twice as many as in September. For every soldier killed, Pentagon officials estimate, another seven are wounded.[13]

Some of the relatives of soldiers killed in Iraq shared their feelings with the newspaper's reporters. Andrea Brassfield of Texas recalled that her husband had told her that, 'They (Iraqis) don't want us here. They throw rocks at us. They shoot at us. I don't know what we're doing here.' Meanwhile in Alabama the cousin of another dead soldier lamented that, 'The President don't care. You see him on TV. He says this, he says that. But show me one tear, one tear.'[14] These feelings of resentment were exacerbated by the fact that media were banned from covering the arrival at Dover Air Force Base of coffins of US soldiers killed in combat in Iraq. Nor were the media permitted to film the constant trickle of serious casualties from Iraq (over 10,000 in total now) who are evacuated to a US base in Germany, or back home to America for medical treatment. The US government, having learnt some lessons from Vietnam, doesn't want the public to see the true cost of the war being waged in their name.

There was also growing unease in the United States about some of America's allies in the war on terror. Two days before the second 9/11 anniversary, Robert Scheer of the *Los Angeles Times* pointed out the obvious. Fifteen of the nineteen hijackers on September 11 were from Saudi Arabia. Osama bin Laden is Saudi and his family are closely connected to Saudi Arabia's ruling royal family. The enduring official incantation from Washington, however, is that the Saudis are our staunch friends and allies in the war on terror.[15]

Yet, it seems obvious that the United States, Britain and Australia's current 'friends' in the Middle East and Central Asia — meaning those rulers prepared to back a US-led war against the Taliban, Al-Qaida and Saddam Hussein — are mostly corrupt despots ruling over states desperately in need of 'regime change' themselves. Saudi Arabia is a dictatorship where women are forbidden to drive cars and homosexuals are beheaded. Pakistan helped set up the Taliban and traded nuclear secrets with North Korea. Both Pakistan and Saudi Arabia have also been long-term sponsors of international Islamic terrorism. Some of the United States, Britain and Australia's allies in this war on terror are actually the people who have the most to lose if genuine democracy did take hold in the Middle East and Central Asia.

America's war against terrorism abroad has also given the US government cause to restrict democracy at home. The Bush administration's *Patriot Act*, with echoes of the anti-communist McCarthyism of the 1950s, provides a legal framework for determining who is, and isn't, patriotic enough in the US of A. At the Skokie public library in Chicago, librarians have put up posters warning 'Big Brother Is Watching You' and notifying patrons that the US government now has the right to monitor what books its citizens read. Reading something suspicious might get you put on the FBI's list. But what is suspicious? Books about 9/11 and Osama bin Laden? Or the Koran? In response to the objections of librarians at Skokie and elsewhere, US Attorney General John Ashcroft denounced their 'baseless hysteria'.[16]

But as ridiculous as this sounds, in 2002 a seventy-four year old woman from Milwaukee called Sister Virgine Lawinger was forbidden to board a plane because the anti-war nun was on a list of suspiciously unpatriotic Americans. At the University of Massachusetts meanwhile, a Sri Lankan student activist was visited by the FBI after he volunteered with an agency responsible for coordinating helpers during state emergencies and natural disasters. His skin colour, Asian name and funny accent obviously concerned someone. Yaju Dharmarajah later told a journalist that:

> They [the FBI] thought I wanted to video [the state emergency agency's] work as part of a terrorist plot …

I am lucky. I have a white American wife. If she was Sri Lankan like me, I wouldn't have said anything for fear they would deport us.[17]

Meanwhile there is one area in which America unquestionably maintains its dominating position as '#1!' — international arms trading. It seems strange that a country which so fears international terrorism (and where handgun shooting sprees by disgruntled employees, high-school children or estranged spouses have become disturbingly routine), should still be the Third World's number one supplier of lethal weaponry. A report by the US Congress found that during 2002 the United States sold US$13.3 billion worth of weapons worldwide (45.5 per cent of the total market share to use the economic jargon). About $8.6 billion worth of these arms sales went to 'developing nations', or in other words, to places and regimes where the chance of those weapons being used against innocent civilians is greatest. Not surprisingly, America's old Cold War nemesis, Russia, was the second greatest supplier of weapons to the Third World, selling $5 billion worth during 2002, while 'peace-loving' France, which opposed the US invasion of Iraq, came third, selling $1 billion worth of arms to developing countries.[18]

At the same time, September 2003, it was announced by the US Census Bureau that the number of Americans living in poverty increased by 1.7 million during 2002. During the year an estimated 12 per cent of Americans were officially living in poverty — 34.6 million people. Poverty was defined as having an annual income of less than US$18,392 for a family of four, or $9183 for individuals. During 2002 the US Census Bureau found that the number of people surviving on incomes less than half this official 'poverty line' income amounted to 14.1 million men, women and children. This again, was an increase on the number of people living in 'severe poverty' (as it is defined) during 2001. For African-Americans the news was even worse. Over 24 per cent of black Americans endure official poverty, and median incomes for African-Americans fell three per cent during 2002.[19]

Imagine what the extra $87 billion that President Bush wants to spend on occupying Iraq — a country which America first armed, then disarmed, then bombed and destroyed, and is now rebuilding — could do to help these Americans who deserve better than this. Imagine how the money could be used to send more medicines and books, rather than cruise missiles and helicopter gunships, to Iraq. If only George W Bush would read more history he might reconsider the folly of his deadly foray into the Middle East.

American Taliban

President George W Bush thinks that he has been chosen by God to lead the world in an apocalyptic struggle against evil. If you don't believe me, read Bob Woodward's *Bush at War*, where Bush discusses his divinely inspired mission with the veteran *Washington Post* journalist. Bush, an evangelical 'born again' Christian, also believes celestial providence is behind his personal rise to power. As Governor of Texas he famously said that he would not have ascended to the position if not for his belief in 'a divine plan that supersedes all human plans.' In 2000 Bush told an interviewer that 'God wants me to run for President,' although it must have made him wonder why God didn't therefore let him win the election.[20] Without a majority of votes Bush had to rely on his brother Jeb, the Governor of Florida, and the US Supreme Court to become US President.

President Bush is not alone in his Christian fundamentalism. Lieutenant General William G Boykin is the US Deputy Undersecretary of Defence who heads the Pentagon's office responsible for hunting down Saddam Hussein and Osama bin Laden. Since 9/11 he has spoken at church groups across the United States, sometimes in military uniform with his chest laden with medals, about the war on terror. For Boykin the enemy is not just 'terrorism' as an abstract concept, or even Osama bin Laden as an individual, but more specifically 'a guy named Satan'. Boykin (like Bush) believes that President Bush was 'appointed' by God to lead America in its time of need and that God is helping the US military defeat its enemies. For Boykin, Christians worship 'a real God' while Muslims supplicate before a false deity. General Boykin described himself, an American soldier, as part of an 'army of God'.[21] Welcome to the world of the American Taliban.

In one of his first speeches on the White House lawn in the days after the September 11 terrorist attacks, President Bush referred to 'evil' and 'evil doers' seven times and commented that 'this crusade, this war on terrorism is going to take a while.'[22] Given Osama bin Laden's attempt to portray 9/11 as a holy war between the Christian West and Muslims, the use of the word crusade was, to say the least, ill advised. While Palestine and 'the Crusades' are moribund issues for most westerners, they are still matters of tremendous historical importance for Muslims around the world.

Few westerners would be aware that when Caliph Umar captured Jerusalem in 638 the Muslim conqueror promised that Christian lives and beliefs would be protected and respected.[23] The Caliph visited the Christian sites of Jerusalem — a holy city in Islam, Judaism and Christianity — and when he was invited to pray in the Church of the Holy Sepulchre, arguably the holiest site in all of Christianity, he declined out of respect for the sanctity of the Christian church. The Caliph feared that future generations of Muslims would want to unroll their prayer mats where the man who won Jerusalem for the Prophet Mohammed had prayed and that the Church of the Holy Sepulchre would be overrun, or annexed, by Muslims. Over the following 450 years the right of Jerusalem's Christians to continue to practise their faith was guaranteed by the city's Muslim rulers. Some of these traditions have survived — the Church of the Holy Sepulchre is still unlocked each day by a Muslim caretaker and protector whose family have apparently been responsible for this task for a thousand years.

Caliph Umar's approach to the issue of religious coexistence was not embraced by the European Christian Crusaders as they invaded Palestine and battered their way into Jerusalem in July 1099. The Crusaders, who had fought their way across Europe and Asia (stopping to massacre Jews in Germany along the way), came not with hearts of love nor with minds full of ideas about the brotherhood of man. They came as Christian conquerors determined to annihilate infidels and Saracens (as they called Muslims) within the Holy City. Jews and Muslims fought alongside one another to defend Jerusalem from these fanatical invaders from distant Western Europe.

As the Crusaders finally hacked their way into the Holy City much of the Muslim population retreated to the Dome of the Rock, a religious site of tremendous importance for Muslims, Jews and Christians alike. The Crusaders laid siege to a large number of Muslims who had taken sanctuary in the al-Aqsa Mosque. Then, in stark contrast to the conduct of Caliph Umar in 638, the Crusaders broke into the Mosque, desecrated and pillaged it, and killed the Muslims sheltering there. By the Crusaders' own boastful accounts, hundreds of religious scholars from across the Middle East were cut down along with ordinary civilians. One Crusader, Fulcher of Chartres, wrote about the massacre of Jerusalem's Muslims:

> Within this temple about ten thousand were beheaded. If you had been there your feet would have

been stained up to the ankles with the blood of the slain. What more shall I tell? Not one of them was allowed to live. They did not spare the women and children.[24]

The Crusaders also set fire to a synagogue in which a large number of Jews had taken refuge. Those who were not killed trying to escape the flames were burnt alive inside. In all, the massacre of Jews and Muslims in Jerusalem took two whole days to complete. Afterwards the stench of death was thick in the nostrils of the Crusaders as the bodies of the dead were dragged through the streets of Jerusalem and burned in piles outside the city gates.

The Crusaders saw their violence as being divinely inspired and morally justified. Rapine was considered sinful, although murdering Muslims and burning Jews as part of a penitential crusade was not. The Crusaders killed because they believed they were doing God's work, and then they gave thanks to Almighty God in the Church of the Holy Sepulchre — ignorant of the religious toleration exhibited by Caliph Umar 461 years beforehand.

To many Muslims today the interaction between the West and the people of the Middle East has been an unbroken history of conquest, colonialism, partition and war, beginning with the fall of Jerusalem in 1099. We have stolen their cultural antiquities (witness the British Museum) and pillaged their natural resources (oil included). In return, in the post-colonial period we imposed governmental models which denied people the very freedoms which we proclaimed as our guiding principles. Given a choice between corrupt and brutal monarchies (Saudi Arabia, etc.) and secular military dictatorships (Egypt, Iraq) an increasingly bitter section of the population clung to Islamic fundamentalist beliefs.

In a videotaped diatribe broadcast on Al-Jazeera on 3 November 2001, Osama bin Laden argued that 'Bush left no room for doubts' as he 'openly and clearly said that this war is a crusader war.' Osama bin Laden declared this to be proof that 'this war is fundamentally religious.' In another message he threatened that America would not know peace until there was peace in Palestine. Osama bin Laden is a religious fanatic, but he is not alone in seeing the West as having a history of intolerance, ignorance and violence in relation to Islam and the Middle East.

To millions of Muslims we remain the barbarians at the gates. To these people we — westerners — lack culture, history and a sense of justice. To these people 9/11 was not just a blow against America, but also against the venal pro-western regimes that still dominate the Arabian peninsula. To these people 9/11, the occupation of Iraq and the fall of Jerusalem in 1099 are linked in a single historical process. And when Bush uses words like 'crusade' and General Boykin speaks of an 'army of God', they confirm these prejudices.

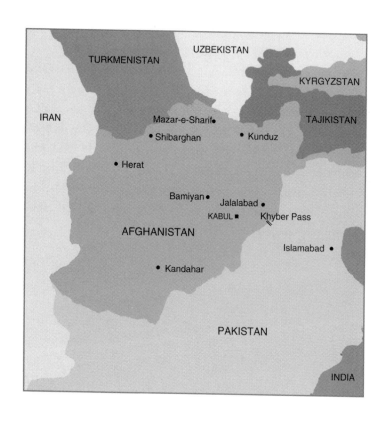

Afghanistan

Afghanistan and
'Those to Whom Evil is Done'

Tragedy has a way of driving people to poetry. After the September 11 terrorist attacks W H Auden's 'September 1, 1939' (written about the Nazi invasion of Poland), with its line about 'blind skyscrapers', was republished in several American newspapers and read on National Public Radio.[25] One section particularly stood out:

> I and the public know
> What all schoolchildren learn,
> Those to whom evil is done
> Do evil in return.

Immediately after the collapse of the Twin Towers in New York there were those in America and in many western countries who wanted to use the United States' unrivalled military strength to strike back mercilessly. This desire for revenge grew as suspicions pointed increasingly to Islamic extremists from the Middle East or Central Asia, and especially to Osama bin Laden's terrorist network. The words of Cofer Black, director of the CIA's counter-terrorism centre, were only an extreme expression of this general sentiment.

> We're going to kill them. We're going to put their heads on sticks. We're going to rock their world.[26]

In this context it is worth remembering that today's 'evil doers' (as President Bush calls them) — Osama bin Laden, Saddam Hussein — were yesterday's heroes. In February 1995 the *New York Times* had even described the Taliban as 'a new force of professed Islamic purists and Afghan patriots' who alone seemed capable of delivering peace to Afghanistan. They were favourably contrasted with the 'warlords' of the ex-Mujaheddin who were accused of establishing 'a reign of terror, pillage and heroin-running.'[27] Of course, the United States had actually funded the Islamic jihad of the Mujaheddin against the Soviet occupation of Afghanistan during the 1980s, and had also supported Saddam Hussein's dictatorship when he was willing to wage a war against Iran that cost half a million lives between 1981 and 1988. This support continued despite US knowledge of Iraq's use of deadly chemical weapons against Iranian soldiers. Similarly, in 1996 when the Taliban took control of Afghanistan's capital, Kabul, a spokesman for the Clinton Administration in Washington said that they could see 'nothing objectionable' about the extremist Islamic laws imposed by the Taliban upon the regions under their military control.[28]

The fierce Taliban emerged from the dust and rubble of Afghanistan in 1994, after a decade of Afghan resistance to the Soviet invaders and five years of civil war. They were virtual unknowns until they conquered Kandahar and advanced north to capture Kabul in September 1996. Arriving at the seat of Afghan political power the Taliban seized former President Najibullah from the United Nations compound where he had been given sanctuary since his pro-Soviet government was overthrown in 1992, and drove him to the Presidential Palace. According to Pakistani journalist Ahmed Rashid:

> There they castrated Najibullah, dragged his body behind a jeep for several rounds of the Palace and then shot him dead. His brother was similarly tortured and then throttled to death. The Taliban hanged the two dead men from a concrete traffic control post just outside the Palace, only a few blocks from the UN compound. At dawn curious Kabulis came to view the two bloated, beaten bodies as they hung from steel wire nooses around their necks. Unlit cigarettes were stuck between their fingers and Afghani notes stuffed into their pockets — to convey the Taliban message of debauchery and corruption.[29]

The Taliban had arrived, establishing themselves as the maimed and brutal rulers of a broken people. Between 1979 and 1992 the Soviets had poured approximately US$3 billion a year into Afghanistan in their war to defeat the Mujaheddin, while the Americans and Saudis each committed somewhere in the vicinity of US$10 billion over the same period to fund the Afghan Muslim guerillas.[30] Even the physical disabilities of the Taliban leadership bore witness to the ferocity of Afghanistan's long internecine conflict. Mullah Omar, the spiritual leader of the Taliban, was wounded during the anti-Soviet jihad and was literally one-eyed — he lost his right eye to fragments from a rocket in 1989. The Taliban mayor of Kabul had only one leg. A number of other senior Taliban commanders and government representatives sported a variety of war wounds and amputations.

With effective control of most of the country by 1997, the Taliban set about establishing the most obscurantist regime in modern history. An extremely fundamentalist version of Islam was instituted with the Taliban expelling girls from school and banning women from paid work — a devastating decision in a country where in 1998 an estimated 98,000 families were headed by war widows.[31] The Taliban prohibited virtually all forms of entertainment including recorded music, movies and television as well as chess and kite flying. Painting, singing, dancing and even the possession of family photographs (idolatry) all became illegal. Women were forced to cover their faces in public. Taliban law banned 'British or American hairstyles' and 'sorcery' and decreed that all men had to have beards at least two fists long. People caught drinking alcohol were publicly flogged. Thieves had their hands and feet amputated. Adulterers were stoned to death.[32]

In the words of Ahmed Rashid, one of the few people to report directly from Afghanistan during this period, the Taliban were mainly boys and their 'simple belief in a messianic, puritan Islam which had been drummed into them by simple village mullahs was the only prop they could hold on to and which gave their lives some meaning.' Rashid found that many were former refugees or war orphans, 'untrained for anything, even the traditional occupations of their forefathers such as farming.' The government they constructed was 'uncompromising in its purist demands to turn Afghan society back to an imagined model of seventh-century Arabia at the time of the Prophet Mohammed.'[33]

In their attempt to impose strict Islamic Sharia law, the Taliban even converted the soccer stadium in Kabul into a forum for public executions — shooting kneeling offenders in the back of the head, or sometimes hanging them from the goalposts. During their five years in power, Taliban law enforcement, via the 'Department for the Promotion of Virtue and Prevention of Vice', became more brutal and bizarre. In January 1999 the Taliban had the severed decaying limbs of six thieves hung from trees in the middle of Kabul as a warning to others.

One Taliban decree, translated into rough English for the benefit of the foreign aid agencies, spelt out how the Taliban expected women to act in the new Afghanistan:

> Women you should not step outside your residence. If you go outside the house you should not be like women who used to go with fashionable clothes wearing much cosmetics … If women are going outside with fashionable, ornamental, tight and charming clothes to show themselves, they will be cursed by the Islamic Sharia and should never expect to go to heaven.[34]

Despite the fact that the Taliban made it nearly impossible for young men and women to meet casually and form relationships, the Taliban reserved a special hatred for homosexuals. Indeed, the Taliban were at a loss trying to decide upon a suitably gruesome punishment. Or as Mullah Mohammed Hassan explained: 'Some say we should take these sinners to a high roof and throw them down, while others say we should dig a hole beside a wall, bury them, then push the wall down on top of them.' The toppling wall faction won the debate. In February 1998 three men in Kandahar found guilty of sodomy were taken to a wall which was toppled onto them with the assistance of a tank. The execution was witnessed by Mullah Omar himself who was obviously impressed because the following month the same grisly punishment was inflicted upon two men in Kabul. To the delight of the Taliban, the accused 'buggerers' were crushed to death. Despite the genuine threat of a horrible death if discovered, irrepressible sexual impulses, and/or isolation from women, clearly affected even the most stalwart soldiers of God. In April 1998 two Taliban in Kabul were caught having sex with one another. They were beaten and humiliated, but spared the wall.[35]

Ironically, it had been the Taliban's ruthless imposition of Islamic law that had initially been their principal appeal to ordinary Afghans. The legend of the Taliban's emergence in Kandahar in the spring of 1994 revolves around their attempt to bring some semblance of decency back to a world of warlords, murder and rapine. As the story goes, two teenage girls had been taken by ex-Mujaheddin fighters to a military barracks where they were raped. A poor local Islamic cleric, Mullah Omar, upon hearing of this, assembled some thirty *talib* (students), collected a few old AK47 rifles and attacked the barracks. The girls were freed and one of the rapists was hanged from the barrel of a captured tank. By the end of 1994 Omar had over ten thousand soldiers (most between the ages of fourteen and twenty-four) under arms and the Taliban were marching to power.[36]

One of the many tragic things about Afghanistan is that September 11 and the Taliban have now forever stained its name. This great country, with magnificent mountains which Marco Polo described as 'the roof of the world,' and whose ruins at Balkh (near Mazar-e-Sharif) mark the remains of one of the most ancient cities in all of human civilisation, has been reduced in the western mind to nothing more than a terrorist training camp for

Osama bin Laden. But Afghanistan is where one of the very first ancient religions, Zoroastrianism, blossomed; a place through which silk traders first carried Buddhism to China; a country where Alexander the Great and Genghis Khan fought during their epic conquests. Bamiyan, in the middle of the country, was already an important trading town at the time of the Roman Empire. It was also the capital of Buddhism in Central Asia for at least a thousand years and the Bamiyan Buddhas — huge stone statues that stood for nearly two thousand years before being destroyed by the Taliban in February 2001 — were one of the wonders of the ancient world.[37]

Islam is actually a comparative newcomer to Afghanistan, only arriving in the middle of the seventh century with invading Arab armies. However, prior to the anti-Soviet jihad of the 1980s, Afghanistan's Islamic traditions — legal, cultural and political — were not at all 'fundamentalist'. Indeed, there was much in Afghan history that was multi-ethnic, multi-cultural and multi-religious, with significant minority communities of Jews, Hindus and Sikhs noticeable in the country's urban economic life. It was the ferocious nature of the anti-Soviet jihad which marginalised moderate Islamicists within the exiled Afghan opposition. Ironically, American CIA funding (as with that from the Pakistanis and Saudis) tended to prefer the more theologically extreme and militarily ferocious elements within the Mujaheddin. And from these seeds grew the Taliban.[38]

Much has been made of the 'clash of civilisations' post-September 11, but Afghanistan has a far greater claim to be a founding place of Western Civilisation than most of the world. The town of Herat was settled 5000 years ago and was praised by the ancient Greek historian Herodotus at a time before Paris, London or New York even existed. An ancient centre of both

Christianity and Islam, by the fifteenth century Herat was still a bustling centre of culture and commerce. The poet Nawai, the 'father of literary Turkic', is buried in Herat. Ulugh Beg, an astronomer whose calendar of the stars was published in 1665, was a native of Herat. And when the poet Lord Byron stood before the tomb of Gowhar Shad at Herat in 1837 he described it as 'the most beautiful example in colour in architecture ever devised by man to the glory of God and himself.'[39]

Afghanistan's path to ruin has been a long and bloody one. It was not until the nineteenth century that Europeans started to seriously meddle in the region. With the Tsar's Russian Empire to the north and Britain's Indian Empire to the east, Afghanistan became a focus for European colonialism's 'great game' in Central Asia. The British made several ruinous attempts to conquer the Afghans before they and the Russians came to the realisation that the country's deadly mountain passes were best left alone. Afghanistan remained a buffer state between the rival empires, with the British eventually bribing their way into a commanding position via competing local kings. It was not until 1919 that Afghanistan officially established its independence and stumbled towards modernisation.[40]

Two kings were assassinated and there were various local revolts against the rulers of the emerging modern Afghan state before a coup and the overthrow of the monarchy moved Afghanistan slowly into the Soviet sphere of influence. During the 1970s, at the height of the Cold War, the Russians invested hundreds of millions of roubles in Afghanistan in order to prop up the nominally leftist, military-backed regime of President Daoud. When Daoud's regime was overthrown in April 1978 the slide towards barbarism accelerated. President Daoud, his bodyguards and his entire family were all murdered in the coup.

The communist coup leaders then fell out among themselves and, facing growing Islamic unrest in the countryside, effective power became more fractured.

Competing factions of the Afghan Communist Party squabbled over who would control the government. The first communist premier was assassinated and the second was executed by the Soviets when they decided they wanted a return on their investment and invaded in December 1979. At the occupation's peak, the Soviets had 104,000 troops in Afghanistan. About 14,000 Soviet soldiers were killed and 50,000 wounded during the Mujaheddin's jihad. When the Soviets withdrew in 1989 they left behind a million dead Afghans and a shattered nation.[41]

With the Soviets gone the West's interest in Afghanistan dissipated. The Afghan civil war continued and the Mujaheddin were left to fight among themselves over which faction would now rule the ruined country. As westerners we have generally been insulated from the consequences of this terrible history of bloodletting by our sheer geographic distance from that part of the world. That is, until September 11.

The Propaganda War:
The Media and 9/11

The best way to get the news is from objective sources. And the most objective sources I have are people on my staff.

George W Bush [42]

Although the rival US networks initially battled over the most horrifying video footage of the two airliners smashing into the Twin Towers on September 11 (CNN reportedly paid US$50,000 to one amateur cameraman), and ran it virtually non-stop for two days after the terrorist attacks, the President of the ABC News network in America eventually issued an order to stop broadcasting the footage as its constant repetition had become 'gratuitous'. Australian networks followed soon after and the harrowing images, which had been replayed perhaps a hundred times over the previous days, disappeared from our screens. When Australia's Nine Network news chief was asked about this, he responded by saying that 'It does distress people and the story has moved on anyway.'[43] The story has moved on?

As terrible as the footage of planes flying into the Twin Towers was, even this was transcended by images of terrified people about to die, frantically waving from the windows of the Towers before they collapsed, or worse still, of people jumping to their deaths. Some of this was shown live on television. The networks, ever conscious of their competitors, agonised over what to do. In America ABC chose not to show people leaping to their deaths, NBC showed the footage but did not repeat it, and CNN pulled its live camera back so that the dying people could easily be confused with falling debris. With every live second on September 11 some new moral and technological boundary seemed to have been irrevocably crossed.[44]

The shocked headlines of major American newspapers in the days afterwards ranged from 'ACT OF WAR' (*New York Post*), to 'BASTARDS!' (*San Francisco Examiner*). Even in far off Australia local papers offered 'IT'S WAR' (*West Australian*) and 'THEY'LL PAY FOR THIS' (*The Australian*). *BBC News Online* received 20,000 emails in the forty-eight hours after the first plane hit the Twin Towers — requests for information, outpourings of grief, confusion and anger. For four entire days after September 11 the major American television networks (ABC, NBC, CBS, Fox) broadcast non-stop news coverage of the tragedy. CNN's website, which usually receives 11 million 'hits' a day, was recording 9 million visitors an hour. There were no commercials on most television channels. Every other news story disappeared. There was no parallel in the entire history of American or Australian television broadcasting. One journalist described 9/11 coverage as exploding 'all previous concepts of a saturation point.' Then slowly, cautiously, there was some regularly scheduled programming, while still allowing for long updates on the situation at New York's smouldering World Trade Center.[45]

Meanwhile, just over the Atlantic in London a professional 'spin doctor' saw her opportunity. At 2.55 pm London time on Tuesday September 11, just after the second airliner had exploded into the side of the World Trade Center, a senior ministerial adviser in Tony Blair's government was emailing her boss. Jo Moore, with an eye on the tragedy that was gripping the entire world's attention, wrote to Blair's transport secretary saying that, 'It is now a very good day to get out anything we want to bury. Councillors' expenses?' Unfortunately for Ms Moore the email was leaked and her career in public relations may well be finished. However, Andrew Rawnsley, a columnist at the *Observer*, made an interesting comment on how the scandal reflected the current state of British politics:

> What icy discipline, what terrifying professionalism must possess someone who can watch the Twin Towers being bombed and, even before they have collapsed, her laser focus is on a brilliant opportunity for manipulating the public. To condemn her is like condemning a fox for biting the heads off chickens. It's in the animal's nature. She was only behaving as should be expected of a creature of the culture of spin.[46]

He had a point, but in the aftermath of September 11 it was hard to accept such things as ... normal. Suddenly, all the political rules had changed. The September 12 edition of the *New York Post* carried no gossip column for the first time in twenty-five years. As the chief gossip writer explained, 'It's not possible to write about canoodling supermodels or dyspeptic pop divas when terrorists are killing our friends and relatives and scaring our children.'[47]

Which is not to say that the new journalistic world was all compassion and handshakes. Two American newspaper columnists — Dan Guthrie from Oregon's *Grants Pass Daily Courier*, and Tom Gutting from the *Texas City Sun* — were fired for criticising President Bush for not returning to the White House immediately after the September 11 attacks. In both cases the editors or publishers issued front page apologies and explanatory editorial columns detailing why they had sacked the journalists. The publisher of the *Texas City Sun* went so far as to say that simply reading the offending column had made him feel physically sick. Indeed, in the aftermath of September 11 it was clear that anyone in the public eye who implied the President of the United States might have been acting in anything other than a brave warrior-like fashion was in for big trouble.[48]

Another person who learnt these new rules the hard way was American comedian Bill Maher whose television show 'Politically Incorrect' had previously been lauded for its political satire. Maher responded to the fact that the September 11 hijackers had been described as cowards by President Bush by saying that, 'Staying in the airplane when it hits the building, say what you want about it, it's not cowardly.' Worse still, he said that with regard to the United States' previous retaliatory military assaults against such people: 'We have been the cowards, lobbing cruise missiles from 2000 miles away. That's cowardly.'[49]

The reaction was not positive. Two days later Sinclair Broadcasting, a major ABC Network affiliate, announced that it was suspending all future broadcasts of 'Politically Incorrect'. Several other affiliates did likewise. Two of the show's major sponsors, Sears and FedEx, pulled their advertising. Maher also found himself pilloried in the press where his comments were presented as being downright treasonous. Attempts by Maher's producers to justify his comments within the framework of vigorous dissent being an important part of American democracy, fell on deaf ears. His once popular show dangled by a thread.

The Maher controversy extended all the way to Washington where White House spokesman Ari Fleischer commented that: 'There are reminders to all Americans that they need to watch what they say, watch what they do, and this is not a time for remarks like that; there never is.' On the contrary, I would have thought that the weeks after the worst terrorist attack in United States history would have been exactly the right time to begin discussing, critically analysing, and vigorously debating the method and effectiveness of previous US military retaliation against its perceived enemies. Moreover, to the unaccustomed ear, Fleischer's comments sounded a little like a call for censorship.

It was much harder to shed a tear for Ann Coulter, whose syndicated column is carried by several websites and fifty newspapers across America. In a piece entitled 'This Is War' published on the *National Review Online* on 13 September, Coulter argued that 'this is no time to be precious about locating the exact individuals directly involved in this particular terrorist attack.' By her estimation, those deemed responsible should include 'anyone anywhere in the world who smiled' in response to the destruction of the Twin Towers. Her proposed form of retaliation? 'We should invade their countries, kill their leaders and convert them to Christianity.' It was too much even for the editors of the conservative *National Review Online*. Coulter was let go.[50]

However, lest you get all misty-eyed over Coulter's sacrifice on behalf of a free media, she was immediately hired by *FrontPage*, another conservative internet magazine. Nor was she chastened by the controversy around her 'This Is War' piece. Two follow-up columns referred to 'suspicious-looking swarthy males' and the fact that 'Not all Muslims may be terrorists, but all terrorists are Muslims.' Her new bosses at *FrontPage* appeared pleased with her work. David Horowitz, himself a well-known conservative columnist, described her writing as 'articulate, forceful — and cheeky.' Horowitz denounced the sacking of Coulter as a form of 'PC McCarthyism'. Not that Coulter seemed worried by any of this, or in the least concerned that her comments, even if we assume they were meant in what passes for jest in the 'cheeky' right-wing circles she moves in, might have been the sort of blather that the American-Arab Anti-Discrimination Committee claimed was encouraging an alarming rise in attacks on Americans of Middle-Eastern origin. As she told the *Washington Post*, 'frankly, I'm getting a lot of great publicity.'[51]

With the question of patriotism dominating the public agenda, the Media Research Centre, a conservative media monitoring group, began exerting greater pressure on American newscasters and reporters to rally around the flag. Even mainstream broadcasters started to become concerned about how quickly, and how narrow, the 'stream' suddenly became. In the words of the President of MSNBC, Erik Sorenson:

> Any misstep and you can get into trouble with these guys and have the Patriotism Police hunt you down. These are hard jobs. Just getting the facts straight is monumentally difficult. We don't want to have to wonder if we are saluting properly.[52]

A January 2002 survey by two American media specialists found that of all the US reporting of September 11 and its aftermath, 'less than 10 per cent of the coverage of administration policy offers significant dissent.' Most coverage contained 'no dissent at all.' In all of this the alleged central precept of the mainstream press — objectivity — was unceremoniously discarded. Or as Brit Hume, the Fox News 'anchor', told the *New York Times*, 'Look, neutrality as a general principle is an appropriate concept for journalists who are covering institutions of some comparable quality. This is a conflict between the United States and murdering barbarians.'[53]

Meanwhile the West had deployed its shock troops, its foreign correspondents, to Pakistan as soon as it became obvious that the Americans were preparing for a war against Afghanistan. Even before the first cruise missile took flight, there were over 500 foreign journalists (including a few Australians) in Pakistan and another 200 in Tajikistan, where they competed for seats on a helicopter into the section of Afghanistan not under Taliban control at the time.[54] Earlier, on 17 September, the Taliban began expelling all foreign journalists from their territory — exiling cameramen, sound recordists and reporters to the gaudy hotels of Peshawar and Islamabad.

The reality was that the western journalists were constantly getting scooped by the competition anyway. Al-Jazeera (The Lighthouse), the Arabic language satellite news show with 35 million viewers and based in the Gulf state of Qatar, had the only live camera link inside Taliban-controlled Afghanistan. It was permitted by the Taliban to stay after all other reporters were expelled, and Osama bin Laden had a habit of delivering his videotaped diatribes exclusively to them. In the days after September 11 most of the quality footage from inside Afghanistan, or of Osama bin Laden, was borrowed from Al-Jazeera.[55]

Not surprisingly, US Secretary of State Colin Powell, touring the Gulf to drum up support for America's war on terror, urged Qatar's ruling emir to curtail the alleged anti-Americanism of Al-

Jazeera. The station's pro-Arab bias was attacked by the *New York Times* (which obviously didn't think it suffered from pro-American bias) and by Britain's *Daily Telegraph* which referred to Al-Jazeera disparagingly as 'bin Laden TV'.[56] Politicians in the United States, Britain and Australia joined the chorus of disapproval. However, as two writers from the American-Arab Anti-Discrimination Committee later argued, Al-Jazeera's real merit was that it was the sole news source inside Afghanistan that was 'not beholden to US officials for "access".'

> Trying to vilify or censor it sends the worst possible message to Arabs — that free debate and, by implication, democracy in the Arab world are threatening to the West. Al-Jazeera represents the best trends of openness and democratisation in the Arab world. It is a long-overdue two-way street in the global flow of information and opinion. It should be celebrated and encouraged, not smeared and censored.[57]

Whether by coincidence or design, Al-Jazeera's Kabul office was bombed by the Americans during their overthrow of the Taliban.

As 35 million Arabs crowded around their televisions watching Al-Jazeera, and millions more 'Westerners' sat transfixed watching CNN, it seemed the only group of people in the entire world who weren't able to observe the Taliban approach their impending doom were the Afghan people themselves. Under the Taliban all photography of living things was banned. Thus Afghanistan constituted the only nation on the planet where possessing a family photograph was a criminal offence. Most

Afghan children born after 1996 had never even seen photos of what their own country, let alone the people, animals and places of the rest of the world, looked like.[58]

Depressingly, in the West where people did have access to a previously unimaginable array of media images, the general level of understanding of our 'enemies' was woeful. American-Palestinian intellectual Edward Said wrote about the deep estrangement many Arab-Americans felt from a society which viewed them as alien and malevolent. He was similarly worried by President Bush's 'Axis of Evil' analysis of the world:

> Anyone reading the world press in the past few weeks can ascertain that people outside the US are both mystified by and aghast at the vagueness of US policy, which claims for itself the right to imagine and create enemies on a world scale, then prosecute wars on them without much regard for accuracy of definition, specificity of aim, concreteness of goal, or worst of all, the legality of such actions. What does it mean to defeat 'evil terrorism' in a world like ours?[59]

Edward Said also commented on the tremendous 'moral blindness' in the US media, whose columnists treated September 11 as the ultimate act of human cruelty, reducing all other injustices and suffering to the periphery, 'as if the lives lost elsewhere in the world were not worth lamenting quite as much or drawing as large moral conclusions from.' He criticised prominent Americans who refused to accept that the world 'is moved and can be understood by politics, not by huge general absolutes like good and evil, with America always on the side of good, its enemies on the side of evil.'[60]

Critics of the war on terror were generally reluctant to turn the moral debate into a numbers game. And yet numbers did provide some perspective. Three thousand innocent people died on September 11. That compared to an estimated eight hundred to three thousand innocent Afghan civilians who were killed during America's subsequent bombing campaign, but whose lives were viewed as regrettable, but necessary, 'collateral damage'.[61] There was no special concert for them and no visits by Hollywood celebrities to their terminal 'Ground Zero' somewhere in a forgotten corner of Afghanistan. These were lonely, unimportant deaths. They were mourned in private, not on CNN.

Howard Zinn commented in *The Nation* that it was not until ordinary Americans saw the direct impact of American policy in Southeast Asia on their television screens — body bags, young dead Americans, napalmed children and burning villages — that the anti-Vietnam war movement gained momentum in the late 1960s.

> … if people could see the consequences of the bombing campaign as vividly as we were all confronted with the horrifying photos in the wake of September 11, if they saw on television night after night the blinded and maimed children, the weeping parents of Afghanistan, they might ask: Is this the way to combat terrorism?[62]

The US media, however, was generally unwilling to confront these issues. For instance, in October 2001 the *Panama City News Herald* in Florida warned its editors in an internal memo:

> DO NOT USE photos on Page 1A showing civilian casualties from the US war in Afghanistan. Our sister paper … has done so and received hundreds and

hundreds of threatening emails ... DO NOT USE wire stories which lead with civilian casualties from the US war on Afghanistan. They should be mentioned further down in the story. If the story needs rewriting to play down the civilian casualties, DO IT.[63]

Similarly, Walter Isaacson, the Chair of CNN, actually told his staff that it 'seems perverse to focus too much on the casualties or hardship in Afghanistan.'[64]

In this context it is also worth remembering the half a million innocent Iraqi children which UNICEF (hardly a source of Arab propaganda) claimed perished between the end of the 1991 Gulf War and 2002 due to the combined results of US bombing and sanctions. Some of this bombing, as revealed in declassified documents from the Pentagon, was deliberately designed to destroy Iraq's clean water supplies, its waste disposal centres, and to increase diseases amongst the general population. The progress of this war against innocent civilians was dutifully documented by US officials dedicated to rendering daily life in Iraq so miserable, and pestilent, that people would rise up and overthrow Saddam Hussein (who, of course, did not have to endure any of this from inside his plush presidential palaces). As a result, diarrhoeal diseases became the main cause of death for Iraqi children by the late 1990s.[65]

When in May 1996 the then US Ambassador to the United Nations, Madeleine Albright, appeared on the American '60 Minutes' program, it was pointed out to her that the main victims of US sanctions against Iraq appeared to be children and she was asked if overthrowing Saddam Hussein was worth the price being paid in innocent lives. Albright replied that it was 'a very hard choice' but 'we think the price is worth it.' Remarkably, even though Albright made these chilling comments on national television, there was no media campaign of moral outrage calling for her resignation. Even more remarkably, six years later, and although this unconscionably cruel strategy had patently failed to remove Saddam Hussein from power, Iraqi children continued to pay for his sins. At the beginning of 2002 UNICEF estimated that the infant mortality rate for Iraqi children under five had increased 160 per cent since 1990 — the worst increase out of 188 countries surveyed.[66]

An Iraqi child is no more responsible for a brutal dictator like Saddam Hussein than an American air hostess is for the dispossession of the Palestinians. The one thing that truly made September 11 unique was not the number of innocent lives lost, but the fact that for once this was occurring in a western country, live on television, to people CNN actually cares about.

At the same time the Pentagon was trying to utilise the global media to its best propagandist advantage. During February 2002 it was revealed that the Pentagon had been planning an 'Office of Strategic Influence' whose purpose, according to critics inside the US Congress, was to plant favourable, and if necessary fictitious, stories in the international press. When the Office of Strategic Influence plan was dumped after media exposure, it seemed as if the US press corps had won a great battle in defence of journalistic integrity.[67]

However, the reality was that the entanglement between the US military and the US media was already extensive. At the most obvious level retired generals were a regular feature of most American TV network coverage of the war on terror, providing a pro-Pentagon spin on events while appearing as specialist commentators. Off camera there were other connections. For instance, in February 2000 it was revealed that several officers from the US Army's 'Psychological Operations Command', or PSYOPS, had been employed at CNN's Atlanta headquarters during the war in Kosovo as part of an internship program. CNN later conceded that their employment had been 'inappropriate'.[68]

More importantly, most of the US media was so amenable to the Pentagon's perspective on the war on terror that any domestic version of the Office for Strategic Influence was unnecessary. For instance, the *Guardian Weekly* reported that the Pentagon had 'done a deal' with the ABC Network to produce a documentary about the lives of US soldiers in Afghanistan. The planned series was to be co-produced by Jerry Bruckheimer (who worked on the popular film about the US intervention in Somalia, *Black Hawk Down*) and Bertram Van Munster (the producer of the pro-police 'reality-TV' show, 'Cops'). With the war on terror the subject of a proposed reality-TV show, the final barrier between war and entertainment appeared to have been breached. With such potential propaganda opportunities on offer, the Office of Strategic Influence's pedestrian plan to lie to the international press seemed, by comparison, somewhat quaint.[69]

Meanwhile those journalists, American or otherwise, who tried to step beyond the sanitised boundaries of the Pentagon's news frontier inside Afghanistan found the experience potentially lethal. Tragically, eight foreign journalists were killed by Afghan bandits and/or Taliban during the early weeks of the war and this curtailed reporting in remote areas. However, even in US-controlled zones journalists were clearly only welcome as long as they asked the right questions. One such example was provided by the *Washington Post's* Doug Struck who claimed that US soldiers actually threatened to shoot him when he asked what would happen if he ignored their orders to desist in his attempt to investigate a remote site (near Zhawar) where it was claimed innocent Afghans had been mistakenly killed by a US missile. When the Pentagon later made the Orwellian claim that Struck had only been held at gunpoint for his own safety, the *Washington Post* journalist described it as 'an amazing lie' which revealed 'the extremes the military is going to keep this war secret.'[70]

And yet despite the potential repackaging of war as 'reality-TV', one of the most horrifying things about September 11 was how many people commented that it had looked 'just like a movie.' And without a doubt, the tragedy shook Hollywood profoundly. In October 2001 the *Australian* reported that forty-five films had already been 'altered or had their release dates changed' because of September 11. These included the shelving of the US$100 million film *Collateral Damage* starring Arnold Schwarzenegger, the unfortunate plot of which involved a fireman out to avenge the murder of his family by crazed terrorists.[71]

Just as worrying from Hollywood's point of view, academics like Kyung Hyun Kim from the University of California addressed the film industry's culpability in the way people responded to September 11.

> I feel very strongly about the reduction of images of mass destruction for entertainment value. Hollywood has prepared us to take these images with popcorn, laughter and cheers. This has been a problem. Images of mass destruction are not for entertainment.[72]

Previously it may have been possible for movie producers to dismiss the learned professor as a whining killjoy. Post-September 11 the issues were more starkly posed. Or as one New Zealand media commentator argued:

We have seen *Armageddon, Deep Impact* and *Independence Day.* We have seen New York laid waste in the movies. As that great cloud of smoke, paper, masonry dust and human remains teemed down from [the] Trade Center towers, then stormed towards the cameras, it followed a visual syntax familiar to us all. But this time it was real and that was what was so hard to grasp. This time it wasn't Godzilla.[73]

This time it was Osama bin Laden and sometimes the attempt to understand his motivations in the media scarcely lifted above Hollywood's attempts to comprehend what might compel a giant lizard to stomp a city to dust. Indeed, just attempting to make sense of September 11 could result in accusations of pro-terrorist sympathies. The former Mayor of New York, Rudolph Guliani, told the United Nations General Assembly that trying to understand the motives of the hijackers was an insult to their victims. Remarkable as it may seem, even in far off Australia some journalists, as well as Labor and Liberal politicians, endorsed the content of the Mayor's comments, partially stifling what should have been, and was, the basic human response to the tragedy — why?

To simply dismiss September 11 as the senseless actions of deranged terrorists was to miss the crucial point — that these were people motivated by extremist theology and with a serious political grudge against America. Asking why did not imply that you agreed with the hijackers, just as seeking to understand the rise of fascism during the 1930s or how Social Darwinism contributed to the Holocaust, does not make you a Nazi. There were, however, voices of reason. Scott Burchill, writing in the *Sydney Morning Herald,* provided one of the better examples as he attempted to undo the 'logic' of America's justification for bombing Afghanistan.

> When Timothy McVeigh blew up the Alfred Murrah Federal Building in Oklahoma City in 1995, much thought was given to the personal motivation of a 'home grown terrorist'. No-one suggested that Washington should retaliate by bombing Montana or Idaho, where his ultra-right militia supporters are based ... Disparaging the efforts to understand these horrific events [September 11] is myopic and undemocratic ... Refusing to understand why the US is so hated and feared in the Middle East and Central Asia is also a profoundly immoral stance because it increases the likelihood that these crimes will be repeated.[74]

Indeed, it was virtually the only thing the media could do to guarantee it. And then the cruise missiles will fly once more, and the cameras will roll again.

Palestine and Israel

Palestine and Israel: The Angry Generation

We want an angry generation
To plough the sky
To blow up history
To blow up our thoughts.
We want a new generation
That does not forgive mistakes
That does not bend.
We want a generation of giants.

Arab poet Nizar Qabbani, 1967

On 27 January 2002 a young Palestinian woman called Wafa Idrees blew herself up in Jerusalem, killing an elderly Jewish man and horribly wounding dozens of other innocent bystanders. Journalists exploring this new cruel twist to the all-too-familiar story of Arab–Israeli violence reported that Wafa Idrees was the first woman suicide bomber of the Palestinian intifada (uprising).

Wafa Idrees' life and death seemed to represent everything that was wrong in Israel/Palestine. She was a refugee from the al-Ama'ri camp outside Ramallah who felt very sharply the defeat, humiliations, poverty and hopelessness of her people. While she had worked as a volunteer nurse with Red Crescent, she had also been beaten by Israeli soldiers and drawn into the nexus of the intifada. Finally she chose a horrible death, her body literally torn to pieces, her only hope that killing innocent Israelis might somehow liberate Palestine.[75]

Her death, along with that of the innocent Jewish man she murdered, were but two in a sickening spiral of violence in the Holy Land shared by Islam, Judaism and Christianity. Over one weekend at the start of March 2002, twenty-one Israelis, including seven soldiers, were killed in Palestinian attacks. Israeli soldiers backed by tanks, helicopters and F-16 fighter jets then killed seventeen Palestinians on the Monday. In the week that followed the Israeli Army used tanks and troops to batter their way through refugee camps in the West Bank, while Palestinian militants continued a terrifying campaign of suicide bombings outside Jewish cafes and restaurants. On 12 March Israeli soldiers, backed by US-supplied helicopter gunships, killed thirty Palestinians in their largest military assault since their invasion of Lebanon in 1982.[76]

In response to this final ignoble collapse of the Middle East peace process, US President George W Bush repeatedly called on the Palestinian leader, Yasser Arafat, to end the killing. Arafat, who seemed increasingly alienated from his own people, had been confined by the Israeli Army to his own compound for over two months at the time of President Bush's comments in late February 2002. Arafat responded to the demands of a US president whom he called 'Bush the Son' that he hadn't done enough to stop the violence, by arguing that 'I didn't send my helicopters and my F-15s and my F-16s and my tanks to any Israeli city.'[77]

He had a point. The Americans have provided over US$92 billion in aid to the Israelis since 1967 — more than they have given any other country. The illegal Israeli occupation of the West Bank and Gaza, regularly denounced by the United Nations, is funded with American taxpayers' dollars and largely carried out with American weapons. While Israel possessed a sophisticated air force and navy, as well as an army with access to tanks, heavy artillery, a missile defence system and even nuclear weapons, Palestinians were forced to rely upon stones, Islamic militias and the corrupt Palestinian police for armed protection. What Arafat didn't mention was that the Palestinian groups who were carrying out the horrific suicide bombings increasingly viewed him as an irrelevancy and a collaborator anyway. In this sense the Israeli siege of his compound was about all Arafat had left to restore his public reputation amongst Palestinians as a freedom fighter rather than a compromised and corrupt bureaucrat within a failed 'peace settlement'.

Palestine is a holy land for the followers of three great religions (Judaism, Christianity and Islam) whose theologies and histories are deeply intertwined. Palestine, and the holy city of Jerusalem, were of course the ultimate destination and military objective of the Christian Crusades, which began in 1095 and caused much violence and residual antipathy between Muslims and Christians for centuries afterwards. Nevertheless, from 1516 until the end of the First World War, Palestine was part of the crumbling Ottoman Empire. The region was extremely heterogeneous, with Muslims, Christians and Jews living together in reasonable harmony. However, increased numbers of European Jews resettled in Palestine during the late nineteenth century. They did so partly because of the Jewish Zionist movement which encouraged migration of Jews to the Holy Land in response to the virulent anti-Semitism of Europe and in order to create a Jewish national homeland. Still, at the time of the outbreak of the First World War in 1914, Jews only numbered about 13 per cent of the total population of Palestine. Moreover, the tens of thousands of Jewish migrants to Palestine during this period were insignificant as compared to the almost three million European Jews who went to the United States between 1880 and 1929.[78]

It was in the midst of the First World War, and after incessant petitioning from Zionist organisations, that Britain, possessor of the most powerful empire in the world, issued the Balfour Declaration. The declaration supported 'the establishment in Palestine of a national home for the Jewish people.' But what was Palestine? — a vague geographical notion which had not been represented as a single administrative unit under the Ottoman Empire. Palestine had no distinct national borders or identity and no independent government. In addition the British had also made sure that the Balfour Declaration recognised the 'civil and religious rights of existing non-Jewish communities in Palestine.' Not long afterwards Jerusalem was 'liberated' by the British Army and with Middle Eastern oil starting to be a matter of significant geopolitical interest (Middle Eastern oil was first discovered in Iran in 1908 and the British Navy converted to oil use in 1911), Britain secured Palestine as a mandated territory in the post-war peace settlement.[79]

Zionists had always viewed Britain as being central to their plans for a Jewish state. Or as the Austrian Jewish founder of modern Zionism, Theodor Herzl, argued:

> England with her possessions in Asia should be most interested in Zionism, for the shortest route to India is by way of Palestine. England's great politicians were the first to recognise the need for colonial expansion

... And so I believe in England the idea of Zionism,
which is a colonial idea, should be easily understood.[80]

The details of the multiple nefarious plots hatched by the British to secure 'British interests' in the Middle East during the 1920s could fill several books (and have). Borders were drawn up and rulers appointed and removed depending upon the competing interests of the various colonial powers (for example, when the French expelled King Faisal from Syria in 1920, the British simply made him the King of Iraq instead). Importantly, under the British Colonial Secretary, Winston Churchill, Palestine was subdivided into two mandates, one of which became Transjordan (now Jordan), while the other remained 'Palestine'. Jewish settlement was prohibited by the British in Transjordan, but permitted in Palestine in keeping with the Balfour Declaration.

In response to all of this Arabs in Palestine started developing a more distinctly Palestinian nationalism. In the same way that the Jewish Zionist national movement was largely a response to chauvinistic European nationalisms and the injustice of anti-Semitism, Palestinian nationalism was largely a response to Zionist settlement and the imposition of the colonial authority of the British Mandate.

During the 1930s the rise of Hitler in Germany was a powerful motivator for renewed Jewish migration to Palestine, especially given that the western powers were less than enthusiastic about accommodating Jewish refugees. Questions of whether Palestine should belong to the Jewish Zionists, to Arab nationalists, or to both, became increasingly vexed and politically contentious, especially in Britain where there was a strong Zionist lobby. For example, in one of his more infamous quotes, in 1937 Winston

Churchill shared his views on Jewish settlement and Arab land rights with the Palestine Royal Commission:

> I do not agree that the dog in a manger has the final right to the manger even though he may have lain there for a very long time. I do not admit that right. I do not admit, for instance, that a great wrong has been done to the Red Indians of America or the black people of Australia. I do not admit that a wrong has been done to these people by the fact that a stronger race, a higher-grade race, a more worldly wise race to put it that way, has come in and taken their place.[81]

By the outbreak of the Second World War in 1939 the Jewish population of Palestine had grown to almost 30 per cent. Despite sectarian violence and tension in Palestine, they were lucky. During the Holocaust six million Jews were rounded up and exterminated in Europe. Jewish Zionists became more convinced than ever of the urgent necessity for a sovereign independent Jewish state. As they lobbied western governments it became increasingly clear that at the end of the war there would be renewed conflict in Palestine. The British government had essentially promised the same territory to two competing, and seemingly irreconcilable, nationalisms — one Jewish and the other Arab Palestinian.

As Jewish diplomats lobbied governments, Zionist terrorists increased their attacks on the British Mandate authorities. In November 1944 they successfully assassinated the British Ambassador in the Middle East. In June 1946 they blew up the King David Hotel in Jerusalem (the centre of the local British military command) killing ninety people, including British soldiers and both Jewish and Arab civilians. Nevertheless, with the end of the war the western powers, including the United States, openly favoured partition and a two-state solution in Palestine. Zionist terrorism did not deter them from this course. It was western support for partition which led the newly formed United Nations to allocate 55 per cent of the land of Palestine to Jewish Zionists, who constituted only 30 per cent of the population in 1947. Due to renewed fighting, the Zionists controlled most of Palestine within a year and prepared to declare statehood. Britain, the Soviet Union, the United States, and the new United Nations all acquiesced to the establishment of the state of Israel on 14 May 1948.

War broke out almost immediately between Jewish Zionists fighting to consolidate their new state, and the Palestinians and other Arab armies fighting to destroy it. There is widespread disagreement amongst rival historians about almost everything that happened from this point onwards. Suffice to say the Jewish Zionists (now called Israelis) won and occupied about 80 per cent of Palestine by the end of the war. By 1949 the United Nations estimated there were 720,000 Palestinian refugees from what were now Israeli-controlled territories. These refugees constituted the overwhelming majority of the Arab population of Palestine and they found sanctuary in makeshift camps constructed on the periphery of Israel, or in neighbouring Arab states. Palestinians refer to the 1948–49 war and exodus as al-Nakba, the catastrophe, and it is from these refugee camps that many of the current generation of suicide bombers (like Wafa Idrees) have come.

Since 1948 Israel has fought numerous wars against its Arab neighbours and has expanded its territory significantly. The most dramatic Israeli victory was during the Six Day War in 1967 when the Israeli armed forces humiliated their enemies and seized

East Jerusalem, all of the Sinai desert and the entire West Bank. They also conquered the strategically vital Golan Heights on the northern border with Syria. Although the Israeli land seizures of 1967 were condemned by the United Nations Security Council, nothing concrete was done to force an Israeli withdrawal, nor to protect the one million Palestinians now living under Israeli military occupation in the West Bank or Gaza.

One result of the 1967 defeat was increased militancy in the exiled Palestinian Liberation Organisation (PLO) which lurched towards terrorist tactics — hijacking planes, assassinations and hostage taking. The Palestinian movement fractured into competing terrorist groups. Most infamously, Palestinian guerillas took nine Israeli athletes hostage at the 1972 Olympics in Munich, a situation which ended in a disastrous gun battle and loss of lives. Palestinian terrorism ensured the issue of Palestine stayed in the headlines, but also thoroughly discredited their cause internationally. During the 1970s the words 'Palestinian' and 'terrorism' became almost synonymous in western minds.

Ironically, another war between Israel and Egypt in 1973 helped foster an eventual peace treaty between the two countries by 1979. Among other things, the Israelis relinquished control of the Sinai. Nor were the Egyptians alone in dealing with the Israelis. Each of the Arab states neighbouring Israel came to terms, one way or another, with the reality of a powerful pro-western, US-backed Israeli state on their border. Each continued to talk of Palestinian liberation but quietly accepted the status quo of Palestinian dispossession.

It was the first intifada that put the issue of Palestine back on the world's agenda. By 1987 an entire angry generation of Palestinians had come of age in the occupied territories who had never known anything but Israeli military rule. They distrusted promises to liberate them by Arab politicians and they resented the western countries for ignoring their plight. The PLO, which still had sentimental influence over Palestinian hearts and minds, was increasingly viewed by this younger generation as being irrelevant to the material reality of life under Israeli occupation. In December 1987 the rage of young Palestinians ignited in Gaza in a popular uprising against Israeli occupation. For the rest of the 1980s the West Bank and Gaza burned. Although Israeli military superiority meant there was no chance of an outright Palestinian victory, the Israelis found themselves incapable of stemming Palestinian resistance.

It was this political and military stalemate which allowed the exiled, corrupt and ageing PLO bureaucrat Yasser Arafat to re-emerge internationally as the official face and voice of Palestinian nationalism. Arafat managed to manoeuvre into a position where he could credibly present himself in front of western news cameras as the spokesman of the disenfranchised masses in the occupied territories. He also ingratiated himself with both local Arab despots and western politicians increasingly nervous about the regional instability caused by seemingly continuous Israeli–Palestinian violence. Increased western pressure on Israel to negotiate with Arafat and the PLO resulted, eventually, in the Oslo peace accords of 1993. The accords created a provisional Palestinian government (the Palestinian Authority) and were supposed to lead to an Israeli withdrawal from the occupied territories as a prelude to the foundation of a Palestinian state. In return the Palestinians had to renounce terrorism and control the rebellion of their own people.

The Palestinian 'occupied territories' which border Israel are, in theory, still made up of two discrete strips of land in Gaza and along the West Bank. In reality they are actually '63 noncontiguous cantons, punctuated by 140 Jewish settlements with their own road network banned to Arabs.' Meanwhile the Palestinians remain under the nominal control of, in the words of Palestinian-American intellectual Edward Said, 'the corrupt Vichy-like Authority of Arafat.' Yasser Arafat's Palestinian Authority rules with the consent of the Israelis who have the power to confine or imprison the people of the occupied territories virtually at will. Poverty and dispossession still define life in occupied territories for Palestinians. According to the World Bank, half the current population of Gaza and the West Bank (nearly two million people) survive on an income of less than US$2 a day and unemployment is over 50 per cent. It is this material deprivation, inequality and political oppression which caused, and has sustained, the second Palestinian intifada which erupted in September 2000.[82]

In March 2002 the Israeli prime minister, Ariel Sharon, explained his strategy regarding the renewed Palestinian intifada and the horrible suicide bombings to reporters outside the Israeli parliament: 'The aim is to increase the number of losses on the other side. Only after they've been battered will we be able to conduct talks.' With Washington on side, Sharon felt no compulsion to mask his disdain for Palestinians or the 1993 Oslo peace accords. Earlier, in January 2003, Sharon publicly regretted he hadn't killed Arafat in 1982 during the Israeli invasion of Lebanon — an invasion during which Sharon was 'indirectly responsible', according to an official Israeli inquiry, for the horrifying massacre of nearly two thousand unarmed civilians (including children) at the Sabra and Shatila refugee camps. Sharon was forced to resign his position as Defence Minister because of the massacre, and there have been more recent attempts to indict him for war crimes in an international court.[83]

No country in the world has supported Israel more — politically, economically and militarily — over the last fifty years than the United States of America. It is widely assumed that this US support is the result of unceasing lobbying on the part of Jewish-Americans. Not withstanding the importance of Jewish votes (and campaign dollars) to American domestic politics, such an argument neglects the fact that the US has a long-term strategic interest in supporting Israel. The United States has always viewed Israel as an important, trusted and stable pro-western ally in the Middle East — a region with resources (namely oil) of crucial importance to America, where Arab politics are seen as being treacherously anti-American and prone to instability. While Israeli and American interests have not always coincided and there have been moments of genuine diplomatic friction, their overall strategic goals in the Middle East are generally convergent.

In this context is it any wonder that most Arabs do not view the United States as a neutral arbitrator in the region? Post-September 11, despite President Bush having a 'vision' for peace in the Middle East, the reality was that Israel's US-supplied missiles, helicopter gunships and fighter planes spoke louder than words. Such solid US support for Israel also rendered the United Nations irrelevant. For instance, UN Secretary General Kofi Annan made a strong public statement on 12 March 2002 against Israel's ongoing 'illegal occupation' of Gaza and the West Bank (in violation of UN Security Council Resolution 242), and called for an end to Israeli 'bombing of civilian areas, the assassinations, the unnecessary use of force, the demolitions and the daily humiliation of ordinary Palestinians.' But Sharon wasn't listening. One of the western world's greatest grievances with Saddam Hussein was his defiance of the United Nations. And yet, despite having wilfully ignored the UN Security Council for more than thirty-five years, there was little substantive US pressure on Israel to end its military occupation of Palestinian lands.[84]

Which is not to say the Israelis were 'winning the war'. Gun battles and suicide bombings continued. More people were dying on both sides but especially worrying from the Israeli perspective was the fact that the 'death ratio' was closing. The *New York Times* pointed out that during the first seventeen months of the first intifada, which started in 1987, roughly one Israeli died for every twenty-five Palestinians. This was because in 1987 Palestinians armed with stones usually fought heavily armed Israeli soldiers in the streets. However, by March 2002, after seventeen months of the second intifada, 'the overall ratio' killed had 'steadily narrowed to about one to three' due to the fact that Palestinian militants were now better armed and had proved willing to blow themselves up in order to inflict casualties. Thirty-one Israeli soldiers were killed during February and March of 2002 — virtually unthinkable a decade before. During the first seventeen months of the first intifada only seventeen Israelis died as compared to 424 Palestinians. During the first seventeen months of the second intifada 340 Israelis and over one thousand Palestinians were killed. Ariel Sharon's strategy for Israeli 'security' was not only morally flawed, it wasn't even working within its own twisted military logic.[85]

Then, in a final paroxysm during April 2002, Sharon ordered an all out assault on the West Bank. Bulldozers and tanks were driven through refugee camps in pursuit of 'terrorists'. When the dust settled the *Guardian Weekly* reported that:

> ... the heart of the Jenin refugee camp was a silent wasteland, permeated with the stench of rotting

corpses and cordite. The evidence of lives interrupted was everywhere ... The scale is almost beyond imagination: a vast expanse of rubble and mangled iron rods, surrounded by the gaping carcasses of shattered homes.[86]

The United Nations Middle East envoy, visiting the remains of the flattened section of the refugee camp, described the destruction of Jenin as 'horrific beyond belief'. Despite the stench of death at Jenin, President Bush still publicly declared Sharon to be 'a man of peace'. Not surprisingly, the Palestinian suicide bombings continued, proving that people with nothing have nothing to lose. With Palestinian–Israeli relations at an all time low, in May 2002 opinion polls revealed that 40 per cent of Israelis now supported the potential forced 'transfer' (that is, expulsion) of the entire Palestinian population from the West Bank and Gaza.[87]

There were, however, marginal moments of hope. In October 2000 Noam Kuzal was one of the first Israeli military conscripts to refuse to serve in the occupied territories. He was jailed briefly and then discharged from the Israeli Army. By February 2002 he had been joined by 400 other Israelis, including 187 *refusenik* reservist officers. The officers publicly declared their opposition in a petition published in Israeli newspapers in early February, proclaiming, 'We will not continue to fight beyond the green line [the pre-1967 border] in order to rule, expel, destroy, blockade, assassinate, starve and humiliate an entire people.' This was followed by another petition, signed by 2795 civilians, supporting the refuseniks and with a rally by 5000 people in Tel Aviv. Leaflets at the rally called on Israeli soldiers to refuse to serve in the West Bank and Gaza.[88]

Despite the small numbers of people involved the petition caused a major debate in Israeli society. It also undermined the fiction in the West and throughout the Arab world that all Israelis support their army's occupation, in defiance of the United Nations, of Palestinian lands. Arguably, the refusenik phenomenon can only weaken the ability of a Jew-hater like Osama bin Laden to present himself as a champion of the Palestinian cause. It could also potentially politically weaken Hamas, al-Aqsa Martyrs and Islamic Jihad, who organise the bulk of the Palestinian suicide bombings, in a way that air strikes and assassinations have not. The emergence of the refuseniks should therefore strengthen the hopes of those who believe that a just solution to the Israel/Palestine conflict can be found. However, whether it will result in tangible improvements on the ground, and save lives, will depend not only on the tremendous courage of ordinary Israelis and Palestinians, but upon the willingness of the western world to support the refuseniks against both the Yasser Arafats *and* the Ariel Sharons of the world.

The war in the occupied territories has corrupted Israel's soul and has so hardened Palestinian hearts that a twenty-seven year old volunteer nurse would blow herself to pieces in the hope she might inflict suffering on ordinary Israelis. The next steps towards peace must involve the West refusing to continue funding the Israeli Army's attempt to strangle the Palestinian desire to be free. Otherwise, to borrow the words of one refusenik:

> We are the Chinese young man standing in front of the tank. And you? If you are nowhere to be seen, you are probably inside the tank, advising the driver.[89]

It is nearly four years since the second intifada began and there seems little hope of genuine peace between Palestinians and Israelis in the near future. The construction of a massive 'security fence' by the Israeli government — which will permanently partition Israel and the occupied territories — evoked memories of both the Berlin Wall and apartheid. Hopelessness continues to breed reciprocal violence and hate. Although the Israeli government has committed itself, in theory, to President Bush's 'road map to peace', their 'vision' of a Palestinian state (one of the essential outcomes of the road map) is hardly going to satisfy the Palestinian desire for national self-determination. Or as Ariel Sharon explained in December 2002:

> This Palestinian state will be completely demilitarised.
> It will be allowed to maintain lightly armed police and
> interior forces to ensure civil order. Israel will continue
> to control all entries and exits to the Palestinian state,
> will command its airspace, and not allow it to form
> alliances with Israel's enemies.[90]

Or in other words, this Palestinian state will be a state in name only — it will have no army, and it will not control its own borders. Its armed police will 'ensure civil order', a polite way of saying they will be expected to repress their own people should the need arise. This will be a vassal state.

In response to this dismal vision, the political centre of gravity in occupied Palestine has shifted more and more towards the suicide bombers of Hamas and Islamic Jihad. On the Israeli side, the Sharon government declared to the world that it was contemplating exiling or killing Yasser Arafat. On 10 September 2003, the day before global 9/11 commemorations regarding the horror of terrorism, the influential *Jerusalem Post* editorialised *in favour* of a rolling series of assassinations and urged the government not to get squeamish about the deaths of innocent Palestinian civilians:

> We must kill as many of the Hamas and Islamic Jihad leaders as possible, as quickly as possible, while minimising collateral damage, but not letting that damage stop us. And we must kill Yasser Arafat, because the world leaves us no alternative.

Washington declared its opposition to the plan, but did not publicly denounce the Israelis as 'state sponsors of terrorism' or threaten immediate and crippling sanctions if the Israelis carried out the assassination threat. Israel remains central to the United States' vision of a pro-western, post-Saddam Middle East. Had the UN-recognised Palestinian Authority in the occupied territories similarly declared that it was planning to assassinate Ariel Sharon, the US attitude would have undoubtedly been different.

To many Israelis the Palestinians are now, simply, the enemy. To the western world the Palestinians have similarly ceased to be people with minds, hearts and hopes of their own. To us they are 'terrorists' and 'suicide bombers'. They are defined and judged by the violent terror of Hamas and Islamic Jihad, the hideous consequences of which we watch on television, or by the bureaucratic antics of Yasser Arafat. We know very little about Palestinian life, culture and history. The official response in the West to the endless suicide bombs and Israeli assassinations (innocent civilians making up the majority of victims in both cases) has been dismal. Despondency and diatribe have almost entirely replaced informed public debate.

For example, in distant Australia during November 2002 a Labor backbencher in the Federal parliament, Julia Irwin MP, put forward a motion calling on the Australian parliament to note Israel's ongoing occupation of the West Bank and Gaza in violation of UN Security Council Resolution 242 of 1967. While recognising Israel's 'right to exist', Irwin's motion called for a UN peacekeeping force to be sent to the occupied territories. In Irwin's words, 'When the world community looks at the ongoing tragedy in the Middle East, is it too much to ask that the United Nations take a leading role in bringing peace to that troubled region, after all, Israel is a creation of the United Nations.' In response Irwin was attacked by Labor and Liberal MPs and accused of 'destroying bipartisanship over Israel' in the Australian parliament. Parliamentary reporters described 'fiery scenes' in the debating chamber, with Irwin being accused of pandering to Muslim constituents as well as leading an anti-Israeli alliance of the 'extreme left', 'Bolsheviks' and the 'unprincipled right' inside the Labor Party. Irwin later commented that:

> While I was disappointed that those opposing my motion in the debate chose to ignore the issues and make a personal attack on me instead, I do feel that we have broken the ice. For the first time in half a century the taboo on discussing Israel and Middle East peace in the Australian Parliament has been lifted.[91]

Regrettably, Irwin's motion sank almost without trace and a stifling pessimistic conformity returned to the Australian parliament as the Palestinian suicide bombings and Israeli assassinations increased during 2003. Thankfully, however, the level of public debate in Israel and Palestine itself, where the risks and consequences were much greater, did not dissipate.

On 25 September 2003, two weeks after the second anniversary of 9/11 and in response to the Israeli Army's ongoing campaign of assassinations of leading Palestinian militants, it was reported that twenty-seven Israeli Air Force pilots had signed a letter pledging not to participate in 'illegal and immoral' air strikes against civilian areas in the Palestinian occupied territories. This was partly in response to reports that 123 Palestinians had already been killed in attempted assassinations launched by the Israeli Air Force, with eighty-four of the dead (70 per cent) being civilian 'bystanders'. In one particularly notorious case, an Israeli F-16 fighter dropped a one-tonne bomb on a house where a senior Hamas official was living. The bomb not only killed the Hamas leader, but also ended the lives of fourteen civilians, including women and children. Israeli human rights organisation B'Tselem argued that such activities were illegal under international law and constituted 'war crimes under Article 147 of the Fourth Geneva Convention and Article 85 of the 1977 Additional Protocol to the Geneva Convention.'[92]

Significantly, the Israeli media reported that one of the twenty-seven air force refuseniks was Yiftah Spector, a brigadier general and famous Israeli air force hero who had participated in the bombing of a nuclear reactor in Iraq during 1981. This brought the number of Israeli draftees, reservists and serving soldiers who were refusing to serve in the occupied territories up to 1200. Not surprisingly, the pilots were denounced as traitors by the Israeli government and most of the Israeli press.[93]

In the occupied territories meanwhile there was a cautious response to the bravery of the refusenik pilots. Khamees al-Alawi, a shopkeeper whose nephew had recently been shot and killed by the Israeli Army, described the pilots' letter as a 'noble effort'.

Interestingly, what Al-Jazeera described as 'a prominent member of Hamas,' also described the refuseniks' action as 'admirable' and commented that, 'Frankly, if they even tried to do this in any Arab country, they'd execute them before they got the chance.'[94]

The brave and hopeful few continue to struggle to have their voices heard over the fearsome roar of Hamas suicide bombers and Israeli fighter jets. They know that without justice there can be no peace.

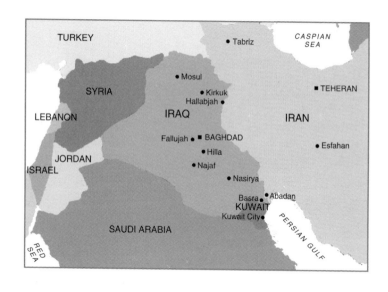

Iran and Iraq

Poison Gas and Diplomacy: Iraq, Iran and the United States

There are things we are not supposed to mention about the United States led invasion and occupation of Iraq.[95] Like the fact that Australian troops were participants in the most unpopular war in modern history. Even before a single shot was fired an estimated eight million people on five continents protested over the weekend of 15–16 February 2003. And after the 'Coalition of the Willing' invaded on 21 March, literally millions more people around the world took to the streets in opposition to the war.[96] The Vietnam War was never this immediately and globally unpopular. Not even after years of napalm, not after My Lai, not ever.

While the initial stage of the invasion, with tanks racing across the desert, facilitated a partial boost in approval of the 'support our troops' variety in the US, Britain and Australia, even this was quickly undermined by the growing death toll of Iraqi civilians, as well as British and American soldiers. The shocking and awful missile barrage of Iraq's cities and the ongoing 'pockets of resistance', which proved much deeper than anyone imagined, did not help either. Vietnam must have haunted the dreams of US President George W Bush and Defence Secretary Donald

Rumsfeld back in Washington. When Bush's father oversaw the 1991 Gulf War he said it shattered forever America's 'Vietnam Syndrome'. What then, do we make of the quagmire that his son has now immersed America in?

I'm old enough to remember when Saddam Hussein was America's comrade in arms. I lived in America between 1979 and 1983. I recall the yellow ribbons we tied around trees at my school — a ribbon a day, for each of the 444 days the American hostages remained prisoners of fanatical Muslim students in Teheran. Old enough to recall when Iran's Ayatollah Khomeini was public enemy number one. Old enough to remember learning that we (meaning the Americans and I, a foreigner) had allies in the Middle East and that one of the greatest of these was the nation of Iraq whose armies were marching against the evil Iranians.

When Iraq invaded Iran in 1980 Iraqi President Saddam Hussein was considered a powerful potential ally in a treacherous region. His brutal regime was secular and his Ba'ath Party had wiped out the Iraqi Communist Party. Like the Americans, Saddam hated and feared Iran's Islamic revolution. He seemed like the kind of guy Washington could do business with. The fact that Saddam's regime brutalised and tortured its own people was a peripheral matter. Bigger issues of geopolitics and American hostages were at stake. In 1982 President Reagan removed Iraq from the US State Department's list of states that supported terrorism.

In supporting Saddam Hussein's regime the US government was sticking with its Cold War policy of finding pliable military strongmen, no matter how noxious, throughout the Third World, who could be relied upon to act in 'American interests'. The Americans were not alone in this. In November 1969 the British Embassy in Baghdad described Saddam as 'a presentable young man' whose Ba'athist star was on the rise. A month later the

British ambassador in Baghdad, reporting on a meeting with Saddam, described his 'engaging smile' and commented that 'I should judge him, young as he is, to be a formidable, single-minded and hard-headed member of the Ba'athist hierarchy, but one with whom, if only one could see more of him, it would be possible to do business.'[97]

By the middle of the 1970s Saddam was positioning himself to take total control of Iraq's government. On 28 April 1975 US Secretary of State Henry Kissinger met with his policy advisers to discuss the Middle East. One of his senior staff offered an analysis of Saddam Hussein:

> Hussein is a rather remarkable person. We have to look more closely into his background ... He's the Vice President of the Command Council, but he is running the show; and he's a very ruthless and — very recently, obviously — pragmatic, intelligent power. I think we're going to see Iraq playing more of a role in the area than it has for many years.[98]

Throughout the Iran–Iraq War from 1980 to 1988 America was openly with Saddam Hussein against Iran. The links between Washington and Baghdad extended to the Americans sharing sensitive satellite intelligence with the Iraqi Army so they could wage war on Iran more effectively. The US Navy provided armed escorts for Iraqi oil tankers. And in December 1983 US President Ronald Reagan even sent a special envoy — a certain Mr Donald Rumsfeld — to meet Saddam Hussein and establish a closer relationship with the Iraqi dictator. Rumsfeld and Saddam were photographed shaking hands and smiling in a cordial diplomatic meeting that was filmed for Iraqi national television. Not that you'll hear Rumsfeld mention this in public any more. These days Rumsfeld works for President George W Bush as Secretary of Defence. He speaks continually of Iraq's elusive 'Weapons of Mass Destruction' and Saddam's appalling human rights record. The lines between trusted ally and evil tyrant were apparently a lot less clear in 1983 than they are today.

President George W Bush, in arguing in favour of an invasion of Iraq, sometimes recalled Iraq's use of chemical weapons against the Kurds in the north of the country, like the appalling incident in March 1988 when Iraqi forces gassed over four thousand Kurds in Halabja. Bush called this an act of attempted genocide. The problem was that none of it was news. The American State Department and the CIA were aware of the Iraqi military's use of chemical weapons throughout the 1980s while Iraq was a US ally. On 5 March 1984, for example, the US State Department issued a public statement criticising Iraqi use of chemical weapons against Iranian soldiers. Behind the scenes, however, US diplomats implied to the Iraqis that the statement was something of a formality.

Two days after the release of the State Department's statement on chemical weapon use, senior US and Iraqi diplomats met in Baghdad. The confidential US cable about this meeting on 7 March 1984 reported that the Iraqi Under Secretary of Foreign Affairs, Ismet Kittani, 'noted the alleged chemical use had been on Iraqi soil and he compared it to use of nuclear weapons to shorten the war with Japan.' (Had Kittani known how well Winston Churchill was still regarded in American political circles, he might also have quoted the former British prime minister: 'I do not understand this squeamishness about the use of gas. I am strongly in favour of using poisoned gas against uncivilised tribes.'[99] Churchill was referring to the potential use of chemical weapons by the British against the Kurds in 1919.) Less than two weeks later Kittani was in Washington where he met with the US Undersecretary of State Lawrence Eagleburger. According to a classified US cable reporting on this meeting:

> The main message of the US side: our condemnation of Iraqi CW [chemical weapon] use was made as part of strong US commitment to long standing policy, and not as a pro-Iranian/anti-Iraqi gesture. Our desires and our actions to prevent an Iranian victory and to continue the progress of our bilateral relations remain undiminished.[100]

At this same meeting Kittani also thanked the Americans for an 'apology' from one US official regarding the attempts by some within the US Congress to 're-impose anti-terrorism controls on exports to Iraq.'

A few days later on 20 March 1984 US intelligence sources reported that they had 'incontrovertible evidence that Iraq has used nerve gas in its war with Iran and has almost finished extensive site for mass-producing the lethal chemical agent.' And yet even this did not stop the United States from establishing full diplomatic ties with Iraq in November that year. Nor did it stop the United States from continuing to support Saddam Hussein's war against Iran. Indeed, when the US Senate and the United Nations attempted to constrain Iraq, the Reagan administration intervened. In March 1986, for example, the President of the UN Security Council proposed a declaration against Iraq's use of chemical weapons. The United States voted against the declaration while Britain and Australia abstained.[101]

The Iran–Iraq war continued. As did the trade, according to a 1994 US Senate Committee Report, in materials used in manufacturing chemical weapons. From 1985 to 1989 about a dozen US companies were involved in exporting biological agents to the Iraqis, assisting them in making, among other things, deadly anthrax. The US Department of Commerce licensed this trade.[102] That is, until the end of both the Iran–Iraq War and the Cold War altered the structure of allegiance in the Middle East.

The Iran–Iraq War ground on until 1988, by which time approximately 105,000 Iraqis and 262,000 Iranians had been killed. It is now a matter of public record that the Reagan administration secretly traded weapons for hostages with the Iranians in the early 1980s. What was largely overlooked in the resulting 'Iran–Contra Scandal' however, was the fact that Washington had therefore militarily supported both sides of the Iran–Iraq war, possibly prolonging the killing. Over one million people had been wounded or killed by the time the war ended.

This is only a small part of the history not mentioned on CNN. And certainly not on Fox News where the disgraced cold warrior Oliver North, the Pentagon's 'fall guy' during the Iran–Contra Scandal (in which the US government was also discovered lying to its own Congress about its support for pro-US terrorism in Latin America), now works as a frontline reporter.

Finally, it is also worth remembering that until the mid-1970s the United States was itself a major possessor of chemical and biological 'weapons of mass destruction'. The 1925 Geneva Protocol banning chemical weapons was quickly ratified by several countries whose armies had suffered massive poison gas attacks during the First World War — France (1926), Belgium (1928), Germany (1929) and Britain (1930). Australia and New Zealand 'acceded to' the Protocol in 1930 and by the 1960s more than eighty countries had signed up to the international ban on chemical weapons. The United States did not do so until 1975, and when it finally got around to destroying its deadly inventory of chemical weapons it was discovered, among other things, that the US had stockpiled 23,000 cartridges of botulinum toxin and 200 pounds of deadly anthrax. Moreover, a later US government inquiry discovered that the CIA kept a secret supply of biological and chemical weapons (in violation of a US Presidential order of 1969) for use in potential political assassinations (Fidel Castro was one intended target). The United States also continued a US$10 million a year program in research and development of chemical and biological weapons for 'defensive purposes', although there has been no suggestion that the United Nations might want to send arms inspectors to the White House and Pentagon to verify (as they insisted they be allowed to do in Iraq) that the US military or CIA is still not secretly producing and hiding chemical weapons for potential offensive use.[103]

Interestingly, in 1969 when US President Richard Nixon was debating whether to publicly announce that the United States was halting its chemical and biological weapons program, one of his key scientific advisers wrote to National Security Adviser Henry Kissinger commenting that:

> If the President should decide to forgo offensive BW [Biological Weapons] as a policy, the timing and the phrasing of a public announcement will be of crucial importance insofar as public reaction, domestic and international, is concerned. There is a large reservoir of scepticism, cynicism, and incredulity that has developed as a result of our past lack of policy and the inconsistency of past statements in this area.[104]

These words are as relevant today as they were thirty-five years ago.

Weapons of Mass Destruction
— Who's Got Them?

	Nuclear weapons	Chemical/ biological weapons	Medium/ long range missiles	$ spent per person on military	% GDP spent on military **	% popn below poverty line
USA	√	√	√	$986	3.2	13
Israel	√	√	√	$1,487	8.7	18
Pakistan	√	√	√	$17	4.6	35
China	√	√	√	$15	4.3	10
Russia	√	√	√	N/A	N/A	40
UK	√	?*	√	$530	2.3	17
North Korea	?	√	√	$230	34	N/A
Iran	?	√	√	$145	3.1	53
Libya	X	√	√	$242	3.9	N/A
Syria	X	√	√	$53	5.9	20
South Korea	X	√	√	$264	2.8	4
Egypt	X	√	√	$57	4.1	23
Iraq	X	X	√	$54	N/A	N/A
Saudi Arabia	X	X	√	$778	13	N/A
Cuba	X	X	X	N/A	4	N/A
Australia	X	X	X	$475	2.9	13

*   Some countries, like Britain, deny having 'offensive' chemical weapons but are known to have chemical and biological weapons 'research facilities'.

**   Annual spending based on the most up-to-date figures available.

N/A Figures not available.

All figures are in US dollars. Some percentages have been rounded.

(Sources: Human Rights Watch, Federation of American Scientists, *CIA World Fact Book*, 2002, 2003)

The Big Picture?
Terrorism, Imperialism and the Iraq War

On a lonely road about ten kilometres east of Baghdad during the American led invasion of Iraq, a group of US Marines established a roadblock and began stopping civilian cars.[105] One vehicle attempting to leave Baghdad (then still under Saddam Hussein's tenuous control and under attack from US air strikes) failed to stop. The US Marines shouted at the driver in English and fired warning shots. The vehicle accelerated. The Marines, suspecting a suicide bomber, opened fire.

When the bullet-riddled vehicle finally halted the US Marines found no fanatical bomber inside. Instead they found three dead adult civilians, three dead children and a fifteen year old boy called Omar. Among the dead were two of Omar's sisters, a brother, his uncle, and both his parents. The children were aged three, six and ten. Omar's baby brother, Ali, miraculously survived despite being shot in the face. Omar was orphaned and he was photographed by a journalist standing over the body of his dead father crying, his pants soaked with blood, as a US Marine tried to lead him away from the scene of horror. (According to one report, some US Marines also sat at the side of the road weeping.)[106]

It occurred to me when I read about what happened to Omar and his family, that if Omar could ask US President George W Bush why his parents, his sisters, his brother and his uncle died on some dusty road outside Baghdad, then President Bush would probably reply that such deaths were tragic, but that the car should have stopped and that civilian deaths are a regrettable but necessary price to pay in the war on terror. President Bush would probably also say that the death of Omar's family tells us little about what is happening in Iraq and in the world today. It's a personal tragedy, but it is *not* part of the 'big picture'. I suspect Omar wouldn't see it that way.

'Imperialism' is a dirty word. It conjures up images of the nineteenth century — of the British Empire in India and Africa. Of the 'white man's burden'. Of the colonial arrogance with which Europeans sought to uplift the backward portion of humanity (meaning everyone not originally from Western Europe) via the three Cs — Christianity, commerce and civilisation. Certainly, we don't use the word empire when discussing the United States, at least not on CNN or in parliament in Canberra. The reason we don't use the words 'imperialism' and 'United States' in the same sentence is not just because it would be rude, or un-academic, but because such usage is so at odds with the way most Australians, along with America's own citizens, have been taught to think of the Great Republic.

The United States was, of course, founded in 1776 in an armed democratic revolution *against* imperialism. Moreover, for at least the first century of its history the United States saw itself as the natural and instinctive ally of any country fighting for liberation from tyranny. Truth, Justice and the American way. Life, liberty and the pursuit of happiness. These were the advertising slogans of the American republic — not empire. At a time when even the most backward European principality held imperial ambitions, America clung tenaciously to its 'isolationism' in foreign affairs.

Thomas Jefferson, the author of the US Declaration of Independence, famously called for the United States to avoid 'entangling alliances' and reckless overseas military adventures. Another former US President, John Quincy Adams, warned against going 'abroad, in search of monsters to destroy.' The great hearts and minds of the early American republic were vocal opponents of empire. However, by the 1890s American politicians were openly flirting with imperial ambition. The US government's military interventions in Cuba and the Philippines are two early cases in point. And yet the US assiduously avoided any attempt to formalise a direct imperial relationship between core and periphery. Even though the rise of the US to the status of global superpower at the end of the Second World War — and self-appointed defender of democracy and capitalism from the onslaught of godless communism — represented a whole new departure in the exercise of *Pax Americana*, empire remained an ideology to be formally avoided.

Until now there have been polite conventions which have constrained Washington and discouraged the outright flaunting of naked imperial might. Even in Vietnam the US made sure to rule, and fight, with the assistance and consent of local proxies. However, as Jonathan Freedland wrote in the *Guardian Weekly* at the time of the US-led invasion of Iraq, President Bush 'is seeking, as an unashamed objective, to get into the empire business, aiming to rule post-Saddam Iraq directly through an American governor-general, the retired soldier Jay Garner. This is a form of foreign rule so direct we have not seen its like since the last days of the British Empire.' Despite journalistic flourishes the plan did have a whiff of the old British viceroy about it.[107]

There were other worrying signs. Why, for instance, did the Americans allow the Iraqi National Museum to be looted and ransacked — leaving its priceless collection of artefacts from the past 5000 years of civilisation unprotected — while the Iraqi Ministry of Oil was guarded by Marines as soon as US tanks rolled into Baghdad? An Iraqi archaeologist, surveying the destroyed museum, told a western reporter: 'A country's identity, its value and civilisation resides in its history. If a country's civilisation is looted, as ours has been here, its history ends. Please tell this to President Bush. Please remind him that he promised to liberate the Iraqi people, but that this is not a liberation, this is a humiliation.'[108]

The unprecedented US military presence in so many dark corners of the globe also hints at empire. One is reminded — and the public rhetoric of President Bush in his 'clash of civilisations' speech after 9/11 reinforced this image — of Roman forts marking out the frontier between the delights, wealth and majesty of the Roman world, and the world of the unwashed heathen *barbari* (the barbarians). There are currently 98,000 US soldiers in Europe, including 56,000 stationed in Germany (a legacy of the Second World War). There are more than 12,000 US soldiers in Italy and 9000 in Britain. There are 7000 US soldiers in the Balkans. There are still 18,000 US soldiers in Japan and 35,000 in South Korea guarding the border with the 'Axis of Evil' power, North Korea. There are approximately 10,000 US soldiers still fighting in Afghanistan, 130,000 in Iraq and several hundred in the Philippines. Saudi Arabia and Kuwait still have thousands of US soldiers within their borders. Not to mention Diego Garcia, Australia and other irrelevant territories where the US currently has small numbers of soldiers, technicians or 'advisers'. In fact the

US has more soldiers stationed overseas than most countries have stationed at home; more than 350,000 by some estimates.

According to the Pentagon's own figures the US military rents 702 overseas bases in 130 countries in addition to its six thousand military bases on US soil.[109] On the seas there are also currently thirteen 'naval task groups' built around massive aircraft carriers that form virtual floating US military bases (or cities) encircling the globe. The largest aircraft carriers, like the USS *Abraham Lincoln,* have about five thousand crew aboard and are supported by destroyers and nuclear submarines that follow them everywhere. In short, the US has a military presence in every major region of the world (on land and sea) protecting and projecting its interests.

On 11 September 2001 President Bush explained the attacks on the World Trade Center and Pentagon by saying that 'America was targeted for attack because we're the brightest beacon for freedom and opportunity in the world.' Bush's words were in keeping with the way most Americans see their country. Opposition to America's dominance over global trade and finance is perceived by many Americans to be either a case of jealousy or bad manners on behalf of foreigners, extremists or (in the case of those who come from their own country) misinformed liberals and unreformed hippies. Rejecting claims that the US dominates global politics, in June 2002 President George W Bush delivered a speech at the military academy of West Point where he told graduates, 'America has no empire to extend or utopia to establish.'[110]

However, we are currently witnessing the most important reconstruction of power and international relations since the collapse of communism in 1989. As Chalmers Johnson has argued, what is distinctive about modern empires is that they 'normally lie concealed beneath some ideological or juridical concept — commonwealth, alliance, free world, the West, the Communist bloc — that disguises the actual relationships among its members.'[111] All empires rely on both consent and the threat of force to rule effectively. This is as true of the United States now as it was of the relationship between the Soviet Union and its satellites before the collapse of 1989. The current Bush administration has abandoned the post-1945 polite fiction of the 'free world' operating as an international community of democratic equals. The modus operandi of American power has altered. Sole superpowers, like dominant empires, expect obedience. Especially when they are wounded and angry.

The US-led invasion and occupation of Iraq will be popularly remembered for the televised toppling of statues of Saddam Hussein in Baghdad. It should be remembered instead for the image of poor Omar standing at the side of a dusty road, splattered with his dead parents' blood, orphaned so that the United States government can assert its will on Iraq and re-create the world as it sees fit.

Iraq and the Ghosts of Vietnam

I only met Sergio Vieira de Mello once. It was July 2001 when he attended the opening of a new church in the small East Timorese village where I was staying. At the time he was the United Nations' top man in East Timor and he flew in by military helicopter to attend mass. The whole village turned out to get a glimpse of the world community's most powerful representative on the tiny half-island as he walked calmly to an official ceremony. Later on we shook hands and passed a few bland pleasantries.[112]

When it was announced that Mr Vieira de Mello was the most senior official killed in the August 2003 suicide bombing of the UN headquarters in Baghdad, I remembered the two things which had most surprised me about him in 2001. Firstly, in the midst of the dirt and poverty of East Timor he appeared casually crisp and debonair. Secondly, I was genuinely surprised by the extent to which José Ramos Horta and other leading East Timorese politicians deferred to him. This was not just a question of power. Vieira de Mello was admired and respected both inside and outside the United Nations.

Sergio Vieira de Mello's death, along with those of twenty other UN workers in Baghdad, probably crippled what remaining hope still existed in Washington that the Iraq War really ended when President Bush proclaimed it over on 1 May 2003. On that day Bush made a triumphant appearance on the deck of the US aircraft carrier *Abraham Lincoln*, working the *Top Gun* imagery for all it was worth in his pilot's jumpsuit, and declared that 'combat operations' in Iraq had ceased. A banner proclaimed, 'Mission Accomplished'. Several hundred US soldiers have been killed since then. Indeed, by the end of 2003 a total of 513 US soldiers had been killed, more than in any other year since 1972 when 640 US military personnel were killed in Vietnam. And still the Americans keep desperately clutching at straws — Iraqi resistance will end with the death of Uday and Qusay Hussein, it will end now that Saddam has been captured, it will end when they wipe out the few remaining supporters of the old regime.

It will not end. American soldiers will continue to die in Iraq as long as the US continues to occupy the country. They will die because they are seen as the most recent invaders of Iraq in an ancient history of conquest and resistance that stretches back across the rise and fall of several civilisations. They will die because they are viewed by many Iraqis as armed colonisers, not as liberators. They will die because the US has so far mightily failed to deliver on its pre-invasion promise to bring peace, prosperity and democracy to Iraq. The longer they stay, the more bitter the Iraqi resistance to American occupation will become.

One of the crucial things that the August 2003 suicide bombing of the UN headquarters in Baghdad revealed is the difference of perception between 'the West' and 'the rest' regarding the United Nations. To the American, British and Australian governments the UN was an impediment to 'regime change' in Iraq. The UN Security Council refused to give its blessing to a unilateral strike by the United States and leading

UN figures were critical of the relentless US drive to war. UN arms inspectors publicly challenged US and British claims that Iraq possessed extensive weapons of mass destruction that could be deployed at forty-five minutes notice. As a result, the 'blue helmets' were regarded as libertarian hand-wringers in Washington and as an obstacle to making the world a better place post-9/11. Viewed from this perspective, the bombing of the UN's Baghdad headquarters was an unprovoked terrorist attack on innocent humanitarian aid workers.

In many Islamic countries, meanwhile, the United Nations is viewed as little more than an appendage of US foreign policy. It should be recalled that it was under the aegis of the UN that the Gulf War against Iraq was fought in 1991; that the country was divided with its 'No Fly Zones' and Kurdish autonomous region; and that the sanctions, arms inspections and 'Oil for Food' programs were managed. To literally millions of people in the Arab world and beyond, the United Nations is not a neutral humanitarian organisation but a key participant in the US-led campaign against Iraq. For these people the Baghdad suicide bombing was a blow struck against sanctions, humiliation and acquiescence to the western occupation of an Arab country.

Writing in the *West Australian* at the time of the US-led invasion of Iraq, I argued that the ghosts of Vietnam would haunt Washington. I was criticised by some readers for my defeatism. And yet, watching US Secretary of Defence Donald Rumsfeld and his polished generals at a press conference held after the UN suicide bombing as they fielded questions regarding a potential increase in the number of US ground forces in Iraq, one couldn't help but think that the scenario was faintly reminiscent. Already people were wondering how many more US soldiers it would take before Iraq was pacified. US Senator John McCain, a Republican, was actually in Baghdad on the day the UN building was bombed. In an interview broadcast on national television in America, and reported in the influential *New York Times*, he called for another division of about 18,000 men to be sent to Iraq immediately to join the 130,000 US soldiers already in the country. He commented that, 'Time is not on our side.'[113] During the Vietnam War, with its escalating enemy 'body counts' and US body-bags, the same issues of spiralling troop levels and lost lives were politically contentious and publicly divisive.

Similarly, US popular support for the continuing occupation of Iraq is weakening, along with the morale of the soldiers. On 16 July 2003 'Good Morning America' broadcast a controversial interview with soldiers from the US Third Infantry Division. The soldiers spoke of their disappointment at becoming an occupation force. One called for Donald Rumsfeld's resignation. Another, a sergeant, said that US soldiers were 'mentally and physically exhausted to the point that some hoped they would get wounded so they could go home.' According to *Newsweek*'s polling, 69 per cent of Americans were concerned that the US was becoming bogged down in Iraq. The same poll revealed that 38 per cent of Americans believed the war in Iraq had actually increased Al-Qaida's power in the world. *Newsweek* also reported that one twenty-one year old private serving in Iraq had told them that on his good days he felt the occupation might be helping ordinary Iraqis, but that there 'aren't many good days.' So how did he feel on the bad days? 'I feel like getting my machine gun and opening up on every one of them.' Again, the ghosts of Vietnam.[114]

If George W Bush is wondering about the future of his occupation of Iraq he only needs to look back to the Vietnam War. Only this time the resistance to US occupation is fuelled by nationalism and Islam rather than nationalism and communism. It scarcely matters how many more US troops he sends — Iraqi resistance will not end because it is created by the humiliations and disappointments associated with occupation itself. This war, which was allegedly fought to prevent Iraq from becoming a terrorist training camp, has actually succeeded in turning it into one. Iraq is now a nation where foreign Islamic extremists are able to infiltrate across borders to come spill 'Crusader blood' (to quote the statement claiming responsibility for the UN bomb attack). It is a nation where legitimate domestic grievances can easily feed into illegitimate acts of terrorism like the suicide bombing which killed Sergio Vieira de Mello and his UN co-workers.

President Bush's statement that the attack on the UN was the work of 'enemies of the civilised world' does nothing to bridge the political gulf between so many Iraqi people and their US occupiers.[115] Even under Saddam Hussein's dictatorship people still had some semblance of personal security (as long as they did not criticise the regime) and access to basic services (water, electricity, etc.). Many Iraqis are now asking what the point is of liberation from Saddam if they are to suffer rampant lawlessness, the collapse of essential services, and an occupying army which is rapidly coming to the conclusion (as in Vietnam) that every civilian is a potential enemy or suicide bomber. The resulting cycle of violence will further poison both American and Iraqi hearts and minds.

As I am writing this (May 2004) the first anniversary has just passed of US President George W Bush's appearance on the deck of the USS *Abraham Lincoln* where he posed in front of a banner proclaiming 'Mission Accomplished' and declared the war in Iraq to be over. No such heady scenes of martial triumph this year. Despite the relentless optimism (or denialism) of the White House in continually claiming that the situation in Iraq is improving, the US occupation forces have just suffered their worst month of violence ever. A total of 134 US soldiers were killed and 900 wounded in Iraq during April 2004. Indeed, more US troops were killed or wounded in Iraq last month than during the initial invasion when they were fighting an Iraqi army equipped (in theory) with heavy artillery, anti-aircraft batteries, missiles, tanks and still undiscovered 'weapons of mass destruction'. In total, 722 American soldiers have died in Iraq since the invasion began last March.[116]

As I write, the siege of Fallujah continues into its fifth week. Hundreds of Iraqi civilians have been killed as US Marines attempt to batter the town of 300,000 people into submission. Outside Fallujah western civilian hostages have been executed and daily ambushes and bomb attacks on the occupation forces continue. Spain has announced that all its troops will be withdrawn from Iraq by the end of the month and fifty-two former British diplomats have written to Tony Blair urging him to abandon his support for the United States' policies in the Middle East. These policies, they claim, are 'doomed to failure.' Honduras, Nicaragua and Dominican Republic have announced they will join Spain in beating a hasty retreat from Iraq. Other countries with small military contingents have also indicated they may leave. Australia alone, via John Howard, has said it would be willing to potentially increase its 'modest' troop commitment in Iraq. The 'deputy sheriff' has, alongside Tony Blair, remained loyal to the cause even when all Bush's other friends in the 'Coalition of the Willing' appear to be deserting him.[117]

The deserters are not alone. In Iraq a battalion of the new US-funded Iraqi Army mutinied last month when it was ordered to move to Fallujah and take part in US-led operations there. In Fallujah itself a section of 36th Battalion of the Iraqi Civil Defence Corps also mutinied after fighting inside the city for a week. According to the US Military Command, at the start of the uprising in Fallujah in early April about 40 per cent of the US-trained Iraqi security forces 'walked off the job' and 10 per cent 'actually worked against us.' Four ministers of the US-appointed Iraqi Governing Council have resigned their positions and an estimated 50 per cent of Iraqis working within the 'green zone' in Baghdad (that is, those doing menial jobs for the occupation forces) have stopped turning up for work inside the heavily fortified US citadel.[118]

Meanwhile opinion polls in the United States reveal that a majority of the American public no longer support the war. A *New York Times*/CBS News Poll of over one thousand Americans at the end of April 2004 revealed that only 47 per cent still believed the US had 'done the right thing in taking military action against Iraq.' (This figure had been 63 per cent in a similar poll conducted in December 2003.) When asked 'whether the results of the war with Iraq were worth the loss of American lives and other costs,' 58 per cent of respondents believed they were not (up from 49 per cent in December 2003). About 46 per cent of people believed the United States should withdraw its forces from Iraq immediately. The poll was particularly bad news for Bush, facing an election in November, as it revealed approval for his presidency has fallen from 89 per cent at the time of the 9/11 terrorist attacks in 2001, to just 46 per cent. As in Vietnam, the guerilla war in Iraq is sapping America's confidence in its president and his global 'vision'.[119]

There was a moment when Baghdad first fell to US Marines in

April 2003 that was broadcast live around the world. A small crowd of Iraqis were attempting to pull down a statue of Saddam Hussein and they were eventually assisted in doing so by a US tank crew. As the assembled Iraqis watched, and the world's media zoomed in, one of the US soldiers clambered to the top of the statue and rubbed a US flag in the face of the bronze Saddam. After a few seconds the US flag was taken down and an Iraqi flag was diplomatically handed up to take its place. Arguably, the entire US occupation of Iraq was revealed — and lost — in that moment.

'No Iraqi Ever Called Me Nigger'

*I ain't got no quarrel with the Vietcong ... No Vietcong ever
called me nigger.*

So spoke Muhammad Ali, the famous African-American Muslim
boxer, in 1966, explaining why he refused to be drafted into the
US Army. Ali officially declared himself a conscientious objector
to America's war in Vietnam and denounced racism in the United
States instead. Ali was furiously criticised in the press, convicted
of draft evasion and stripped of his boxing championship.

Times change. A week after 9/11 the *New York Times* ran an
article called 'Calm needed during time of anger', the first line of
which read: 'Perhaps the greatest sports hero in America, and
possibly the world, is a Muslim. His name is Muhammad Ali.' It
was pointed out that Ali lit the Olympic flame in Atlanta in 1996
and that he had become an international 'symbol of peace'. Ali's
post-9/11 statement that, 'Whoever performed, or is behind, the
terrorist attacks in the United States of America does not
represent Islam' was also used to reassure readers that good
Muslims, and good African-Americans, were appalled by what
happened in New York on September 11.[120] All of which was true,

although as the war on terror began in late 2001, opinion polls started showing that race was a factor in determining the attitudes of Americans.

For example, Jonathan Farley, a black American academic, pointed out that 20 per cent of surveyed African-Americans 'opposed Bush's response' to 9/11, as compared to only 6 per cent of whites. As Farley argued:

> As bombs fell, opposition rose. We're less enthusiastic about America's wars in the developing world because we are aware, as has often been said, that no Iraqi ever called us nigger.[121]

Farley was not alone in his reworking of Muhammad Ali's famous quote, nor was he the only American concerned about issues of race as the United States launched its war on terror. During the invasion of Iraq in March 2003 the *New York Times* reported on the racial composition of the US forces fighting there.

> A survey of the American military's endlessly compiled and analysed demographics paints a picture of a fighting force that is anything but a cross section of America. With minorities over-represented and the wealthy and the underclass essentially absent, with political conservatism ascendant in the officer corps and Northeasterners fading from the ranks, America's 1.4 million-strong military seems to resemble the makeup of a two-year computer or trade school outside Birmingham or Biloxi …[122]

While African-Americans make up about 12.7 per cent of the age-group amongst the civilian population able to serve in the US military, they are about 22 per cent of its enlisted personnel. I got to visit the USS *Abraham Lincoln* when it was anchored off Fremantle during 2002 and I found that the composition of the 5200 people aboard the ship reflected the broad ethnic diversity of US society. For instance, 63 per cent of the *Abraham Lincoln*'s crew are white, 14 per cent are black, 12 per cent Hispanic, and 3 per cent Native American. However, 90 per cent of the warship's officers are white. And of the seventy-nine fighter pilots, the most prestigious job on the ship, only three pilots (or 4 per cent of the total) are black.[123]

Are African-Americans treated equally inside the US Armed Forces? Many blacks don't think so. Compare, for example, the cases of Jessica Lynch and Shoshana Johnson. Both are young female American soldiers from the same unit (the US Army's 507th Maintenance Company) who were wounded in the exact same battle in Iraq and taken prisoner. When Lynch was dramatically freed by US special forces she returned to a hero's welcome in America. She secured a book and movie deal in which her war experiences will potentially be shared with an audience of millions (the book, published in November 2003, was entitled *I Am a Soldier Too*). Meanwhile Shoshana Johnson, who was shot through both legs and held captive for over three weeks before being freed by US forces, received no such star treatment. Shoshana was placed on 30 per cent disability benefit and was being paid about US$700 less a month than Jessica Lynch by the same US government that they both served. Jessica Lynch is white and Shoshana Johnson is black. Right or wrong, Johnson's family and African-American politicians like Jesse Jackson believe that skin colour determined Lynch and Johnson's different treatment.[124]

Also, one cannot help but wonder about the motivations of some of the men and women who are currently serving with the US military in Iraq. When I went to high school in America most of the people I knew who were signing up for the armed forces were doing so in order to get their college tuition paid, or to learn a trade. The *New York Times* spoke to US soldiers in Iraq about why they joined:

> Lt. James Baker, 27, of Shelbyville, Tenn., who is white, enlisted in the National Guard. The Tennessee Guard had no infantry units, so he chose artillery instead. 'Artillery is exciting,' he said. 'I get to blow a lot of stuff up and play in the woods. The Army is the biggest team sport in the world.'[125]

Another soldier, Sergeant Sprague from West Virginia, interviewed by the British *Guardian*, gave the following assessment of his trip through Iraq as part of the invasion force: 'I've been all the way through this desert from Basra to here and I ain't seen one shopping mall or fast food restaurant. These people got nothing.' Sergeant Sprague's comments would not have been so shocking if not for the fact that he was stationed near the ancient ruins of Ur, a town founded 8000 years earlier, allegedly the birthplace of Abraham and a centre of civilisation more than seven thousand years before Sprague's first European ancestors staggered ashore in the Americas. Not quite a shopping mall, but surely not nothing. Meanwhile Staff Sergeant Larry Simmons, a member of a US Marines reconnaissance unit, was similarly unimpressed by his presence on the banks of one of the mighty rivers where human civilisation was founded. 'You learn about the Euphrates in geography class, and you get here and you think:

"This is the Euphrates? Looks like a muddy creek to me.'"[126]

These are some of the people fighting for democracy in Iraq. This is the army that we are supposed to trust to be sensitive to the history, culture and civilisation of Iraq's vast multi-ethnic citizenry.

It is America's poor who continue to fight and die in America's wars. The children of America's wealthiest 5 per cent of the population appear almost absent from the country's armed forces. This is something which seems to cut against the very idea of the United States of America — land of liberty and democracy. It certainly worries the *New York Times*:

> Confronted by images of the hardships of overseas deployment and by the stark reality of casualties in Iraq, some have raised questions about the composition of the fighting force and about requiring what is, in essence, a working-class military to fight and die for an affluent America.[127]

The newspaper was not alone. Democrat Representative Charles B Rangel, a Korean War veteran himself, said 'It's just not fair that the people that we ask to fight our wars are people who join the military because of economic conditions, because they have fewer options.' Similarly, a university professor who worked with US Army recruiters commented that the one thing that would really help the morale of US troops, and make the US population feel like the war in Iraq really was a cause worth dying for, would be if Jenna Bush (the President's daughter) enlisted to fight. In fact, only one of the 535 current members of the US Congress has a child currently serving with the American occupation forces in Iraq.[128]

Statistics about the class and racial composition of the US armed forces in Iraq were published around the same time that the US Bureau of Justice revealed that there are currently two million Americans in prison. The United States now imprisons more people than any other country on earth. In fact the United States, a democratic nation of 286 million people, had more people in prison (both proportionately and in overall terms) than Communist China, where an undemocratic Stalinist oligarchy rules over a nation of 1.3 billion people with 1.4 million prisoners. On a per capita basis the United States had three times more prisoners than Iran in 2002, and five times more than Tanzania. When America, the 'land of the free', is locking up more of its citizens than corrupt Third World dictatorships, you have to question whether something is wrong with US society.[129]

The total number of people in prison in the United States is now four times higher than it was in the 1970s. But again African-American men topped the chart in incarceration rates. According to recent figures 12 per cent of African-American men aged 20 to 34 are currently in prison. This compares to 1.6 per cent of the white male population in the same age group. Although blacks only make up 16 per cent of New York's population, 50 per cent of prisoners in the state are African-American. The US Bureau of Justice estimates that 28 per cent of black men in the United States will spend some time in jail during their lives.[130]

Many former prisoners with felony convictions are now ineligible to participate in the formal processes of American democracy. In November 2002 the American Civil Liberties Union estimated that 25 per cent of all African-American men in New York had lost the right to vote because of a previous felony conviction. Another organisation estimated that 1.4 million

African-Americans in the United States (13 per cent of all black men) had been disenfranchised because of laws prohibiting 'felons' from casting ballots in elections.[131] The question is inescapable: can a nation that doesn't allow a substantial portion of its own population to vote because of crimes they have already been punished for really be trusted to bring freedom and democracy to Iraq and the rest of the world?

Meanwhile another report by the US government, based on Census Bureau data, lamented the fact that although 65 per cent of adults and 13 per cent of children in America are alarmingly overweight, some 34.6 million Americans live in poverty.

> Despite the nation's struggle with obesity, the Agriculture Department says, more and more American families are hungry ... Nearly 3.8 million families were hungry last year to the point that someone in the household skipped meals because the family could not afford them. That is 8.6 percent more families than in 2001, when 3.5 million were hungry, and a 13 percent increase from 2000.[132]

This poverty and hunger also falls disproportionately upon African-American families. For example, an April 2003 report from the Children's Defense Fund, also based on US Census Bureau data, revealed that in 2001 about one million black children in America were living in families with an after-tax income that was less than half the amount used to define official poverty. While the percentage of black Americans living in poverty is falling (from 41.5 per cent in 1995 down to 30 per cent in 2001) the number of black children living in 'extreme poverty' is increasing. On top of this, median incomes for

African-Americans actually fell three per cent during 2002.[133]

It therefore seems reasonable to ask why it is that nearly 150 years after the end of slavery so many black children are still poor and hungry in America? Wasn't the civil rights movement of the 1960s supposed to change all of this? Especially given that 2003 was the fortieth anniversary of Martin Luther King's famous 'I have a dream' speech.

There was another significant anniversary in 2003, one that passed virtually unnoticed in most of the media despite the enormous controversy it caused at the time. Thirty-five years ago two Olympic 200-metre medallists, John Carlos (bronze) and Tommie Smith (gold), participated in a famous Olympic protest. After receiving their medals the athletes raised their clenched and black-gloved fists in the black power salute and bowed their heads as the American national anthem was played. Between them was a white Australian, Peter Norman, who supported their silent act of defiance. While the black fists got the media's attention at the time, few noticed that the two African-Americans also stood on the winners' platform without shoes and that Carlos wore beads around his neck. What did it all mean? On the thirty-fifth anniversary of the 1968 Olympics, John Carlos explained that:

> We wanted the world to know that in Mississippi, Alabama, Tennessee, South Central Los Angeles, Chicago, that people were still walking back and forth in poverty without even the necessary clothes to live. We have kids that don't have shoes even today. It's not like the powers that be can't provide these things. They can send a space ship to the moon, or send a probe to Mars, yet they can't give shoes? They can't give health care? I'm just not naïve enough to accept that.[134]

As for the beads:

> The beads were for those individuals that were lynched, or killed that no-one said a prayer for … It was for those thrown off the side of the (slave) boats in the middle passage. All that was in my mind … We were trying to wake the country up and wake up the world too.

John Carlos and Tommie Smith were pilloried by the mainstream media for bringing America's domestic politics into the sacred apolitical arena of international sport. They were suspended from the US athletic team and expelled from the Olympic village. Interestingly, their protest was inspired by an organisation called Olympic Project for Human Rights.[135] Among the OPHR's main demands were for Muhammad Ali's boxing championship title to be restored. Looking back with the benefit of thirty-five years reflection, John Carlos was asked if he thought black athletes in America should still speak out on social issues. 'Yes,' he said, 'because so much is the same as it was in 1968 especially in terms of race relations. I think things are just more cosmetically disguised.'

With two million Americans currently locked up, 1.4 million Americans in the armed forces and the legacy of institutional racism still painfully evident in US society, perhaps it is truly time for black Americans to reformulate the famous words of Muhammad Ali in opposition to another military occupation of a Third World nation — 'No Iraqi ever called me nigger.'

2

'OUR BACKYARD':
AUSTRALIA, INDONESIA
AND EAST TIMOR

The Anzac Legend and the Deputy Sheriff

In London on 10 November 2003 the prime minister of Australia, the Honourable John Howard MP, rose to his feet in front of a room of wine-sipping distinguished guests and political dignitaries to speak on the topic of 'Australians at war'. It was an important moment for the prime minister. It had been John Howard who had led the nation during Australia's largest military deployment since Vietnam when he sent troops to join the United Nations' peacekeeping mission to East Timor in late 1999. Two years later, on 11 September 2001, Howard had actually been in Washington as a plane slammed into the Pentagon and the first reports filtered in of the attacks on the World Trade Center in New York. Howard, ever conscious of the role he had given himself as America's 'deputy sheriff' in the Asia–Pacific region, immediately pledged Australia's support for any US military retaliation against the perpetrators of the 9/11 terrorist attacks. He stuck to his word. Howard saw to it that his government committed small numbers of Australian troops to participate in the overthrow of the Taliban in Afghanistan, and in the invasion and occupation of Iraq two years later.

Therefore by November 2003 Howard had arguably proven himself as a reliable ally in US President George W Bush's war on terror. He was not afraid to send Australian troops into potentially unpopular wars. He said he was prepared to suffer casualties if necessary (although, luckily, no Australians were killed in East Timor or Iraq). He had reinvigorated the Anzac legend. And now Howard was in London to join Queen Elizabeth and Tony Blair in opening a war memorial for those Australians killed while fighting to defend Britain during the twentieth century's two world wars.

The night before the opening of the memorial, 10 November, Australia House (as the Australian Commission in London is called) hosted a function where John Howard would talk to his guests about Australia's martial feats. His speech started off confidently and on familiar territory — Howard talked about the long and intimate cultural and historical ties between Australia and Britain. He spoke of 'those moments when the very survival of liberty seemed in peril' during the Second World War and of Australia's role in the 'final victory' over Nazism. And then Howard uttered words which were partly factual, partly wishful thinking, and overall so strangely at odds with Australia's actual history that I downloaded a transcript to make sure I hadn't misheard him when excerpts of the speech were broadcast on national television.

> Australians are not by nature a war-like people. There is no tradition of conquest or imperial ambition. We've had no history of bloody civil war, of winning our independence through armed insurrection or fortifying our borders against some constant military threat. Indeed, there's something revealing in the fact that only two statues of individuals are placed outside our national War Memorial in Canberra. The

Memorial contains relics, artwork and historical records that tell the story of Lone Pine, Beersheba, Villers Bretonneux, Kokoda and Tobruk, Kapiong, Long Tan and the hundreds of other places where Australians have performed some of the finest feats of arms in the history of warfare. And yet it's Simpson with his donkey who brought wounded from the firing lines of Gallipoli and Sir Edward 'Weary' Dunlop ... both unarmed and unlikely warriors — that stand in bronze as symbols of the Australian military tradition and character.[1]

Although this version of 'Australians at war' reflects the way most Australians would like to think about 'the Anzac legend' and our country, it contains within it numerous contradictions and myths. Firstly, while most Australians would agree with Howard that we are not a 'war-like people' it is, however, entirely plausible that others might see us differently. For an isolated island with no 'natural predators' in our immediate region, Australians have demonstrated a remarkable propensity to go overseas in search of wars to fight. Even before Australia was federated in 1901, about 2500 Australian colonial soldiers had already fought against the Maori in New Zealand in the 1860s, 770 fought in the Sudan during 1885, and 16,000 Australian soldiers were eventually dispatched to the Boer War after it broke out in 1899. More than 600 Australian soldiers died in South Africa. Around 500 Australian soldiers even managed to make their way to China in 1900, where they participated in the suppression of the Boxer Rebellion, although they arrived too late to play any real combat role and were relegated to guard duty. Nevertheless, six Australian soldiers died and were buried in China.[2]

In addition, Australia's armed forces have participated in two world wars, as well as fighting in Malaya, Borneo, Korea, Vietnam, both Gulf Wars and Afghanistan. Even at the end of the First World War, following the greatest loss of Australian lives in any foreign conflict, about 150 to 200 Australians volunteered to fight in Russia and participate in the British Army's attempt, in alliance with 'White Russians' from the old Tsarist regime, to overthrow the new revolutionary Bolshevik government. Two Australian soldiers won Australia's highest military honour, the Victoria Cross, while fighting in North Russia in 1919. One unfortunate Australian Captain, Allan Brown, was killed by the Russian troops he was commanding when they mutinied and went over to the Bolsheviks in July 1919.

In short, Australian soldiers have never been shy of foreign conflicts. This is reflected in the list of battlefields mentioned by John Howard in the middle of the quoted passage where he discusses the 'relics' and such at the Australian War Memorial in Canberra. The listed battles took place in Turkey, Palestine, France, New Guinea, Libya, Korea and Vietnam. It is worth contemplating how the citizens of these countries might differently remember these 'finest feats of arms in the history of warfare.' Additionally, it is simply not true that there 'is no tradition of conquest or imperial ambition' in Australia. Most of these military actions were wars of both conquest and imperial ambition, with many (including the Second World War) carried out in enthusiastic service of the British Empire.

Indeed, Howard admitted as much later on in the same speech when he quoted an Australian newspaper at the time of the outbreak of the First World War: 'The British Empire is our family circle, and we cannot live outside it.' For Howard such comments reflected the fact that 'Australians in 1914 felt themselves intrinsically a part of the then British Empire. They were bound by emotion, economic links, through cultural and blood ties, and by an understanding that Australia's security interests remained absolutely dependent on British supremacy.'

John Howard was not, however, being entirely honest when he argued that, 'We've had no history of bloody civil war, of winning our independence through armed insurrection or fortifying our borders against some constant military threat.' There was one undoubtable truth here, surrounded by two hopeful untruths. It is true Australia has never won independence by force of arms. On the issue of 'fortifying our borders against some constant military threat,' however, it is worth remembering that from its earliest days the British colonial outposts in Australia were intensely fearful of foreign invasion. At first this was confined to European competitors — the French, Russians and so forth. The first major military fortifications in Sydney Harbour, built in the nineteenth century, were constructed for fear of other Europeans coming and stealing Britain's Australian colonies (much as the British had done elsewhere). In 1883 the Queensland government even attempted a pre-emptive annexation of eastern New Guinea, in the name of the British Empire, in order to block Germany out of the region.

By 1888, the centenary of Australia's white settlement, 'invasion fiction', based on popular fear of non-European foreigners, was being published in Australian newspapers. The stories included William Lane's apocalyptic *White or Yellow: A Story of the Race-War of AD 1908*, which predicted that Australia would be overrun by the Chinese. From at least the first decade of the twentieth century Australians became more intensely paranoid of an imminent 'Asian invasion', with the focus of their fear shifting between China and Japan. This was not just a question of the 'White Australia Policy' (the *Immigration Restriction Act*), introduced at the time of

Federation and designed to prohibit Asian migration to our whitening shores. In 1908, the exact year of Lane's predicted Race-War, the United States Navy (or the 'Great White Fleet' as it was unashamedly referred to then) visited Australia with no less than 80,000 Australians lining Sydney Harbour to welcome their American brothers-in-arms. The Americans were increasingly viewed as White Australia's military insurance policy against potential Asian invaders.

From 1908 onwards Australia continued fortifying itself in preparation for what many leading politicians truly considered to be an inevitable and impending 'race war' (and they used this exact terminology) with Japan. Until the end of the Second World War 'race' and a 'White Australia' were terms of pride and articles of faith. And when war with Japan did arrive in 1941, following Japan's dramatic entry into the Second World War, the Australian government intensified construction of the now rusting fortifications which can still be found on coastal headlands around many of Australia's major cities.

Arguably, although Australia does not possess major fortifications against contemporary potential invaders, the fortification mentality is still reflected in our current refugee policy. John Howard's government, after all, won the last Federal election largely on the issue of refugees, 'illegal immigrants' and the need for increased 'border protection'. The day before the October 2001 Federal election the Liberal Party even ran full-page advertisements in major Australian newspapers with a singular defining message — 'A vote for your local Liberal team member protects our borders and supports the Prime Minister's team.' In the words of Peter Mares, an expert on Australia's immigration policy:

Outside observers could be forgiven for assuming that Australia's harsh [mandatory detention of refugees] policies were the product of an assault on the nation's borders by huge numbers of unauthorised migrants. In fact the opposite is the case: Australia's 'problem' with asylum seekers is modest, particularly when compared with poor nations in Africa or West Asia that have been confronted with huge numbers of refugees pouring across their frontiers in a single day. Even when boat arrivals to Australia peaked the largest number to arrive in a single year was 4175 (in financial year 1999–2000).[3]

The August 2001 'Tampa affair' (where the government used armed commandos to prevent a ship carrying 433 refugees, mainly Afghans, from landing in Australia) and current Australian immigration policy neglect the fundamental truth that boat people have been arriving in Australia for some time now. Take the single most famous example, the 216th anniversary of which fell recently. During January 1788 a small fleet of 'queue jumpers' arrived, without visas, on the shores of Botany Bay and rather presumptuously assumed that they should be allowed to stay, regardless of the wishes of local inhabitants and despite the adverse affect this decision would have on the delicately balanced local environment. Although the newcomers were cautiously welcomed by the Eora, as the original Sydneysiders were known, the newcomers clustered together in ghettoes, failed to assimilate to local customs, and refused to learn the local language. Soon they became such a drain on Sydney's welfare resources that mass starvation became a serious concern for both the Eora and the 'settlers' (as this group of immigrants chose to call themselves).

The boat people also brought disease with them and historians estimate that the outbreak of smallpox in April 1789 killed possibly half the Aboriginal population around Sydney.[4] The coastal caves into which many Eora crawled to die are a forgotten memorial to the tragic consequences of this invasion by uninvited boat people.

Nor was the *Tampa* the first ship of unwanted human cargo to be turned around from our shores. In the book *Legacies of White Australia*, historian Ann Curthoys points out that in 1849 huge demonstrations greeted the British ship *Hashemy*, which was carrying convicts. Although many Sydneysiders were themselves descendants of convicts, by 1849 the popular mood had turned decidedly against transportation. The protests and public opposition to the landing of the *Hashemy* meant the ship became the last to carry convicts to New South Wales. Similarly, in 1888 a ship carrying Chinese immigrants (ironically, the ship was called the *Afghan*) was prevented from landing in Melbourne or Sydney. Its Asian passengers were considered a potential racial contaminant to a White Australia: 40,000 protesters marched against Chinese immigration in Sydney. As with the *Tampa* episode more than a century later, the New South Wales premier, Henry Parkes, attempted to rush legislation through parliament to prohibit legal Chinese migrants aboard the *Afghan* from disembarking in Sydney. As Curthoys argues:

> Indeed, the plight of the *Tampa*'s human cargo calls to mind all the many occasions in Australian history where a large majority in a liberal democratic society has expressed a strong desire to exclude others, on the grounds of race, religion, culture or morality, often in the face of international condemnation and opposition.[5]

In this satellite age we only need turn on the nightly news to see tragic scenes of wailing refugees streaming into makeshift camps bordering countries at war. This should compel us to contemplate the role Australia has sometimes played as a safe haven for refugees. After the Second World War Australia welcomed thousands of 'displaced persons' from Europe, and in the 1970s about 2000 'boat people' fleeing communist Vietnam and Cambodia were accepted into Australia. At other times in our past, however, Australian political leaders grasped at the intolerant thread that also runs through our history. For example, during the 1930s a Jewish organisation put forward a plan to purchase several million acres of pastoral land in the far north of Western Australia and use it to provide sanctuary for 50,000 potential Jewish migrants. These people were victims of European fascism who were desperate to flee the hate that would eventually create the gas chambers of Auschwitz. After acrimonious debate and years of delay, the scheme was rejected by Prime Minister John Curtin in 1944.

Indeed, at a time when Jews faced naked persecution in Europe, the response of some Australians was less than welcoming. The president of the Victorian Legislative Council described Melbourne's Jewish refugees of the 1930s as 'slinking rat-faced men under five feet in height.' One can only hope that when the full horror of the Nazi concentration camps was revealed at the end of the war such individuals felt some shame about their role in attempting to protect Australia's borders from these 'undesirable' immigrants. Interestingly, in 1939 the *West Australian* newspaper had actually come out in favour of the Jewish Kimberley plan, with one of its readers agreeing (in a letter to the editor) that the Jewish scheme would 'help us defend the empty north against invaders.' Similarly, historian David Day quotes one West Australian MP's response to the plan: 'In my opinion the proposition can be boiled down to one question, "Are we going to have Jews or Japs?" I say, let us have the Jews.'[6]

We should also remember that perhaps the earliest known contact between Aborigines and seafarers is not Cook's arrival at Botany Bay in 1770, nor even the seventeenth-century Dutch shipwrecks in Western Australia, but the interaction between Macassan fishermen (from what is now Indonesia) and Aborigines in the far north. It was probably the humble wooden boats of these fishermen in pursuit of 'sea slugs' that first explored our northern coastline. And if 'first come, first served' is really going to be all that counts in our heartless new immigration and refugee policy, then those of us of Anglo-Celtic migrant heritage probably qualify as queue jumpers as well.

Perhaps the biggest omission in John Howard's London speech lay in his assertion that Australia has 'no history of bloody civil war.' Howard, the most conservative prime minister in modern Australian history, continues to wilfully ignore the fact that violence between Aborigines and European settlers, soldiers and police on the Australian frontier between 1788 and the early twentieth century constituted a 'war'. If the battle for physical control of Australia between settlers and Aborigines (which features so prominently in the accounts of the early settlers) was not a war of conquest, or a 'bloody civil war', then what was it? Strangely, Australians like John Howard seem to have no problem acknowledging New Zealand's 'Maori wars' or pondering the significance of America's centuries of sporadic warfare with various Native American tribes. The absence of Aboriginal armies, artillery barrages, cavalry charges and naval skirmishes, along with the historical tendency of Australian conservatives to belittle or ignore resistance by various groups of Aborigines to the white conquest of their country, does not change the fact that Australia's first war was with its own native people.

What is strange about all of this is that Howard's failure to acknowledge Australia's Aboriginal wars is at odds with the direction in which many recognised Australian military historians are moving. For example, the well respected *A Military History of Australia*, written by Australian Defence Force Academy lecturer Jeffrey Grey, explicitly argues that:

> In Australia's case the frontier conflict between European settlement and the Aborigines was, for much of our history, greatly downplayed ... Unlike the Maori, the Zulu or the North American Indian, they [Aborigines] were not conceded the dignity due to worthy opponents. We now know that Aboriginal resistance was widespread, consistent and determined, and the debate has moved on to consider whether resistance should properly be called 'warfare'.[7]

While deliberating over the historical and theoretical issues involved, Grey argues that: 'the conflict between native inhabitants and white settlers over the possession and utilisation of land can readily be described as "war". That indeed is where the real analysis begins ... We must ask how it was fought and why the outcome was so decisive.'[8]

So why did John Howard, in a public speech about 'Australians at war', choose to ignore this most significant of all wars fought by Australians — a war which led to whites being able to secure the country in the first place? He did so because tradition has it that only sovereign peoples and formal armies fight wars, and when they are finished they negotiate terms of surrender or armistice. For Howard to officially recognise the conflict on the Australian frontier as a war (civil or otherwise) might have raised questions of land rights, treaties and such. It might also have given succour to those incorrigible Aboriginal activists who would like to see significant battle sites, like Pinjarra in Western Australia, acknowledged and protected. And so Howard, like so many other Australians, chose to deftly ignore this less than noble chapter in our national story.

Instead Howard invoked the statues and stories of Simpson and his donkey, and Weary Dunlop, 'unarmed and unlikely warriors', outside the War Memorial in Canberra. For Howard these were symbols of Australia's 'military tradition and character'. Les Carlyon, in his popular history *Gallipoli*, writes that, 'Australia likes quirky heroes and the Simpson poetry was right … He wasn't a toff; he was one of us.' Simpson's legend 'played to the way Australians like to see themselves,' which is precisely why Howard raised it.[9] What Howard did not mention was that Simpson was very much a 'Britisher'. Born into a working-class family in England, he arrived in Australia at age seventeen. He joined the Australian Army in part because he thought it might be a good way to get back home to England. His politics were not quite the sort of thing John Howard would usually want to endorse either. In a roughly composed letter home to his mother before the war Simpson wrote that:

> I often wonder when the working men of England will wake up and see things as other people see them what they want in England is a good revolution and that will clear some of there Millionaires and lords and Dukes out of it and then with a labour Government

they will almost be able to make their own conditions.[10]

Before he died helping wounded Australian soldiers at Gallipoli, before he became an Anzac legend and a war memorial statue, Simpson had been an active and enthusiastic trade unionist. The supreme irony, however, which Howard seemed blissfully unaware of, was that Simpson had originally entered Australia by jumping ship in Sydney. He had deserted his position in the merchant navy and entered Australia in circumstances that would get him locked in a detention centre these days, or deported to some bankrupt Pacific Island for 'processing' as an illegal immigrant and 'queue jumper'. In short, our most famous Anzac hero was a boat person.

It must be said that any speech by any politician can be picked over and dissected for minor inaccuracies and contradictions. Prime ministers give speeches every day and they should not be held accountable for every insignificant little error they make. However, John Howard's 'Australians at war' speech in London on 10 November 2003 was no ordinary speech. It came at a time when he had committed Australia to fight in the most unpopular war in modern history — the US-led invasion of Iraq, against which millions of people around the world protested even before a single shot had been fired. Moreover, Howard had sent troops to Iraq against the wishes of a majority of Australians; a January 2003 opinion poll revealed only 6 per cent of Australians were in support of an invasion without the explicit approval of the United Nations. One-third of those surveyed were opposed to Australian participation in an invasion of Iraq even with UN support.[11]

John Howard also spoke at a time of increased danger after

the war on terror had claimed its first post-9/11 Australian victims, with Islamic terrorists bombing the Sari nightclub in Bali. And he spoke as a prime minister, more than any other in the last fifty years, who was consciously trying to refashion the way in which Australians thought about themselves, their history and their role in the world.

The Iraq war had played an important part in all of this. Earlier, on 4 February 2003, John Howard had given a lengthy speech in parliament justifying the imminent invasion of Iraq by the United States, Britain and the 'Coalition of the Willing', which included Australia. Howard claimed that Iraq's 'possession of chemical and biological weapons and its pursuit of a nuclear capability poses a real and unacceptable threat to the stability and security of our world.' He claimed that Australia had specific intelligence from its American and British allies confirming Saddam's massive weapons of mass destruction programs. During the course of the fifty-five minute speech the immense danger posed by Saddam's possession of these WMDs was constantly referred to and presented, as in Washington and London, as the primary justification for an invasion of Iraq.

However, only three months later on 14 May it was already clear that the intelligence regarding Iraqi WMDs, as presented in the case for war by Howard, Bush and Blair, was a mixture of exaggeration, guesswork and outright fabrication. Most telling of all, the US-led invasion force failed to find even a single weapon of mass destruction after toppling Saddam Hussein's regime. Howard's 14 May speech, in contrast with the one he gave three months earlier, was therefore noticeable in its attempt to downplay the WMD issue. Howard now conceded that the 'hunt for these weapons will not be easy.' Although he claimed Coalition troops had discovered possible 'mobile biological weapons production facilities,' this later proved to not be the case.[12] It is worth noting that the Iraq Survey Group, commissioned by President Bush to hunt for Saddam's illegal weapons, now believes that Iraqi WMDs simply did not exist at the time of the US-led invasion.

A few years earlier John Howard had implied in an interview with *Bulletin* magazine that Australia would be the 'deputy sheriff' to the United States in the Asia–Pacific region. Howard's comments caused much controversy in Asia, evoking memories of Australia's armed support for the British Empire during the nineteenth century, and the history of White Australia's bellicose preparation for a 'race war' with Asia during the early twentieth century. One of Australia's closest neighbours is Indonesia, the largest Muslim nation in the world. Australia's participation in the invasion and occupation of Iraq was viewed very poorly in Indonesia and throughout Southeast Asia.

In October 2003, a month before Howard's 'Australians at war' London speech, US President George W Bush had been asked if he saw Australia as a deputy sheriff of the United States. Bush responded by saying that he saw Australia 'as a sheriff. There's a difference. Equal partners, friends and allies.' Again, the reaction in Asia was less than favourable. At a summit of Islamic nations being held in Malaysia, the Malaysian Deputy Defence Minister said that, 'I suppose America wants a puppet of its own in this region whom they can trust, who will do whatever they wish.'[13] The image of Australia as a white, rich, arrogant and potentially aggressive country was reinforced in many Asian minds.

Bush briefly visited Australia a short time afterwards, his payback for John Howard's support and Australia's minor role in the 'Coalition of the Willing'. Bush was genuinely grateful. He had desperately needed the participation of less powerful countries like Australia in order to challenge the popular international perception that the invasion and occupation of Iraq was an exclusively US and British affair. In practice on the ground in Iraq it may not have been much of a military coalition, but the idea served its political purpose well enough. In return Bush anointed Howard as one of the trusted few — a genuine ally in America's global struggle against the 'axis of evil' and terrorism.

Australia and the United States certainly go back a long way together, having fought as allies in no less than five major wars. Australia's post-1945 strategic alliance with the United States has its origins in the portentous visit by the 'Great White Fleet' in 1908. While Australia has always retained its constitutional and sentimental links with Britain (as well as the paraphernalia of the Union Jack on the flag and the Queen's head on our coinage), during the Second World War Australia recognised that the United States would be the key Pacific power in the post-war world. The gradual move away from London and towards Washington was simply a reflection of the decline of the British Empire and the rise of American power.

Perhaps the best illustration of the way in which Australia managed this shift in allegiance (with all its inherent contradictions) was reflected in Prime Minister John Curtin's speeches in the aftermath of the Japanese bombing of the US Pacific Fleet at Pearl Harbor in December 1941. On 16 December, in a speech to the Australian parliament, Curtin said that Australians would show their 'determination that this country shall remain for ever the home of the descendants of those people who came here in peace in order to establish in the South Seas an outpost of the British race.' He also said that Australia's war with Japan would be to help maintain 'the principle of a White Australia.' Soon afterwards, Curtin wrote a newspaper article which proclaimed that 'without any inhibitions of any kind, I make it quite clear that

Australia looks to America, free from any pangs as to our traditional links or kinship with the United Kingdom.'[14] Many Australians shared Curtin's belief that the British had turned their backs on Australia as the Japanese invaders drew near, and that only the Americans possessed the might and the motivation to save us.

The idea was that having fought so closely together during the Second World War, the Americans would now guarantee Australia's defence, much as the British Empire had for the previous century and a half. However, the Australians were also determined to develop new weapons and tactics of their own to deal with potential aggressors. For example, recently released secret documents reveal that in the late 1940s Australian scientist Sir Macfarlane Burnet, a Nobel Prize winning microbiologist, was a key advisor to the Australian government on the issue of the development of 'New Weapons'. In 1947 Sir Macfarlane wrote in a confidential report that:

> ... the most effective counter-offensive to threatened invasion by overpopulated Asian countries would be directed towards the destruction by biological or chemical means of tropical food crops and the dissemination of infectious disease capable of spreading in tropical but not under Australian conditions.[15]

Sir Macfarlane sat on the 'chemical and biological warfare subcommittee' where he advised the military and government on the potential viability of an Australian chemical weapons program. Minutes of a meeting in 1948 detail that Sir Macfarlane was 'of the opinion that if Australia undertakes work in this field it should be on the tropical offensive side rather than the defensive.' A study group was even established to examine 'the possibilities of an attack on the food supplies of S-E Asia and Indonesia using B.W. [biological weapons] agents.'[16] Like Britain and the United States, Iraq's other main accusers, Australia has its own dark history of secret WMDs during the Cold War.

The first major test of Australia's post-1945 strategic alliance with the United States came in Vietnam. Popular opinion now has it that Australia was dragged into Vietnam by the United States. Such a view appeals to Australians precisely because it frees us from blame for military failure in Vietnam, and absolves us of any guilt regarding the destruction done to the country. Evoking the ghosts of Gallipoli and Anzac, legend has it that our troops in Vietnam 'did a good job' in a bad war that was lost because of American incompetence. The reality was quite different. Or as Michael Sexton argues in his study of confidential Australian government documents from the period, *War for the Asking: Australia's Vietnam Secrets*:

> [T]he Australian government desired an increased American involvement in the Vietnam conflict at every level, and a significant Australian participation ... These aims already formed the basis of the Australian government's policy ... at a time when the United States itself still had no combat troops in Vietnam.[17]

It was the Australian government, drawing on longstanding fears of Asian invasion, who felt the threat (real or imagined) of communist takeover in Southeast Asia most sharply. For example, shortly before Australia announced it would send combat troops to Vietnam, the Brisbane *Courier Mail* of 19 April 1965 felt compelled to point out that:

Australia's stake in what started out as a Red-engineered dirty little civil war is this: if Communism takes over in Vietnam, then Thailand, Malaysia and Indonesia will surely be swallowed, too, in time. We could be next.

Ten days later, in a speech to parliament, Prime Minister Robert Menzies similarly commented that 'the takeover of South Vietnam would be a direct military threat to Australia.'[18]

Such thinking had caused the Australian government to give strong political support to those in the US administration who were pressing for their government to commit combat troops to Vietnam. The next step was to get the Americans and South Vietnamese to invite Australia to participate, something they did (as Sexton points out) with some considerable reluctance. Nevertheless, on 30 April 1965 Prime Minister Menzies announced that Australia had committed 800 combat soldiers to Vietnam, with the number rising to 8000 by the late 1960s. Just over five hundred of these soldiers were killed in Vietnam. However, Canberra's principal concern during the later stages of the war was that an American defeat in Vietnam would lead to the superpower scaling down its military presence in the Asia–Pacific region. As a result Canberra continued to lobby for military escalation. Again Sexton writes that:

In addition to pressing the Americans to bomb North Vietnam, Australia at this time was concerned to dissuade them from any idea of negotiating with Hanoi. This stand followed automatically from the Australian desire to see the war widened.[19]

Nevertheless, domestic political pressures came to bear and in December 1971 the Australian government announced it was withdrawing its soldiers from Vietnam. By 1973 the majority of US troops had also been withdrawn. In 1975 Saigon fell and Vietnam was reunited. The myth-making started not long afterwards.

John Howard, addressing the nation on 20 March 2003 to inform the Australian public he had sanctioned Australian participation in the invasion of Iraq, asked Australians to 'remember that bin Laden specifically targeted Australia because of our intervention to save the people of East Timor.' He also remarked that the 'Americans have helped us in the past and the United States is very important to Australia's long-term security.' In the face of mounting concern in Asia about the war on terror and the way in which Australia was projecting its power in the region, Howard chose to retreat into the comfortable simplicities of 'the Anzac legend'. In doing so Howard, like many Australians, chose to ignore the complex history of our military past and foreign policy — first as an appendage of the British Empire, and since 1945 as an active supporter of US global hegemony. He also ignored the complicated and often problematic nature of Australia's historical entanglement with Asia.

The essays in this section of the book examine that most vexed issue in recent Australian foreign policy in Asia — East Timor — and how it became a crucible of Australian politics in the region. Related to this is Australia's complex and less than glorious relationship with Indonesia over the last forty years; from supporting General Suharto's military dictatorship to cautiously assisting in the transition to democracy. Through all of these issues Australia has been ever mindful of its powerful allies in

Washington, and of Australia's subsidiary role as a protector of 'western interests' in the Asia–Pacific region. Although the end of the Cold War and 9/11 have altered regional relationships, the net result is an Australian government increasingly confident and aware of what is now expected of it as a 'deputy sheriff' to the world's sole remaining superpower. This section of the book is about the sort of nation that Australian foreign policy in Southeast Asia has made us and the struggles within Australia and the region for a different kind of history.

Australia Goes to War:
Major Overseas Deployment of Australian Soldiers, 1885–2003

	Number of soldiers sent overseas	Number killed
Sudan (1885)	770	9
Boer War (South Africa, 1899–1902)	16,463	606
Boxer Rebellion (China, 1900–01)	560	6
First World War (1914–18)	331,781	61,720
Second World War (1939–45)	575,799	39,366
Korean War (1950–53)	17,164	339
Malaya (1950–60)	7,000	36
Borneo Confrontation (1965–66)	3,500	15
Vietnam (1965–72)	50,001	520
Gulf War (1990–91)	1,872	0
Afghanistan (2001)	1,550	1
Iraq (2003–?)	2,000	0

- Number of foreign wars in which Australia has fought = 12
- Number of countries Australia has gone to war with who have actually attacked the Australian mainland = 1 (Japan)
- Approximate number of Australians killed in foreign wars = 102,600
- Approximate number of Australians killed in foreign wars, excluding the two world wars = 1550
- Number of times since 1945 Australia has gone to war without the support of the United Nations = 4 (Malaya, Borneo, Vietnam, Iraq)
- Number of times since 1945 Australia has gone to war without the support of the USA or Britain = 0

(Source: Australian War Memorial Museum)

Osama bin Laden, Half a Million Dead Communists and the Revenge of History in Indonesia

The past can be cruel. In 1965–66 Australia and the United States quietly supported the Indonesian military's great purge of the Communist Party (PKI) from Indonesian society. Bodies literally clogged the waterways on some islands of the archipelago as hundreds of thousands of people were put to death. This prodigious bloodletting was carried out with the active assistance of the US Embassy in Jakarta who supplied the Indonesian military with lists of PKI members. Glowing reports were sent back to Washington about how General Suharto and the Indonesian Army, with the help of Muslim machetes, had saved Indonesia from the scourge of communism.

The price was high. It was paid not only by the hundreds of thousands of PKI supporters who perished — cut down in village laneways, bayoneted in mass graves, or shot kneeling with a bullet to the back of the head — but by all Indonesians.[20] For the net result of the 1965–66 PKI massacres was the Suharto dictatorship, one of the most nepotistic and rapacious regimes of the second half of the twentieth century — a dictatorship that not only strangled what remained of Indonesian democracy, but also destroyed the small emerging democracies of West Papua and East Timor, forcibly integrating both nations into the Indonesian Republic.

In August 1965, just before Suharto's takeover, the PKI was the third largest Communist Party in the entire world (behind the Soviet Union and China). It had over two million members and controlled various union, youth, peasant, womens' and cultural organisations that claimed ten million additional supporters. The PKI had also won 16 per cent of the popular vote in the 1955 elections.[21] Indonesia's first president, Sukarno, suspended parliament in July 1959, opting for 'Guided Democracy' under his personal leadership. He invited the PKI to join his government in March 1962. This was part of Sukarno's strategy of using the PKI to offset the power of the other main political player in Indonesian society, the army.

In the West the rise of the PKI was viewed with trepidation. Indonesia, made up of over 15,000 islands, was the fifth most populous country in the world and by the 1950s western political analysts were predicting that the PKI would eventually win government there. This would have been, in the midst of the Cold War, the biggest blow to 'western interests' since the fall of China in 1949. As early as December 1954 the United States National Security Council indicated that it would be willing to use 'all feasible covert means' including 'the use of armed force if necessary' to stop the PKI taking power.[22]

By 1965 the US embassy in Jakarta was pressing for a radical solution to 'the PKI problem'. They found it in General Suharto.[23] Sections of the Indonesian Army were deeply divided between those who supported President Sukarno and were sympathetic to (or tolerant of) the PKI, and those who saw the PKI as the army's main rival for political influence in Indonesian society and wanted to crush it. On the night of 30 September 1965 six army generals were murdered, their bodies dumped down a well, by army officers who believed the generals were planning a military coup to overthrow Sukarno. The murder of the generals was blamed on the PKI (this remains a major point of historical contention) and sections of the army based around Suharto realised that their moment had arrived.

According to CIA reports sent to Washington from Jakarta, on 5 October the Indonesian Army decided to 'implement plans to crush PKI.'[24] The 17 December 1965 issue of *Time*, which could hardly be accused of Marxist sympathies, reported what happened next.

> ... Communists, red sympathisers and their families are being massacred by the thousands. Backlands army units are reported to have executed thousands of Communists after interrogation in remote jails. Armed with wide-bladed knives called *parangs*, Moslem bands crept at night into the homes of Communists, killing entire families and burying the bodies in shallow graves. The murder campaign became so brazen in parts of rural East Java, that Moslem bands placed the heads of victims on poles and paraded them through villages. The killings have been on such a scale that the disposal of the corpses has created a serious sanitation problem in East Java and Northern Sumatra where the humid air bears the reek of decaying flesh. Travellers from those areas tell of small rivers and streams that have been literally clogged with bodies. River transportation has at places been seriously impeded.

Although the areas of worst violence were in Java, Bali and Sumatra, blood was spilled throughout the archipelago.[25] The *New York Times* of 8 May 1966 reported one local incident in which about 100 PKI members, 'or suspected Communists,' had been rounded up and murdered. The severed head of the school principal, a PKI member, 'was stuck on a pole and paraded among his former pupils, convened in special assembly.' Similar events occurred in hundreds of other villages. According to historian Gabriel Kolko, the killings were carried out mainly by Muslim extremists and 'right-wing youth, with aid from the army.'[26]

One of the most badly affected areas was East Java where, according to one academic specialist, 'Communist Party efforts to accelerate land reform' had 'deeply antagonised existing landholders and threatened the social dominance of Islamic preachers.' In some regions the pretext of an anti-PKI purge was sometimes a convenient facade for settling other ethnic and socio-economic differences. In West Kalimantan, for instance, an estimated 45,000 ethnic Chinese were expelled from the area with the loss of hundreds of lives.[27]

The response of the western media to all of this was mixed. The *New York Times* of 12 March 1966 described what was happening as 'one of the most savage slaughters of modern political history.' However, the western media were also keen to point out that this same savage slaughter was, 'The West's best news for years in Asia.'[28] But those decapitated, bayoneted or shot in Indonesia during 1965–66, their corpses dumped in rivers or pitched into shallow graves, were not hardened communist guerillas. Literally tens of thousands of those killed were simply teachers, trade unionists or ordinary peasant PKI-sympathisers.

Still, in October 1966 the US Deputy Undersecretary of State, U Alexis Johnson, described the 'reversal of the Communist tide in the great country of Indonesia' as 'an event that will probably rank along with the Vietnamese war as perhaps the most historic turning point of Asia in this decade.' There were some in the business community who also liked what they saw. US exports to Indonesia tripled. Direct American investment in Indonesia rose from US$106 million in 1966, to $1.5 billion ten years later. Meanwhile, ordinary Indonesians remained among the poorest in Southeast Asia and movements for land reform, which the PKI had often led, were all but extinguished.[29]

In December 1976 the Indonesian Army estimated that between 450,000 and 500,000 people were killed in the violence of 1965–66.[30] Some historians argue that as many as a million may have died. All in all it was a horrifying demonstration of the ferocious violence the Indonesian Army was willing to unleash against its own people.

When Indonesia first won independence from the Dutch in 1949 it was led by its charismatic anti-colonial president, Achmed Sukarno. However, President Sukarno's vociferous 'anti-imperialism' became a considerable thorn in the side of the Americans. In 1955 Sukarno had helped organise the 'Non-aligned Movement' within the United Nations — Third World countries that didn't want to follow either Moscow or Washington's Cold War diplomatic dictates. As early as 1956 the CIA's Deputy Director of Covert Operations suggested that 'it's time we held Sukarno's feet to the fire.' (Presumably he didn't mean this literally, although one can never be entirely certain.) In 1958 the US government had secretly supported an armed separatist rebellion on the island of Sumatra against President Sukarno. US support extended to sending arms and aircraft to assist the rebels. In 1975 a US Senate Committee investigating the CIA revealed that it had 'received some evidence' that the Agency had also planned to murder Sukarno and had even identified potential assassins.[31]

The US government's problem with Sukarno was a result of their being, in the words of historian William Blum, 'unable, or unwilling, to distinguish nationalism from pro-communism, neutralism from wickedness.' US plots to oust Sukarno extended to the truly ridiculous. According to Blum's history of the CIA, a 'substantial effort was made to come up with a pornographic film or at least some still photographs that could pass for Sukarno and his Russian girlfriend.' The resulting pornography (produced by the CIA in collaboration with the FBI!) was never actually used to discredit or blackmail Sukarno.[32]

In 1965, prior to General Suharto's bloody ascent to power, the United States had cut off all military assistance to Indonesia. This was not, however, in response to the fact that Sukarno had opted for 'Guided Democracy' in 1959, effectively ending Indonesia's experiment with democracy since a republic was first proclaimed at the end of the Second World War. US military aid to Indonesia was cut off because Sukarno had threatened western business interests in Indonesia, taking over US oil and rubber firms in March 1965. His earlier statement that the United States could 'go to hell with your aid' had also been viewed unfavourably in Washington.[33]

It would be wrong, however, to suggest that the American government orchestrated the overthrow of Sukarno and the massacre of half a million communists in Indonesia during 1965–66. Instead they sat back and watched — supplying logistical support and crucial, but quiet, political encouragement to those organising the killing. The US government, which was about to embark on a major war against communism in Vietnam, wept no tears for the PKI.

As the anti-PKI massacres started in early October 1965 the US Ambassador to Indonesia, Marshall Green, cabled Washington that he believed the Indonesian Army would crush the PKI and move things in a 'direction we would wish to see.' In this regard, Green believed that the army's 'success or failure is going to determine our own in Indonesia for some time to come.' As the killings intensified in late October the US Secretary of State advised the embassy in Jakarta that the 'campaign against PKI' should continue and indicated general support for Suharto's section of the army, which he saw as the 'only force capable of creating order.' A week later Ambassador Green cabled back reporting that the Indonesian Army was now fully involved in anti-PKI mass killings and that the Generals were contemplating ousting Sukarno and establishing military rule. Green indicated that he had 'made it clear that Embassy and USG [United States government] generally sympathetic with and admiring of what army doing.'[34]

Nor did the US embassy in Jakarta restrict itself to encouraging noises. In May 1990 the Kadane Report, published in the *San Francisco Examiner* and *Washington Post*, revealed that:

> The US government played a significant role by supplying the names of thousands of Communist Party leaders to the Indonesian army, which hunted down and killed them, former US diplomats say ... As many as 5000 names were furnished to the Indonesian army, and the Americans later checked off the names of those who had been killed or captured ... They included names of provincial, city and other local PKI committee members, and leaders of the 'mass organisations,' such as the PKI national labor federation, women's and youth groups.[35]

Kadane, whose report was primarily based upon interviews with former high-ranking US officials, including Marshall Green, revealed that the Americans believed that they had better information 'than the Indonesians themselves' regarding regional PKI leaders. The lists were handed over to Suharto's command structure. A former State Department official told Kadane that 'no-one cared' about the resulting death toll 'as long as they were communists.'[36]

The response to the Kadane Report in America was not universally favourable. Senator Daniel Moynihan wrote in the *New York Review of Books* on 28 June 1990 that 'we are poisoning the wells of our historical memory.' Privately, some of those who had given succour to Suharto and had encouraged the massacres must have worried about the historical enormity of the bloodstains. Even a 1968 CIA report argued that, 'In terms of the numbers killed, the anti-PKI massacres in Indonesia rank as one of the worst mass murders of the twentieth century.' The CIA described the killings as 'one of the most significant events of the twentieth century, far more significant than many other events that have received much more publicity.'[37]

The consequences for Indonesia were tragic and far-reaching. The bond between Washington and the new military rulers in Jakarta was a bond of blood. A decade later President Ford and Secretary of State Henry Kissinger met with General Suharto the day before the Indonesian invasion of East Timor and gave advanced blessing to the enterprise. Although Kissinger has consistently denied this (as recently as 1995), this is simply not true. Recently released secret State Department documents reveal that as early as 12 August 1975 Kissinger, discussing the issue of East Timor with his foreign policy advisers, told them 'it is quite clear that the Indonesians are going to take over the island [East Timor] sooner or later.'[38]

On 6 December 1975 the presidents of the United States and Indonesia met face to face in Indonesia and Suharto asked for Ford's 'understanding if we deem it necessary to take rapid or drastic action' with regard to East Timor. In response Ford told Suharto: 'We understand the problem you have and the intentions you have.' The documents reveal Kissinger attempting to ease the US president's apprehensions over the potential illegality of the impending invasion (under US law the Indonesian Army's US-supplied weapons were only meant to be used for self-defence), noting that 'it depends on how we construe it.' Kissinger also told Suharto that, 'It is important that whatever you do succeeds quickly' and warned against launching an invasion before Ford had left Jakarta. In a final chilling exchange on the matter, Kissinger asked Suharto if 'you anticipate a long guerilla war' in East Timor? Suharto's response was that there 'will probably be a small guerilla war.' The meeting then turned to issues of trade. The fateful invasion took place the following day.

In the West, Suharto continued to be praised by politicians for bringing peace and stability to the region. British Prime Minister Margaret Thatcher described the General as 'one of our best and most valuable friends.' Every Australian government from 1965 to 1998, Labor and Liberal, from Menzies to Howard and from Whitlam to Keating, did business with the dictatorship in Jakarta. Every Australian prime minister from 1965 to 1998 praised Suharto's leadership and vision. From the perspective of the western governments, the human and national rights of ordinary Indonesians (not to mention East Timorese) were a peripheral issue. The Indonesian government remained the West's most important Cold War ally in Southeast Asia. American military aid to Indonesia actually increased from US$83 million in 1975 to US$146 million a year by 1982.[39]

In a fair and just world General Suharto will be remembered not only for what his army did in East Timor, but for the terror of 1965–66. His name should go down in the darkest chapter of the history of Southeast Asia alongside that of Pol Pot. The names of several notable Australian and United States officials of the period probably deserve to follow him there.

Indonesia is the largest Muslim country in the world and in the 1965–66 anti-PKI massacres Muslim extremists had participated widely in the killing. In rural villages throughout the archipelago local Muslim militants were suddenly catapulted into the role of judge, jury and executioner — identifying PKI members, rounding them up, handing them over to the army, or putting them to death themselves. In the process many other Indonesians, perceived as being hostile to Islam or as simply too secular-minded, were also eliminated.

With the main nationalist, progressive and secular political forces under threat, under arrest, or under sentence of death, the more extreme proponents of Islam tried to fill the power vacuum in Indonesian society. However, having trudged over the corpses of the PKI, Islamic militants discovered, to their surprise, that the official corridors of power were closed to them. The 'New Order' proclaimed by General Suharto was not going to be expressly Islamic. In the bitter words of one Muslim activist, having done the army's dirty work, they were now treated by Suharto 'like cats with ringworm.'[40]

For Suharto the army's alliance with Muslim extremists was only ever a temporary affair. It was Golkar, the army-dominated political party, that was promoted as the official expression of national aspirations in the years after 1965–66, not the Islamic movement. Indeed, several Muslim political organisations remained banned under Suharto. Throughout Suharto's long tenure of power (1965–1998) the aging general recognised that Islamic fundamentalism posed a potential danger to his regime. The growth of Islamic extremism in many predominantly Muslim countries during the 1980s was generally anti-western, literal in its religious interpretations, and backward-looking (in the sense of longing to return to the certainties of a pre-industrial world). By comparison, the Suharto dictatorship was umbilically linked to both modernising western capital and US military aid.

The social dislocation caused by Indonesia's rapid rush towards industrialisation brought growing numbers of Indonesians back into the mosques. What worried Suharto was that besides spiritual solace, there was no guarantee that they would not also find, especially amongst the urban poor, growing numbers of aggrieved Islamicists there. Indeed, like the Communists during the 1960s, it was militant Muslim activists who revealed the cleavages in Indonesian society and became confident enough to take their protests into the streets. In 1984 a dozen protesters were killed when soldiers opened fire on an Islamic demonstration in the Jakarta port area of Tandjung Priok. The protesters had apparently been angered when soldiers had visited a mosque and not removed their shoes. In the aftermath of the killings, Muslims attacked and burnt a number of shops, banks and government offices. During the 1980s Islam increasingly became a language of dissent in Indonesia, conveniently providing the security forces with someone new to blame for acts of subversion.[41]

In response to these problems General Suharto relaxed restrictions on moderate Muslim political activity, made some comments in support of the Palestinians, and in 1991 embarked upon a pilgrimage to Mecca. Suharto's re-embrace of Islam was not universally accepted. Abdurrahman Wahid, the then popular and widely respected leader of the Islamic movement Nahdlatul Ulama (NU), emerged as a trenchant critic of the Suharto regime. Meanwhile, Muslim extremists continued to promote an Islamic fundamentalist state as the only workable solution to the social decay and poverty caused by Indonesia's growing industrial economy.

And so it was that when the discredited Suharto dictatorship collapsed in 1998 the Islamic movement did not fall with it. Indeed, Wahid became the first democratically elected president of the new Indonesia and all major parties continued to tread carefully around Muslim political sensitivities. Even the new president, despite his theological credentials, had to watch himself. When Wahid apologised to the victims of the 1965–66 massacres while leading Friday prayers at a mosque, and made other comments critical of Muslim involvement in the PKI massacres, he was visited at the presidential palace by protesting Islamic militants carrying swords.[42]

Which brings us to September 11. In the weeks after the destruction of the Twin Towers, American and Australian politicians decried the growth of Islamic fundamentalism and chattered nervously about pro-Taliban sympathies throughout the Muslim world. Even Abdurrahman Wahid had publicly denounced the United States as a 'terrorist nation'.[43] With trepidation some reporters wondered aloud what, if anything, the new Indonesian president, Megawati Sukarnoputri, would do to restrain those who were selling Osama bin Laden t-shirts in the dirty back alleys of Jakarta, or who marched in the streets calling for US hands off Afghanistan and, in the words of one placard featured on CNN, for 'Death to US Jews'.

Millions of westerners wondered what we had done to create this hate. The media pondered learned responses from retired US army generals, former Australian diplomats and such. And yet not one of them mentioned that the US government had supported the Indonesian Army and Islamic fanatics as they overthrew President Sukarno (Megawati's father) and soaked the country with the blood of half a million people during 1965–66, effectively eliminating the most powerful secular forces in Indonesian society at the time.

Under intense pressure, in October 2001 Megawati Sukarnoputri stated, in response to US plans to capture or kill Osama bin Laden by attacking Afghanistan, that 'no individual, group, or government has the right to try to catch terrorist perpetrators by attacking the territory of another country.'[44] Meanwhile extremist groups like Laskar Jihad and the Islam Defenders Front threatened to 'sweep' Americans out of Indonesia. There was a genuine fear that previous Muslim attacks on commercial symbols of 'Western decadence' could potentially become real attacks on real people. Laskar Jihad had already been involved, with the connivance of the Indonesian Army, in violent attacks on non-Muslim Indonesian citizens in West Papua, Maluku and Central Sulawesi. Even the moderate Ulemas Council, which eventually backed away from its call for jihad in solidarity with Afghanistan, criticised Megawati's tepid support for America's war on terror. Ironically, one Ulemas Council spokesman argued that 'Indonesia should be more independent from world powers', just as Sukarno 'always strived for.'[45]

However, the legitimacy of the West's fear of mysterious Indonesia seemed truly vindicated with the Bali bombing of October 2002 in which 200 people, including 88 Australians, lost their lives. The bombing was blamed on Muslim extremists from

Jamaah Islamiyah and a number of arrests were made. When two of the accused bombers later appeared in Indonesian courts they smiled at the cameras and shrugged off the imposition of death sentences. One, Imam Samudra, punched the air and shouted 'God is Great!' as the judge read the court's verdict. He was later confronted by an Australian man who had lost friends in the Bali bombing. Mr Laczynski, from Melbourne, waved an Australian flag and told Samudra that, 'I'm proud to be Australian.' In response Samudra, 'wide-eyed' according to the *Sydney Morning Herald*, yelled out 'Calm down infidel' and proclaimed that he was not afraid to die.[46]

In a video message broadcast on Al-Jazeera television a month after the Bali bombing Osama bin Laden had argued that 'reciprocal treatment is part of justice' — 'you will be bombed just as you bomb.' 'We warned Australia before,' Osama bin Laden raged, 'not to join in [the war] in Afghanistan, and [against] its despicable effort to separate East Timor. It ignored the warning until it woke up to the sounds of explosions in Bali.' Bali bomber Imam Samudra's message was somewhat more direct: 'Australia go to hell.'[47]

There are 140 million voters in Indonesia, which is now the world's third largest democracy. In 2004 they will elect a new president and attempt to consolidate Indonesian democracy. Western election analysts are predicting that Islamic fundamentalists may win as much as 15 per cent of the popular vote. How the country will continue to deal with the legacy of 1965–66 and the ongoing struggle between secularism and those who wish to turn Indonesia into the world's largest Islamic state, will determine the political future of our region for some time to come. We are witnessing the revenge of history in Indonesia today. And it is an ugly, ironic and cruel thing.

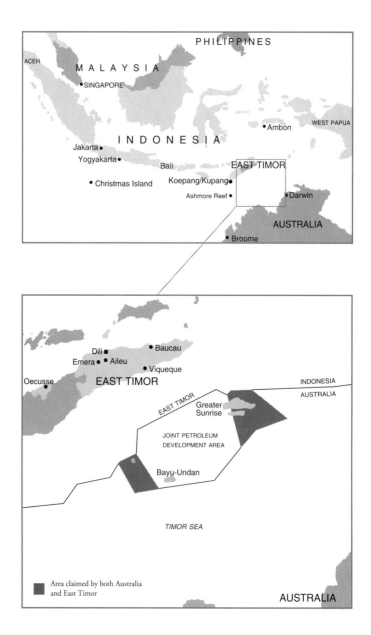

East Timor, Indonesia and Australia

Student Politics in Southeast Asia: In Memory of Kamal Bamadhaj

Whether total genocide occurs in East Timor or not depends not only on the remarkably powerful will of the East Timorese people, but also on the will of humanity — of us all.

Kamal Bamadhaj, 1991[48]

We showed eleven students who were travelling to East Timor as part of the University of Notre Dame's 'service learning' program a video about Kamal Bamadhaj, a Malaysian-born student who was studying at university in Sydney in the early 1990s. Kamal was almost ten years dead when we showed the video, and was only twenty when he was killed. He was a founding member of Aksi, an Australian organisation dedicated to supporting democracy in Southeast Asia and he went to East Timor to work as a translator for Community Aid Abroad. The video, called *Punitive Damages*, is about how Kamal's mother, Helen Todd, sued Indonesian Major-General Sintong Panjaitan, who commanded the troops responsible for the 1991 Dili massacre, in a US Federal Court. She was able to do so (eventually being awarded US$14 million in damages) under a law that makes violators of human rights anywhere in the world accountable if they are living in the United States. Appropriately enough, the law had originally been framed to punish pirates and slave traders.[49]

After the Dili massacre in East Timor on 12 November 1991 the international outcry was so great that the Indonesian regime felt compelled to punish Panjaitan. It did so by sending him to Boston so that he could study at Harvard University. Thus, fortuitously, the court case was able to be brought. In her declaration to the court Ms Todd said that:

> I bring this case not only as Kamal's mother but on behalf of hundreds of East Timor mothers who are forced to grieve in silence for their dead children. Our grief and anger is the same, but, unlike them, I can bring a case against a military officer without putting the rest of my family in danger. Whatever compensation is awarded by the court in this case will belong to the mothers of all the victims of the Dili massacre, and I will find a way to get it into their hands.[50]

The last time I spoke with Kamal was in Esme's Cafe at the University of New South Wales when we were both second year undergraduate students. It would have been late September or early October 1991, I suppose. He was about to depart for East Timor and his visit was planned to coincide with the arrival of a UN/Portuguese government delegation. I had a hot chocolate as we discussed East Timor, a country I knew very little about. I stupidly remember telling Kamal (as you might tell a friend about to drive home in the rain) to be careful, to stay safe. We made some vague agreement to try to meet up and have coffee when he got back so he could tell me all about his experiences. The next time I saw Kamal was on the front cover of a newspaper. Local Student Shot Dead in East Timor, or some such headline.

Helen Todd told the US court about how Kamal's death affected her:

> He was my only son, one of three children I raised as a single parent. When we [were] together, we shared a closeness which I treasured ... I watched him grow into an intelligent and caring young man with much to offer the world in the field of human rights — perhaps as a scholar, perhaps as a diplomat, perhaps ... we will never know.[51]

Even now I remember what the then Australian Foreign Minister, Gareth Evans, said of the November 1991 Dili massacre. He described the killings in Dili's Santa Cruz cemetery as 'an aberration by a section of the military.'[52] There had been about four thousand demonstrators at Santa Cruz when the shooting began. Most were young and many were wearing Catholic school uniforms. One of the few western eyewitnesses to the massacre, Russell Anderson, submitted a report to the Australian Department of Foreign Affairs and Trade with details of how the Indonesian Army had advanced on the demonstrators outside the cemetery gates.

> Suddenly a few shots rang out, followed by an explosive volley of automatic rifle fire that persisted for two to three minutes. It sounded like the whole fifteen

in the front row had their fingers pressed firmly on the trigger. They were firing directly into the crowd.[53]

In one of the photographs taken inside the small white concrete chapel at the centre of Santa Cruz cemetery on the day of the massacre, you can see people huddled in fear. Blood is splattered across the floor and up the wall. Rays of sunlight are shining through while a young man in jeans is lying on his side, wounded and quietly dying. Beside him another young man is sitting on the floor holding his friend in his arms. The second man has lost his shoes in the attempt to escape and his white socks are stained with dirt and blood. His friend is shot in the chest and will probably die. And yet the second man appears to be making no attempt to escape. It was reported by Bishop Belo that many of those who stayed in the chapel, with wounded friends and such, were later 'disappeared' by the Indonesian Army.

Of course there are those who still think it melodramatic to call what happened in Dili on 12 November 1991 a 'massacre' rather than simply 'aberrant behaviour'. In all, 271 innocent people were killed, 278 wounded and 250 reported missing. In the diplomatic language of the United Nations Special Rapporteur the events of that day were a 'planned military operation designed to deal with a public expression of political dissent in a way not in accordance with international human rights standards.'[54] But such words now appear as inadequate and shallow as the hasty graves the Indonesians dug for Kamal and his friends.

Prior to the arrival of Europeans the island of Timor had been part of an Asian trading network which reached as far as India and China. In particular, Chinese merchants collected various spices throughout the eastern regions of the modern-day Indonesian archipelago and brought them to Malacca for sale and onward shipment. Timorese involvement in this loose network was based principally around the trade in sandalwood. In return the traders introduced the horse, the buffalo and new crops to Timor.[55]

It was the developing European taste for exotic Asian spices that eventually drew Europeans to the archipelago. Portuguese entry into the Indian Ocean in 1498 opened up the opportunity to supplant earlier Muslim trade networks. In 1511 the Portuguese seized Malacca, an 'opulent city of 50,000 inhabitants and emporium of the spice trade' (in the words of economic historian Eric Wolf), and took over the trade themselves. Principally, the Portuguese were after pepper. During the sixteenth century pepper was at the top of the spice hierarchy. According to Wolf it was actually used as money in some parts of Europe: 'Like gold, it was durable and easily devisable, and it was often demanded in payment for taxes.'[56]

While the Portuguese were the first European maritime power to establish a trade monopoly in Southeast Asia, establishing forts and small settlements, they were soon challenged for control of the lucrative spice trade by the Dutch. In 1605 the Dutch succeeded in displacing the Portuguese from the Spice Islands, in what is now eastern Indonesia. Blood was spilt as the Dutch and Portuguese continued to battle over the Asian trade, with the Dutch eventually achieving dominance and establishing their headquarters at Batavia, modern-day Jakarta. With the Dutch in control of most of the archipelago, the coast of Timor remained under tenuous Portuguese command.

The Portuguese had initially landed on Timor around 1512, the exact date not being entirely clear. Regardless, they maintained only a token presence on the island, seeing it as not especially economically important and finding the mountainous landscape difficult to penetrate. Ongoing conflict with the Dutch resulted in the western portion of the island eventually being ceded to their control (except for the Oecusse enclave, which remained under Portuguese rule). The Portuguese gradually concentrated their colony on the eastern portion of Timor, with their capital at Dili, and with sandalwood and coffee dominating the local colonial economy. Portuguese colonial administration and 'development' were minimal. The first Governor was not appointed until 1701 and during the nineteenth century the famous seafaring writer Joseph Conrad despairingly described Dili as 'that highly pestilential place.' At the time of the outbreak of the First World War Dili still had no paved roads, and as late as 1970 the capital had only 28,000 residents.[57]

Outside the Portuguese hamlet of Dili and the Dutch base at Kupang (on the western end of the island), traditional Timorese life continued in the dense mountains and rugged interior of the island. The Timorese were often able to retard the imposition of colonial rule by playing one European power off against the other.[58] It was not until the late nineteenth century, by which time Portugal had declined to the status of a third-rate European power with a second-rate empire, that the Portuguese intensified their efforts to exploit their dwindling possessions. The Portuguese Royal Commission of 1889 argued that the government:

> ... should have no scruples in obliging and if necessary forcing these rude Negroes in Africa, these ignorant Pariahs in Asia, the half savages in Oceania to work, that is, to better themselves by work, to acquire through work the happiest means of existence, to civilise themselves through work.[59]

The resulting efforts by the colonial administration in East Timor to intensify exploitation were not accepted without protest. Between 1910 and 1912 a rebellion against Portuguese rule necessitated the importation of troops from Mozambique and Macau to suppress resistance. Violence was considered a more suitable palliative than colonial reform as about three thousand Timorese were killed. Following this 'pacification' campaign the border negotiations with Dutch West Timor were settled and the formal demarcation of the island — east and west — was agreed upon.[60]

Organised Christianity did not immediately follow the Portuguese to Timor, the first official visit by the Catholic Church occurring in 1561 when a Dominican friar arrived in Oecusse. It was not until 1621 that twenty missionaries arrived in Timor and set about the task of mass conversion of the population. Progress was slow but by 1750 East Timor had about fifty Catholic churches. While the Church was often the only visible institution of Portuguese colonialism in many rural areas, the majority of Timorese continued to practise animist beliefs. By 1930 the Church could only claim 18,984 adherents, representing a small number of local converts.[61]

In 1941 the Salazar dictatorship handed responsibility for all education in the Portuguese colonies over to the Catholic Church. This decision was the result of a 1940 accord between the Vatican and Salazar's government which argued that Catholic missions not only exhibited an 'imperial usefulness', but also exercised 'an eminently civilising influence' over the natives. Perhaps that helps explain why the majority of East Timorese continued to reject the Church's embrace. By 1973 it was estimated that less than half the population were practising Catholics and illiteracy was still 93 per cent.[62]

Not until after the collapse of Portuguese colonialism and the

December 1975 Indonesian invasion of East Timor did the vast bulk of the population embrace Catholicism. And embrace it they did — by 1999 over 90 per cent of East Timorese were Catholic and the religion was practised with what appeared to western eyes to be an almost frighteningly fervent devotion. The decision to use Tetum as the liturgical language played an important role in this regard. The Catholic Church was one of the few places where East Timorese could still congregate freely and hear their language spoken. Many believed the Church was all that stood between them and annihilation as a people.

In October 1989 Pope John Paul II visited East Timor.[63] An estimated 100,000 people attended the Papal mass at which the Pope appeared beneath a gigantic portrait of himself and General Suharto. There was also a small defiant attempt by the East Timorese to use the opportunity to protest against the Indonesian occupation. According to one of the student protesters, Constancio Pinto:

> As [the Pope] conducted Mass for 100,000 people, a group of the Catholic Boy and Girl Scouts unfurled protest banners hidden in the girls' clothing. It was like a blast bomb. People thought the Indonesians were going to start shooting and began to flee. But the Pope was there and it was difficult for them to open fire. They hurried him away but the media were present and for five minutes or so watched the whole thing.[64]

This constituted one of the first public protests by the East Timorese since 1975. For fifteen years East Timor had been covered in a blanket of censorship with few international journalists permitted to visit the territory. Whatever scant news existed of human rights violations was often fed to the outside world via the Catholic Church, which had become the only public institution in East Timor capable of offering limited opposition to Indonesian rule.

The Pope's visit was followed by that of John Monjo, the US Ambassador to Indonesia, a few months later. Monjo's visit also resulted in another small protest and it seemed that a pattern was forming. Indonesian General Murdani was furious. In a speech in Dili he ominously threatened that:

> There have been bigger rebellions, there have been greater differences of opinion with the government than the small number calling themselves Fretilin, or whoever their sympathisers are here. We will crush them all! ... Yelling in front of an ambassador ... won't solve the problem.[65]

Still, the fact that the Pope and a US Ambassador had both visited East Timor, and that the sky had not fallen, possibly influenced the Indonesian decision to allow a Portuguese delegation, under the aegis of the United Nations, to visit East Timor in October 1991. In Dili pro-independence student activists immediately set about organising a large demonstration to coincide with the arrival of the Portuguese. A few foreign journalists (and some clandestine independence supporters like Kamal) also turned up in Dili to cover the delegation's arrival. According to Bishop Belo the Indonesian Army began threatening individual East Timorese that if they demonstrated while the delegation was in town, they would kill their families 'to the seventh generation.'[66] Kamal, who had just over a week to live, wrote in his diary that:

Youths in Dili and other towns have been secretly painting pro-independence banners, organising demonstrations and, as many have admitted to me, preparing to die for their people if the Indonesians try to stop them. Timorese of all ages and walks of life have been signing up to be on the list of interviewees for this Portuguese fact-finding mission. Considering that talking to foreigners about the situation in East Timor is risky, there are large numbers who have decided to take the plunge and talk to the Portuguese when they come.[67]

When the visit of the Portuguese delegation was cancelled at the last moment, the Indonesian Army moved against local student activists. On 3 November Kamal wrote despairingly in his diary after it was announced the delegation was not coming:

Hearts sank. People could not believe it. The disappointment here today is not only the deflating of many high expectations, but, more worrying still, the indefinite delay gives the Indonesian military the perfect opportunity to eliminate all those Timorese who had exposed their identity while preparing for the visit.[68]

Two days after Kamal wrote those words a young man, Sebastiao Gomes Rangel, was killed. He was buried at Santa Cruz cemetery and on 12 November 1991 independence activists decided to risk everything by organising a public protest to coincide with a procession to Sebastiao's grave. The path to the Dili massacre lay ahead.

It was the students of Dili who organised the demonstration that led to the massacre at Santa Cruz cemetery in 1991. It was they who clandestinely met in darkened houses to paint slogans, turned bed sheets into banners, and risked arrest. Sebastiao Gomes Rangel was one of their friends and on the day of the 12 November protest they paraded with home-made banners that had things written on them like, 'Why the Indonesian military shoot our church'. Young kids in school uniform ran excitedly in front of the demonstration while the older students called for 'diciplina'. When they reached the cemetery many went inside to pay their respects at Sebastiao's grave. Hundreds more congregated outside the cemetery, standing on the walls and holding banners.[69]

Suddenly the Indonesian military could be seen, and heard, marching in formation up the street with their rifles at the ready. American journalist Amy Goodman was standing beside Kamal, himself a student activist at university in Australia, as the Indonesians approached. Nine days earlier Kamal had written in his diary about his fears for the East Timorese activists who had exposed themselves in the lead-up to the proposed visit of the Portuguese delegation. He wrote that 'now that the visit is off' the East Timorese were 'once again in the all too familiar position of being defenceless from arbitrary arrest, maltreatment, or even death.'[70]

While Goodman and another American journalist, Allan Nairn, moved forward in the hope that the unexpected presence of western journalists might prevent the soldiers from opening fire, Kamal stepped back and joined the students in the crowd. Kamal was shot in the arm and wounded in the withering fusillade that followed. Miraculously, he escaped from the cemetery and walked at least half a kilometre before he was shot again, this time in the chest. He was found a short time later by the Red Cross lying on the road. He was then placed in the back of a truck that was detained by the Indonesians before it could reach the hospital. By the time Kamal eventually made it into the hands of doctors, he was dead from loss of blood. The Indonesians buried him in a mass grave with the other massacre victims.[71]

In a packed 1995 public lecture in Melbourne, American academic Noam Chomsky pointed out that after the Dili massacre the Yogyakarta Students Association in Indonesia put out a public statement calling on their government, 'for the sake of humanity and our common wellbeing, to reconsider the fake process of integration in East Timor.' Soon after, eleven Javanese student councils called on the Suharto dictatorship to withdraw its troops and allow the people of East Timor a 'full and free "right of self-determination".'[72] Chomsky argued that the Indonesian students who released that public statement did so at considerable risk. At the time Suharto was still firmly in power and when Indonesian students publicly challenged the fiction that East Timor was Indonesian, they were risking arrest, prison and accusations of treason.

What all of this reflected was a remarkable transformation that was slowly taking place in Indonesian society. By the 1990s about 100 million Indonesians, almost half the population, were under the age of twenty. They had never known anything but the Suharto dictatorship and they became the key political force in fighting for an end to the corrupt and authoritarian system they had grown up in. It was university students who led growing public opposition to the Suharto dictatorship, especially after the 1997 crash of the Indonesian rupiah, whose value fell from 2400 to the US dollar in August 1997 to 10,000 to the dollar by 1998. It was estimated that the real value of Indonesian wages declined by 77 per cent during 1997. For the urban poor the price of essential foodstuffs rose disastrously — the price of rice increased by 38 per cent in less than a year, chicken by 86 per cent, cooking oil by 110 per cent.[73]

Student-led demonstrations, along with food riots, became a focus for the festering discontent with Suharto's regime. A protest at Gajah Mada University in Yogyakarta on 11 March 1998 was the largest student demonstration in the country in twenty years. The students organised a series of rolling demonstrations which lasted over three months. Strikes by Indonesia's burgeoning and super-exploited industrial working class also intensified. Workers at Nike and Barbie Doll factories, producing goods they could never afford which were intended for the US domestic market, went on strike and protested. Under relentless pressure, and with Indonesia lurching towards economic and political chaos, on 21 May Suharto finally resigned the presidency. Indonesia began its slow, but explosive, transition to democracy.

At the Indonesian parliament, where student protesters had occupied the building, the response to Suharto's resignation was effusive. Or as CNN reported:

> In a scene of absolute jubilation, the students revelled at the news of the resignation — hugging, singing, dancing and giving high-fives. They formed a conga line in a ceremonial pool outside the legislative building. Others prayed. Some students demand that Suharto be punished for his rule and the wealth that he, his family and his allies accrued. Other students chanted: 'Hang Suharto!' or 'Give his property back to the people!'[74]

The intimacy and complicity within the relationship between

successive western governments (especially Australia and the United States) and those Indonesians who oversaw crimes against humanity in Indonesia and East Timor is the principal reason Suharto will never be tried as an international war criminal and violator of human rights. He may not rule Indonesia anymore, but watching television at night, Suharto must be amazed by his luck in escaping even Saddam Hussein's, Jean Kambanda's (the former president of Rwanda, found guilty of genocide by the UN) or former Serbian president Slobodan Milosevic's fate.[75]

Suharto's removal was achieved at a terrible price. Six students were shot dead by the Indonesian security forces at Trisakti University on 12 May 1998. Hundreds more were tear-gassed or severely beaten during anti-Suharto protests. In Jakarta special 'security volunteers' (Pam Swakarsa) were deployed during May to defend Suharto and the parliament. Although the vigilantes were allegedly motivated by their desire to protect the integrity of the Indonesian nation, it was later reported that they were 'largely destitute men' who had been bussed in and paid 10,000 rupiah a day 'to attack student demonstrators.' The Indonesian Army and Police utilised 'security volunteers' in the same way their colleagues would secretly pay, train and arm the deadly militias in East Timor a year later.[76]

Nevertheless, the fact that Suharto was eventually overthrown, that East Timor is now free, and that Indonesia is experiencing a democratic awakening is the greatest possible tribute to the East Timorese and Indonesian student movements. It was a movement that Kamal Bamadhaj worked tirelessly to help organise, politically nourish and build ties with beyond the arbitrary borders imposed by governments. Kamal was born in Malaysia, educated in New Zealand and attended university in Australia where he studied Indonesian and was heavily involved in the international student movement. Kamal was killed in East Timor, the only foreigner to die in the Dili massacre — an event that brought the issue of Indonesian human rights abuses to the attention of the world for the first time. He never got to see a free East Timor and the democratic Indonesia that his death helped create.

A Debt of Blood:
Australia and East Timor

In December 1941 Australian commandos landed in Portuguese Timor (as East Timor was then known) to prevent the Japanese building air bases which could then be used to launch attacks on Australia. Notwithstanding Japanese imperial designs in Southeast Asia, without the presence of the Australian commandos the Japanese may never have invaded East Timor. They were certainly under pressure from their allies in Nazi Germany not to violate Portuguese neutrality.[77] With 400 Australian commandos in the mountains however, everything altered and over 20,000 Japanese soldiers occupied Timor. The Australian commandos then organised a guerilla campaign against the Japanese in which about 1500 Japanese and forty Australian soldiers were killed.

For the Australians survival depended on Timorese peasants providing food, shelter and sympathetic guides. Harry Levy, an ex-commando, spoke passionately of the support offered by the local population:

> Never once did the Timorese betray us. They were unbelievably loyal to us. That loyalty is why we survived

and why I am able to stand here more than five decades later, to tell you of the debt my comrades and I owe the Timorese people. It is a debt that we owe unto the third and fourth generations, and all the generations to come.[78]

At the time Australia had a 'whites only' immigration policy and some of the commandos carried their racism with them to East Timor. In the words of John 'Paddy' Keneally:

Everyone was inferior to us, we were the white people. Now some people might resent what I'm saying, but if they cast their mind back, people my age, cast their mind back, if they're honest with themselves, they'll admit that anything wasn't white was considered inferior. Now there was a lot of that attitude with us. We referred to the Timorese as 'Boongs,' in fact I noticed a situation report going out there in the records and the officer there said, 'I'm sending you a wireless, and a battery charger. Make sure you have Nig[ger] porters to carry it, and make sure you've always got Nig porters to look after it and get it away from danger.' Now the battery charger and the wireless were considered far more valuable than the Nig porter who was a Timorese.[79]

The Australian commandos eventually retreated from East Timor in January 1943. Many, like Paddy Keneally, were traumatised by the experience.

I tell you, that night on the beach, when we withdrew, broke my heart. We were all crying our eyes out, the Australians and the Timorese. We went to their country and we brought nothing but misery down on those people. They sacrificed their lives to prevent the Japanese invading Australia and we deserted them.[80]

Indeed, afterwards it was estimated that as many as 60,000 Timorese may have died during the Japanese occupation. More civilians died in tiny East Timor during the Second World War than died in Britain. More Timorese civilians died than all the Australian war dead killed across the entire globe during the war. The Allies bombed the island to ruins while the Japanese violently repressed the native population in their attempts to subdue them. During the war leaflets had been dropped from Allied planes, which promised:

> Timorese! Your Friends Do Not Forget You!
>
> For you, Timorese, the day of liberation is drawing nearer. The day is not far off when we shall go back there, counting on your friendship and goodwill to work with us and help us in driving out forever from your country these cruel pygmies.[81]

Of course when the so-called 'cruel pygmies', the Japanese, were finally expelled from the island, the Allies assisted the return of the cruel colonials, the Portuguese. For the Australian government the known evil of an unfree East Timor under the exploitative control of the Portuguese was preferable to an independent indigenous government. Despite their differences during the war, the Australian government shared with the Portuguese a historical sense of the need to bring the three Cs ('commerce, civilisation, and Christianity') to the 'natives' of Asia and the Pacific.

During the Second World War Portugal had been officially neutral. Unofficially, the sympathies of Antonio de Oliveira Salazar, Portugal's dictator, were with Hitler and Mussolini. In 1940 when the Nazis were winning the war, Salazar had openly proclaimed that he and Hitler were 'linked by the same ideology.'[82] Portugal also made a great profit selling tungsten, used in armour-piercing shells, to both sides during the war, only cutting off the supply to Germany after June 1944 when it was clear that the Nazis were beaten. It would take another thirty years for Salazar's military dictatorship in Portugal to fall and for East Timor to experience its first trembling moments of freedom.

Much has been made of the fact that as an independent East Timor emerged in 1974–75 after the fall of the Portuguese dictatorship, local politics were dogged by disunity. This is hardly surprising. Timorese disunity merely mimicked the centuries of rivalry amongst the Portuguese and Dutch colonials (with Japan thrown in for good measure) who not only continually fought each other for control of the tiny island and its resources, but had also intentionally undermined the possibility of Timorese unity. Under the Portuguese those independent-minded East Timorese who could not be bought off with jobs in the colonial administration were imprisoned and silenced. Under the Japanese they were tortured and killed. The Australians had deliberately raised expectations of political independence in order to secure Timorese support for their war against the Japanese, only to abandon East Timor to the Portuguese when the war ended.

The Australian government also gave its tacit approval to Indonesia's 7 December 1975 invasion of East Timor — an invasion designed to liquidate East Timor's desire for national independence and to forcibly incorporate the territory into the Indonesian republic. Australian journalist Roger East wrote in

1975 that, 'moral reasons are necessary to wage an immoral war.'[83] For Canberra and Jakarta those reasons included the alleged unviability of an independent East Timor. Australia's support for other small, and arguably much less economically viable, Pacific island microstates was all but ignored. Not to mention Australia's support for tiny, economically successful Asian states like Singapore (forty times smaller than East Timor) and Brunei.

Additionally, the Australian and Indonesian governments attempted to generate public fear that East Timor might become 'another Cuba'. The left-leaning rhetoric of Fretilin, the most popular party to emerge from the quagmire of East Timor politics after the collapse of Portuguese rule, was a particular concern. In this sense, Indonesia's invasion of East Timor was quite possibly Australia's most paranoid piece of Cold War foreign policy — justifying the invasion of a small half-island nation on the grounds that a desperately impoverished peasant population of less than one million people constituted a grave threat to regional stability and Australia's national security.

At least Richard Woolcott, the Australian Ambassador to Indonesia at the time of the 1975 invasion, was privately honest. He sent a secret telegram to Canberra in August 1975 that advised the government to allow 'events to take their course,' by which he meant for Canberra to keep quiet about growing Indonesian military intervention in East Timor. With brutal honesty he cabled that, 'I am recommending a pragmatic rather than principled stand but that is what national interest and foreign policy is all about.'[84] Or in other words, it was necessary to sacrifice the East Timorese in order to maintain Australia's strategic alliance with the Suharto dictatorship.

As for Roger East, he was murdered by the Indonesians on the first day of the invasion. He paid for his support for East Timor's independence with his life. According to some witnesses, East was captured by the Indonesian Army in the centre of Dili, his hands were tied with wire and he was dragged to the wharf. Along the way East could apparently see Timorese being executed and pushed into the sea. Standing on the wharf, with seconds to live, he allegedly abused the Indonesian soldiers before he joined the dead Timorese floating in the tide.[85] The Australian government did not officially protest Roger East's death. Instead it continued to appease his murderers, with Richard Woolcott advising the Australian government that:

> Finally, we believe the emphasis should now be on accepting the inevitability of Timor's incorporation into Indonesia, letting the dust settle and looking ahead while taking what steps we can in Australia to limit the further growth of hostility towards Indonesia within the Australian community.[86]

To the surprise of both Canberra and Jakarta, it took the Indonesians several years to gain military control over East Timor. The popular pro-independence party, Fretilin, and its armed wing, Falintil, tenaciously held on to small liberated enclaves. And when the end came in 1978 and the last of the liberated zones fell, the shattered remnants of Falintil went deeper into the mountains where they continued a desperate low-level guerilla war.[87]

Legendary East Timorese resistance leader Xanana Gusmao and his Falintil comrades fought in isolation and with no hope of military victory. Falintil guerillas realised that in all likelihood the future offered them nothing but defeat and despair, possibly cut short by death at the hands of the Indonesian Army. They had no international military backers, no liberated zones or friendly countries to retreat to, no supply of weapons or medicines other than those they took off dead Indonesian soldiers, and no easily defendable bases. Anyone who helped them faced death, and they were unable to see or protect their families. And still Falintil fought on in the mountains, far from home, for years on end — mountains that Xanana described as being 'mournfully dressed with bones.'[88]

The military strategy of Falintil recognised that they did not have the ability to seriously contest Indonesian military control over what Xanana called, 'our prison-island'. Instead they had to content themselves with small skirmishes, occasional ambushes, and with the knowledge that their very survival as a guerilla army, against all odds, was as much a source of inspiration to their people as it was a source of intense irritation to their enemies. Xanana's slogan, 'to resist is to win,' reflected Falintil's belief that their greatest weapon was simply endurance.

In 1997 an Australian journalist, John Martinkus, made it to a Falintil camp in the hills outside Baucau. There he met twelve Falintil fighters including the local commander, David Alex. According to Martinkus, 'All except for two of them had bullets inside their bodies. They all had malaria and they all had kidney infections from the bad drinking water.' The doctor who secretly travelled with Martinkus was the first doctor the guerillas had seen in a decade. Several had been fighting in the mountains since 1975, almost all had been wounded at some point, and had been forced to let bullets heal inside them. Martinkus wrote that, 'Sitting there, I could also see that it would just keep going on like this until all these men were dead.' After twenty years of resistance, David Alex was finally killed by the Indonesians in 1997.[89]

The abandoned and resilient East Timorese people would have to wait until 1999 before they would get the chance to vote on their country's future. It was only then, following the collapse of the Suharto dictatorship and in response to mounting international pressure, that Indonesia agreed to hold an independence referendum in East Timor. In the lead-up to the referendum vote of 30 August 1999 the Indonesian Army actively encouraged pro-Jakarta militias to attack independence supporters and destabilise the territory.

Nevertheless, there are few things as powerful as an idea whose time has come. On 30 August 1999 people voted overwhelmingly to reject Indonesian rule. In response the pro-Jakarta militias were good to their promise, destroying East Timor's public infrastructure and murdering any political opponents they could get their hands on. By the time the United Nations peacekeepers arrived in the country at the end of September it had been reduced to ashes. Dili was gutted. It was only then that the Indonesians withdrew, the remaining Falintil guerillas came down from the mountains, and East Timor's future began.

It had been the Australian Labor Party's left-wing reformist hero, Gough Whitlam, who, when still Prime Minister, had met with General Suharto in September 1974 and indicated that he believed 'Portuguese Timor should become part of Indonesia.' Whitlam never explicitly encouraged an invasion. What he said to Suharto was that absorption 'should happen in accordance with the properly expressed wishes of the people of Portuguese Timor.' However, Whitlam must have realised that he was talking to a military ruler who had overseen the deaths of half a million of his own people when seizing power during 1965–66, and had also completed the 'integration' of West Papua into the Indonesian

Republic. Technically speaking, West Papua had been voluntarily absorbed into Indonesia according to the properly expressed wishes of its people. The reality was that the place had been militarily occupied and then annexed, all with the blessing of the United Nations and with hardly a word being raised internationally in defence of the West Papuan independence movement. Essentially, Whitlam was indicating to Suharto that Australia had no objection if a similar process were quietly embarked upon in East Timor.[90]

It is easy to read duplicity and malevolence into the actions of Whitlam where there was quite possibly only ignorance and a complete lack of compassion for the East Timorese. According to former Australian diplomat James Dunn, during the 1960s most Australian politicians and government bureaucrats considered East Timor to be an 'untidy colonial relic'.[91] Whitlam simply thought it made sense for East Timor to become part of Indonesia and so he told Suharto that. From then on the Australian government sat back and tried to keep a respectful distance just in case things got ugly.

When Whitlam spoke to Suharto on the issue of East Timor again, in April 1975, he was much more direct. He voiced his concerns over public reactions to rumours of an impending Indonesian invasion of East Timor, which Whitlam believed showed ordinary Australians to be 'overly nervous and fearful of Indonesia.' He stressed how important the relationship between his government and the Indonesian dictatorship was to him. And he commented that he 'could not help feeling the majority of the people of Portuguese Timor had no sense of politics, and that in time they would come to recognise their ethnic kinship with their Indonesian neighbours.'[92]

While Whitlam and his most important adviser on the issue,

Richard Woolcott, might be able to claim that they had no way of knowing that the Indonesians would commit widespread human rights abuses in East Timor (although, again, their knowledge of Indonesian history should have caused them to see this was a strong possibility), their excuses could not be utilised by subsequent Australian governments. Malcolm Fraser was caretaker prime minister at the time of the 1975 invasion and implemented policy which effectively isolated the East Timorese resistance from their support networks in Australia and through them, their access to the world. Among other things, all radio contact between Australian supporters and the Fretilin resistance was cut.[93]

The United Nations never formally recognised the Indonesian occupation of East Timor. Malcolm Fraser's government had no such qualms. In 1979 Australia accorded *de jure* recognition of Indonesia's occupation of East Timor. And yet, by the late 1970s it was already clear that serious crimes against humanity were being perpetrated by the Indonesian Army there. During 1979 independent observers reported widespread famine and were already using words like 'near genocide'. Agricultural output had fallen from 42,100 tons before the invasion to 12,600 tons in the first year afterwards. An estimated 90 per cent of Timorese livestock was killed, lost or stolen during the first three years of war. By 1979 an Indonesian Jesuit priest working in the village of Ainaro was burying up to four people a day and estimated the local population had decreased from 9600 in 1976 to only 4600 three years later. Approximately five thousand villagers had been killed, starved, or had otherwise disappeared. Across the half-island, an estimated 300,000 people were dead, displaced, or missing.[94]

Although Australian officials may have been able to claim that they were ignorant of specific atrocities, the general outlines of the situation were not beyond their comprehension. Recent evidence has emerged that in January 1979 the Australian Joint Intelligence Organisation (JIO), using signals intelligence, had compiled an extensive secret report on 'The Indonesian Integration of East Timor'. According to revelations published in the *Sydney Morning Herald*, Chris Jones, an army major who worked at JIO and saw the secret eight-chapter report, commented, 'You'd cry if you read it.' Detailing the full horror of the Indonesian occupation, sixteen copies of the report were circulated amongst 'Australian and allied intelligence services' before being locked away. In other words, if the Australian Intelligence community wasn't giving Australian politicians and the public specific details, it wasn't because they didn't know.[95]

The popular Labor Prime Minister Bob Hawke publicly wept in front of television cameras for the Chinese students killed at Tiananmen Square in 1989. Following the Iraqi invasion of Kuwait in 1990 Hawke passionately argued, 'Big countries cannot invade little countries and expect to get away with it.' And yet, it seemed he never shed a tear for East Timor. Indeed, in August 1985 his government had confirmed the *de jure* recognition of East Timor's annexation. In 1994 Paul Keating, Hawke's successor, said that 'no country is more important to Australia than Indonesia.' In 1995, the year before East Timorese activists José Ramos Horta and Bishop Belo were awarded the Nobel Peace Prize, at a time when international awareness of the East Timor issue was peaking, Paul Keating's government awarded the Order of Australia to Ali Alatas, the Indonesian Foreign Minister. Infamously, Alatas once described East Timor as just a 'pebble in the shoe' of Indonesia.[96]

Even John Howard had an appalling record on East Timor. He liked to present himself as the concerned saviour of East Timor after its 1999 independence referendum (it was Howard who sent the Australian/UN peacekeepers), but in 1996 Howard had said, in defence of the Indonesian regime, that 'you can't always expect countries with whom you want to have good relations to have the same value system as we have.'[97] During 1997, while Suharto was still desperately clinging to power (he was toppled in May 1998), Howard's government initially refused to accept nearly 1500 East Timorese seeking political asylum in Australia, threatening to deport them to Portugal if they didn't want to return to Indonesian-occupied East Timor. The Howard government did not want to embarrass Suharto by accepting the refugees. Such was the respect with which the Australian government continued to treat the aged dictator right up to the last moments of his rule.

Of course, having a disgraceful record on East Timor was not limited to Australian prime ministers. Gareth Evans, Australia's long-serving Foreign Minister, publicly supported, in violation of various United Nations resolutions, Australia's recognition of Indonesia's forced incorporation of East Timor. According to Evans there was 'no binding legal obligation not to recognise the acquisition of territory that was acquired by force.' For a politician who assiduously promoted himself as an accomplished international diplomat, Evans was forced to rely on the basest of cliches to justify his position. After all, Evans argued, 'the world is a pretty unfair place.'[98] It was also Evans who, as Foreign Minister, signed the Timor Gap Treaty in December 1989, by which Australia and Indonesia divided East Timor's rich natural gas and oil reserves between themselves. A photographer snapped a commemorative photo of Evans and Alatas toasting each other with champagne in a jet flying above the Timor Sea.

On the ground in East Timor, Xanana Gusmao, the legendary guerilla leader, was interviewed by Australian journalist Robert Domm from a jungle hideout outside Ainaro. Xanana accused

Australia of being 'an accomplice in the genocide perpetrated by the occupation forces.' When asked specifically about the Timor Gap Treaty he said, 'I think it is a unilateral, illegal decision, illegitimate and criminal, in the context that we are being exterminated by a party to this agreement … It shows the dirty, cynical and criminal policies practised by the Australian Government in regards to East Timor.'[99]

What happened in East Timor between 1975 and 1999 demanded a response from the Australian government. And as John Birmingham has written:

> The response was denial. Denial that the death toll could be that high. Denial that the atrocities could be that bad. Denial that a modern state, with which we sought close relations, could pursue so destructive an end by such vile means. Denial that by recognising its sovereignty over the island we were approving of its actions. And denial that we had been besmirched by our failures, by our foolishness, our clumsiness, our cowardice and our gross moral turpitude.[100]

Put crudely, the Australian government's response to East Timor's tragedy over the twenty-four years from 1975 to 1999 — Labor and Liberal, from Whitlam to Keating, and from Fraser to Howard — was shameful. Although oil, political opportunism and Cold War paranoia were not the only determining factors in Australia's foreign policy on East Timor, they stained everything and diminished us all.

Australia's debt to East Timor remains only partially repaid. Australia is the richest nation in our region, while East Timor remains the poorest. Unemployment and illiteracy are still extremely high on the half-island. Despite desperate attempts to rebuild infrastructure destroyed by the pro-Indonesian militias in 1999, only one in five houses has clean drinking water and one in three has electricity. While former East Timorese guerilla leader, now President, Xanana Gusmao, has praised Australia for its contribution, via the United Nations peacekeeping force INTERFET, in helping East Timor achieve independence, the dispute over ownership of the oil and gas in the Timor Sea remains unsettled.[101]

According to international maritime law, sea boundaries between countries situated close to one another should be drawn at the median line between the two territories. Australia, however, is clinging to a deal it made with the discredited Suharto regime that gave it access to a significant portion of East Timor's rich underwater oil and natural gas fields. Rejecting East Timorese pleas to negotiate a final sea boundary based on international norms (which would place the oil and gas fields in East Timorese territorial waters) Australia has already started exploiting several fields in the disputed region. It is estimated that if Australia continues with this 'oil and gas grab', East Timor might lose up to US$10 billion in much needed revenue. In the words of President Xanana Gusmao:

> How can we prevent poverty if we don't have money? How can we reduce disease, how can we stabilise the country, how can we strengthen the democratic process, how can we strengthen tolerance … if we don't have money?[102]

The obvious solution to the Timor Sea dispute would be to take the matter to the International Court of Justice or the

International Tribunal on the Law of the Sea. However, Australia withdrew from both bodies in 2002, partly because it knew that the international bodies would, in keeping with convention, probably enforce a median line boundary and place the disputed fields under East Timorese control. Since 1999 the amount of tax revenue the Australian government has received from the disputed Laminaria Corallina field alone is approximately $1 billion. This is several times more than the amount of aid given to East Timor by the Australian government since the militia rampage of 1999.

East Timor is free at last. But despite the strong sympathetic ties between ordinary Australians and East Timorese following the events of 1999, it appears that old habits die hard with the Australian government.

The World Is Watching:
The Media and East Timor

In Australian journalist Greg Shackleton's last report from the East Timorese town of Balibo, filmed on the same day in 1975 that he and four colleagues were later executed by Indonesian soldiers, he mentioned that:

> Something happened here that moved us very deeply. It was so far outside our experience as Australians that we'll find it very difficult to convey to you, but we'll try. Sitting on woven mats, under a thatched roof, in a hut with no walls, we were the target of a barrage of questioning from men who know they may die tomorrow and cannot understand why the rest of the world does not care.[103]

He signed off from, 'an unnamed village which we will remember forever, in Portuguese Timor.'

Working under the shadow of what had happened to Greg Shackleton, Roger East, and the other western reporters killed in East Timor, John Pilger was among a select group of journalists who used his international reputation to fight tirelessly for the East Timorese cause. Pilger visited East Timor and secretly filmed a powerful documentary about the country's plight. I remember watching *Death of a Nation* during an activists' conference in Sydney in the early 1990s. There were many East Timorese present in the darkened lecture room and occasional sobs emanated from towards the front. The response of the Australian government was less empathetic. Prime Minister Paul Keating, always a close ally of the Indonesian dictatorship, publicly attacked the veracity of *Death of a Nation*'s evidence regarding the Dili massacre. The fact that Pilger had previously won many international awards for his reporting was ignored. According to Pilger:

> This was a propaganda gift for the Jakarta regime, which published what it called the Australian Prime Minister's 'official judgement' on my film, and released it to the press wherever it was shown around the world. I doubt if there has been another time when an Australian prime minister and a senior Cabinet minister [Gareth Evans] have used their high office vehemently to deny evidence, in a work neither had seen, of murderous violence carried out by a ruthless dictatorship in an illegally occupied territory.[104]

Pilger was joined by journalists such as Allan Nairn, Amy Goodman, John Martinkus, Robert Domm, Max Stahl, and American dissident academic Noam Chomsky, who all played an important role in continually pushing a story that until recently, few mainstream newspapers wanted to publish. In their attempts to expose the truth about East Timor they provided one of the few positive examples of western engagement with the tiny half-island. It was sometimes at tremendous personal risk.

In 1990, for instance, Australian Robert Domm had conducted the first interview with resistance leader Xanana Gusmao from high in the mountains outside Ainaro. Xanana, speaking freely ten years later, placed the interview in historical context:

> Robert Domm's visit was one of the important moments in our struggle, just because he was the first-ever journalist going to meet us in the jungle. It was very exciting; we were very, very worried about the possibility of having combat during his stay in the jungle.[105]

Domm himself later told Radio National about his secret journey through East Timor to interview the resistance leader:

> To meet with Xanana Gusmao we had to secretly leave Dili and travel by car for many hours. We then walked for perhaps twenty kilometres through the rugged mountains. Finally, when I thought I was done for, one of the guerillas pointed ... I looked up and saw this 'mini-Matterhorn' covered with jungle and totally inaccessible ... By the time we reached the camp I was exhausted, climbing on my hands and knees. Suddenly Xanana appeared from nowhere and I scrambled up, shook his hand ... The history of the moment struck me immediately. For fifteen years no outsider had got to them, and they seemed like a lost tribe ...[106]

Domm's interview revealed the East Timorese resistance's authentic voice from deep in the jungle. And in bringing that voice to the ears of radio listeners in Australia (where it was broadcast on

Radio National) Robert Domm undoubtedly risked his life.

No less inspiring example was provided by American journalists Allan Nairn and Amy Goodman. Both witnessed the 1991 Dili massacre and were attacked by Indonesian soldiers. Nairn was smashed in the head with M16 rifle butts, suffering a fractured skull. According to Goodman, Alan was 'covered in blood' and his 'whole body was in spasm' as the soldiers beat him. Then the soldiers apparently couldn't make up their minds whether to finish him and Goodman off. In Nairn's opinion, they only decided not to kill the two journalists after they established they were Americans. The weapons they had fractured Nairn's skull with, the weapons their colleagues were still shooting down demonstrators with, were US-made and supplied. In Goodman's opinion, the soldiers knew 'they would have to pay a price for killing us that they had never had to pay for killing the Timorese.'[107]

Back in America Goodman attended several White House press briefings and on the day it was announced that José Ramos Horta and Bishop Belo had been awarded the Nobel Peace Prize she interrupted a 'Q&A session' about President Bill Clinton's new golf clubs in order to ask a question about East Timor. It was not well received. Goodman also remained a merciless critic of the mainstream US media. According to *Media Lens*, one study of the *New York Times* index between 1975 and 1979 revealed that only 70 column inches were dedicated to the issue of East Timor, as compared to 1175 column inches dedicated to denouncing and detailing the 'killing fields' in Cambodia under Pol Pot. Some media commentators, including Goodman, felt that the explanation for this journalistic oversight was, quite simply, that military dictator General Suharto was a Cold War ally while Communist despot Pol Pot was not.[108]

Amy Goodman claimed that in 1979, when the killing in East

Timor peaked, there was not a single article on the issue in the *Washington Post* or *New York Times*. She also claimed that no major US television network ran a story on East Timor between the time of the 1975 invasion and the 1991 Dili massacre. There was, except for the efforts of alternative journalists like herself, a virtual media blackout in America concerning East Timor. As Goodman told her audience at a lecture in June 1997, the Timorese 'can't march in the streets of the US, they certainly can't march in the streets of their own country, although when they do they get gunned down with US weapons. It is really up to us.'[109]

In 1984 José Ramos Horta spoke to the National Press Club in Canberra. His speech alluded to the recent Falklands war and the fact that Britain (with western support) had sent its armed forces halfway around the world in order to defend the 'principles of self-determination' for 'two thousand settlers in the Malvinas Islands.' Horta commented that when the television pictures of the war revealed 'the terrain of the Malvinas, showing the penguins, the goats, etcetera, I could not help thinking: maybe these wild penguins, these lazy goats, have more rights to self-determination than myself and the people of East Timor.'[110]

It had been Horta that Indonesian Foreign Minister Adam Malik had written to in June of 1974, shortly after the collapse of the Portuguese dictatorship in Lisbon, insisting that 'the independence of every country is the right of every nation, with no exception for the people in Timor.'[111] However, the political ground in Indonesia was shifting quickly. Just over a year later, General Suharto publicly stated that an independent East Timor was simply 'not viable.' Then in August 1975 the Uniao Democratica Timorense (UDT) launched a political coup in Dili with Indonesian backing and the express goal of halting the advance of communism in East Timor. Their real intent was to halt the popular rise of the independence movement represented by young Fretilin militants like José Ramos Horta.[112]

It was the growing mass popularity of Fretilin (which had only been formed in May 1974) that allowed it to militarily defeat the UDT's coup and force UDT's armed supporters over the border into Indonesian West Timor. On 28 November 1975, with the threat of Indonesian invasion looming large, Fretilin declared East Timor to be an independent nation. The Democratic Republic of East Timor lasted just nine days. On 7 December the full-scale Indonesian invasion began. A dawn naval bombardment of Dili was followed by a marine landing and paratroopers being dropped on the outskirts of the city. On 17 July 1976 Suharto declared East Timor to be the Indonesian Republic's twenty-seventh province. Meanwhile, beyond the occupation of Dili, the war for control of the half-island raged on.

After 1977 the Indonesian Army adopted a 'strategic hamlet' or 'encirclement' strategy in East Timor designed to isolate East Timorese guerillas from the local population. The US Agency for International Development estimated that by 1979 about half the population of East Timor (an estimated 300,000 people) had been corralled into designated Indonesian-controlled villages. Civilians were also forced to participate in the 'Fence of Legs', where they were used in gigantic sweeps of the countryside; mass walks designed to flush out guerillas hiding in the jungle. Also in 1979, a Red Cross representative described the famine situation in East Timor as being 'as bad as Biafra and potentially as serious as Kampuchea.'[113] The difference being that the world actually cared about Biafra or Pol Pot's destruction of Kampuchea (Cambodia). East Timor was ignored, a marginalised cause. No television crews were sent to cover the atrocities. There was no moral outrage in the editorial columns of mainstream newspapers in Washington, London or Sydney.

During the long years of Indonesian occupation José Ramos Horta became a sort of combined activist, diplomat and propagandist for the East Timorese cause. He continually moved across the globe petitioning government representatives, speaking at protests, writing articles and lobbying the media. In April 1991 — seven months before the Dili massacre — José participated in a forum in Washington DC on the issue of East Timor. During the discussion, which involved a number of academics and several individuals from the US State Department, a former US Air Force Colonel commented that he had seen no evidence of human rights abuses when he visited East Timor. The Colonel then politely insinuated that international supporters of the East Timorese cause may have been exaggerating about the situation there. These comments were backed up by another retired US Army officer who had also experienced nothing amiss during his visit to Indonesia's disputed twenty-seventh province as a guest of the Indonesians. José asked to say something in response. He mentioned that he had lost a teenaged sister and two brothers to Indonesian soldiers armed with US weapons and that he had no idea where they were buried.

> One day, when I can find their graves, I will say to them, 'You idiots, you were not there because you were not seen. No-one saw you killed so wake up!' … The oil men who came here, the US diplomats who came here, the Third World diplomats who came here, they did not see you. They did not see you killed, so you are not dead.[114]

More than anyone else, José continually pricked the conscience of the West and he remained the voice of those unseen and unreported dead of tiny abandoned East Timor.

It was Max Stahl who actually shot the shaky video footage of the Dili massacre and to him goes the dubious distinction of being the first westerner to film the naked brutality of Indonesian rule in East Timor, and to live to tell the tale. While the army carried out its attack on the crowd at Santa Cruz, Stahl shot video for ten minutes at a time and buried the tapes in the dirt of fresh graves. He was arrested by the Indonesians inside the cemetery but was eventually released and was able to smuggle the videotapes out of East Timor. Because of Max Stahl the Dili massacre became news. In the words of one of the student organisers of the demonstration, because of Stahl's videotape, 'for the first time we were able to break the silence.'[115]

Indeed, from the perspective of the western media, what happened that day at Santa Cruz changed everything. Goodman commented that by the time she and Nairn arrived at a hospital on the island of Guam, where Nairn finally received treatment for his fractured skull, the phones were ringing constantly — 'For the first time in seventeen years the international media was interested in what had happened in East Timor.' And yet, when Nairn and Goodman made it back to the United States three days after Santa Cruz they discovered that only the print media ran with the story. According to Goodman, television reporters explained to her that it was a case of 'no pictures — no story,' a policy, Goodman pointed out, that ensured that military dictatorships would continue to kill journalists and prohibit television reporters from entering their countries when they realised that if you can't see it on CNN, then it never happened.

At that stage Max Stahl's videotapes had still not been smuggled out of East Timor, although they eventually made it on to American television screens on 21 November, nine days after the Dili massacre. Viewers were appalled by the footage of young students gunned down by soldiers carrying US-made weapons. Suddenly East Timor was an issue and a year later when Bill Clinton was running for president he gave a major foreign policy speech in New York. Afterwards, he answered a question on the issue of US military funding for Indonesia. In his careful response he was quite possibly the first US presidential candidate to publicly address the issue of East Timor. He said that Americans had ignored the conflict there in ways that were 'unconscionable'.[116] The power of television.

John Martinkus, who later produced one of the most powerful books ever written about East Timor, *A Dirty Little War*, initially found Australian newspaper editors similarly unwilling to report on East Timor, even after the Dili massacre. According to Martinkus, in 1995 he was told directly by the foreign editor of one major Australian daily that, 'we are not going to publish anything on East Timor' and was asked to 'stop bothering us.' The Indonesian authorities were even less appreciative of his journalistic talents. During 1997 Martinkus was kicked unconscious by undercover Indonesian police. Nevertheless, Martinkus continued reporting directly from East Timor, virtually the only western journalist based there. During 1998 he found evidence of the widespread killing of civilians during an Indonesian Army offensive against East Timorese guerillas. In his own words:

> The newspapers didn't believe it — or didn't care. It was a frustrating situation. People were putting their

lives at risk to give me details of what was happening and that news was still not getting any further than me. I wondered what I was doing wrong or if it was just that nobody really gave a shit about what happened in a small, isolated village in the south of East Timor.[117]

When in late 1999 East Timor suddenly became a big story in the West many of these journalists — including Martinkus, Goodman, Nairn and Stahl — must have marvelled at the hundreds of western media who now suddenly stood blinking in the sunlight at Dili airport. Many of the newcomers quickly abandoned East Timor again when the militias plunged the country into total chaos following the 30 August UN-sponsored referendum. Not that you could blame them. The militias openly threatened to kill journalists (particularly Australians), and a European reporter named Sander Theones was shot dead in Dili.[118]

Nevertheless, Martinkus stayed through most of the militias' reign of terror and was evacuated on the last UN flight to leave Dili. Max Stahl went up into the hills outside Dili, where he filmed the plight of the refugees there, virtually the only western cameraman to do so. Allan Nairn stayed after the final UN evacuation and was arrested by the Indonesian police when he was discovered hiding in the smoking ruins of Dili. He was allegedly the only journalist left in the entire desolate city at the time.

Interestingly, East Timor's first democratically elected government has renamed the street on which Sander Theones was killed, Avenida Liberdade da Imprensa, Freedom of the Press Avenue. It is a fitting tribute to the continuing importance of critical journalism and the power of the written word today.

Big Problems in Our Backyard:
Indonesia and John Howard's Australia

Alone, tired and trapped in Dili — the bustling, dirty capital of East Timor — for a day during July 2001, I managed to find a young boy selling the local newspaper, the *Timor Post*. I bought one and read the English page while I waited for my lift back up to the mountains. The prose wasn't fantastic but one story concerned the ongoing problem on the West Timor border where former militias were still holding 100,000 East Timorese in refugee camps. A spokesman for the militias was quoted as saying that although they had a strong desire to return to East Timor, 'we don't want to go home as loser, while Jakarta hands off, forgetting we have defended the Red and White' (a reference to the colours of the Indonesian national flag).[119]

The other major English language story in the *Timor Post* that day had been lifted from the *Sydney Morning Herald* and concerned ongoing violence in the fractured Indonesian region of Aceh. Like East Timor, Aceh is rich in oil and gas and, also like East Timor, a significant proportion of its residents do not want to be part of Indonesia. According to the article the Indonesian Army had formed 'East Timor-style militias' amongst the 260,000

Javanese transmigrants in Aceh to assist in the suppression of the separatist movement. These militias were backed up by an estimated 30,000 Indonesian soldiers and police, including 800 'specially trained troops' sent to defend the Exxon-Mobil gas fields. About 300 Kopassus (Indonesian Special Forces) soldiers had also been deployed in the region. The results were predictable, with the report noting that sixteen people had recently been killed when the Indonesian Army had thrown a hand grenade into a hut where several suspected rebels were hiding. The Free Aceh movement later claimed that only four of the sixteen were separatist fighters; the rest were innocent civilians.[120]

Given that Indonesia is Australia's largest and most significant Asian neighbour, you may well ask yourself what the attitude of the Australian government was to all this refugees, grenades and dead civilians carry-on. On one level there is no denying that there was an important shift at the highest level of the Australian government regarding Indonesia after the 1996 election of Liberal Prime Minister John Howard. In particular, increased international awareness of the East Timor issue, combined with growing economic and political crisis in Indonesia (the effects of which helped bring down Suharto), caused the Australian government to move cautiously towards a new position. However, Howard's Foreign Minister, Alexander Downer, initially continued the decades-long tradition of dutiful adherence to Australia's 'special relationship' with the Indonesian dictatorship. Tim Fischer, Howard's Deputy Prime Minister, had even gone so far as to describe General Suharto as perhaps the world's greatest figure in the second half of the twentieth century.[121]

In December 1998 John Howard wrote to President Habibie, who replaced Suharto after his resignation, gently suggesting change with regard to Indonesia's occupation of East Timor. This was the first major indication of new thinking inside the Australian government. In January 1999 Habibie, freshly conscious of international criticism in light of Indonesia's increased dependence on IMF funds following the Asian currency crisis, and partly in response to Howard's letter, dramatically announced that if East Timorese people did not accept his June 1998 offer of 'special status' as an 'integrated part' of Indonesia then they might be granted independence instead. While Habibie's initiative was rejected by Indonesian opposition leaders, including Megawati Sukarnoputri, it was clear that a new opportunity was opening. In August 1999 the United Nations held a referendum on East Timorese independence and the half-island slid into chaos as pro-Indonesian militias set about the destruction of East Timor.[122]

Ironically, John Howard's letter to Habibie, which contributed to the Indonesian decision to hold a referendum in East Timor, had actually praised Habibie's 'visionary lead' and emphasised that Australia preferred East Timor to remain part of Indonesia. Alexander Downer also stated that it was still Australia's view that it was more 'convenient' for East Timor to 'remain legally part of Indonesia,' albeit with increased 'autonomy'. This was the real intention of Howard's letter, despite the fact that it inadvertently facilitated the 1999 independence referendum.[123]

In 2001 writer John Birmingham argued that Australia's policy of appeasement towards the Indonesian dictatorship was continued up until the last crucial moments of the Suharto regime. By Birmingham's estimation, Australian policy was one of 'wilful blindness, made possible only because we were always somewhere else when the trigger was pulled.'[124] When the Indonesian-backed militias embarked upon their murderous rampage in September 1999, after the results from the UN referendum were announced, the Australian government moved awkwardly to confront the crisis. Alexander Downer constantly made excuses for the Indonesians — blaming the violence on rogue elements in the army and praising the 'goodwill' of President Habibie.[125]

Throughout Australia the response of ordinary people to all of this was disgust and outrage. Disgust that militias were hacking people to death and outrage that nothing was being done to stop it. Indeed, many ordinary people were appalled by the Australian government's attempt to maintain the fiction that the Indonesian military could somehow be relied upon to bring peace to the situation. Even more potentially dangerous, however, was the belief — which penetrated the highest echelons of the Australian political establishment after the deployment of UN peacekeepers in East Timor — that having 'sorted out' the East Timor problem, and notwithstanding the occasional exchange of gunfire between Indonesian and Australian soldiers on the West Timor border, official Indonesian–Australian relations could, and should, revert to their old pattern. Such a perspective ran the risk of failing to learn the real lessons of East Timor's tragedy.

In June 2001 the Indonesian government released from prison the leader of the pro-Indonesian Aitarak militia, Eurico Guterres. Having led the destruction of East Timor during 1999 Guterres had been taken to Indonesia and sentenced to six months in jail for inciting violence. Hundreds of people were killed in the violence that Guterres helped foment and he served a grand total of twenty-seven days in jail before Jakarta released him. He wasn't even kept behind bars, but was incarcerated in a 'government housing complex' before his release. He immediately returned to West Timor where his followers still controlled the refugee camps on the Indonesian side of the border. About 100,000 refugees were still there at the time and it was assumed that many would have gladly returned to East Timor if the militias allowed them.

At the same time the head of UNTAET (the UN administration in East Timor), Sergio Vieira de Mello, told *Time* that there was 'no precedent that matches the scope of the challenge facing the UN in East Timor.'[126] There was no functioning water or electrical system, no telephones, and almost every significant building had been burned or destroyed. It was principally the pro-Indonesian militias who had created this 'challenge'.

The militias had a penchant for giving their groups fierce names — Aitarak ('Thorn'), Ahi ('Fire'), Besih Merah Putih ('Red and White Iron'), Darah Merah ('Red Blood'), and Mahidi ('Life or Death for Integration') to name just a few. The prevalence of names based around red and white was, of course, a reference to the colours of the Indonesian national flag. The militia strategy, although it depended for its success upon local collaborators willing to do the dirty work, was inspired and directed by the Indonesian security forces. There was a history to this. During the 1965–66 anti-communist massacres which brought General Suharto to power, the Indonesian Army had relied extensively on gangs of civilians (especially Muslim extremists) to do the killing. While the gangs usually operated under army direction or instigation, a great deal of autonomy was also given to them.

Similarly, in East Timor during the early 1990s, as a result of the intractable guerilla war and in response to the growth of the pro-independence student underground, the Indonesian Army set up local paramilitary groups, or militias, as they became more commonly known. One such initiative involved the construction of *Gardapaksi*, supposed youth 'civil defence' groups based in urban areas and responsible for night-time attacks on independence supporters. In Dili, where the Gardapaksi were commonly referred to as 'Ninjas' because of their black clothing and balaclavas, independence activists were routinely 'disappeared' under cover of darkness.

In 1997 Australian journalist John Martinkus was taken to view 'a headless body, no hands, no feet,' that was lying in the tide just outside Dili. He later wrote:

> In another country this would have been a crime scene, cordoned off while the authorities investigated then removed the horrible spectacle. In East Timor at that time, it was the authorities themselves who were responsible. Their point was blunt: support independence and this is what will happen.[127]

Meanwhile in the easternmost regions of East Timor Kopassus were training Team Alpha, a local auxiliary group designed to assist the Indonesians in their operations against pro-independence East Timorese guerillas. The developing relationship between Kopassus, Team Alpha and the fearsome 'Ninjas' was crucial to the later development of Aitarak and all the other 'red and white' militias that the Indonesians set to work during 1999.[128]

Kopassus had been responsible for some of the worst atrocities in East Timor. As a West Australian I was particularly disturbed to discover that in the past Kopassus had sent soldiers to the Australian SAS base in Perth for training in, among other things, 'hostile interrogation'. One can only guess how that training was later put to use in East Timor. It is also assumed that it was Kopassus troops who murdered the five Australian journalists at Balibo in 1975. Interestingly, after East Timor achieved its freedom the former Australian foreign minister, Gareth Evans, wrote about Australia's ties to the Indonesian military, claiming that, 'I am one of those who has to acknowledge, as Australia's foreign minister at the time, that many of our earlier training efforts helped only to produce more professional human rights abusers.'[129]

During 1999, in the escalating violence that preceded the 30 August United Nations referendum on *integrasi* (integration), Eurico Guterres emerged as the public face of the militias in Dili. Eurico claimed to have 800 armed men under his command. During early August he told a rally of pro-integrationists that East Timor would become 'a sea of fire' if people voted for independence. At militia rallies in Viqueque and Aileu pro-integrationists expressed their loyalty to Indonesia and to local militia leaders like Eurico by drinking dog's or goat's blood mixed with wine.[130]

As growing numbers of international media began arriving in East Timor to cover the 30 August UN referendum, Eurico's long hair, youth (he was 28) and penchant for bloodthirsty soundbites all made for a good story. As leader of the Aitarak militia he had both a personal army *and* a mobile phone. He was a media sensation just waiting to happen and John Martinkus described meeting Eurico as being 'a bit like discovering a second-rate celebrity for the first time.'[131] When the television cameras arrived to record East Timor's descent into chaos (over 165 foreign journalists were in Dili for 30 August), Eurico was there to squeeze every murderous second out of his fifteen minutes of fame.

It was a curious and somewhat sad path that led Eurico to the centre-stage of East Timorese politics. He apparently first started out as a pro-independence youth activist, which was why he was arrested and badly beaten by Kopassus in 1988. He was later 'turned' and recruited by the Indonesians to serve as a Gardapaksi leader in 1994. He then apparently participated in 'Ninja' activities in Dili, terrorising the youth movement he once belonged to. The resulting money and power drew him further into the nexus of Indonesian repression. At one point Martinkus travelled by helicopter with Guterres to a pro-integration rally outside Dili.

> Eurico looked like he was having the time of his life. His vanity was stroked by his Indonesian bosses and when they allowed him occasional indulgences — such as a helicopter — he loved it.[132]

The district of Ermera — which includes Ermera town, Gleno, Atsabe, and Letefoho and has a combined population of about 90,000 people — was at the centre of the eruption of militia violence. Militias across the Ermera district were loosely organised into *Darah Integrasi* (Blood of Integration), under the command of two brothers, Miguel Soares Babo and Antonio dos Santos. According to one international observer based in Ermera, Miguel was often drunk and Antonio was an Indonesian Army officer. Both were determined to force through a pro-integration vote.[133]

Although the 30 August ballot was supposed to take place in free and fair conditions, under UN supervision, in Ermera the independence movement suffered murderous repression which made campaigning nearly impossible. The umbrella organisation of the Timorese resistance, Concelho Nacional de Resistencia Timorense (CNRT), had their office in town burnt down and during April local militia and the army killed nine people. A local community leader connected to the CNRT was shot dead in the street. Three other local CNRT leaders were forced to attend a pro-integration rally and to sign a document disbanding the

CNRT in Ermera. One was compelled to drink chicken's blood in an oath of allegiance to Indonesia. Meanwhile in Gleno western journalists were taken to see the badly decomposed corpses of eleven people who had been stabbed to death. The dead were displayed outside the medical clinic. A local priest insisted that the murders were perpetrated by militia, who had also killed six high school students and dumped their bodies in a nearby river.[134]

When the referendum was eventually held on 30 August militia members shot at the UN helicopter that came to pick up the ballot boxes from Gleno. For good measure they also burnt down ten houses and kept 140 UN staff under siege in their compound. In Atsabe an East Timorese man working with the UN was stabbed to death. Under intense pressure, and despite its earlier promises to stay, the UN retreated from Ermera district. An estimated forty pro-independence supporters were killed in the district between 30 August and the end of September, with about half the deaths occurring in Gleno.[135]

It is representative of the bravery and determination of the East Timorese that not even militia violence could stop them from voting for independence. On 4 September at the UN compound in Dili it was announced that 94,388 people had voted for 'special autonomy' within Indonesia (meaning, integration) and that 344,580 had voted against, representing a 78 per cent vote in favour of independence. It was then that the militias put Plan B into effect. Under Indonesian Army supervision, the militias carried out a scorched earth policy. The water, power and communications infrastructure of every major East Timorese town and village was systematically destroyed. People fled to the hills as the militias went on the rampage.

Matt Frei from the BBC saw militias hack a man to death with machetes. He later described the attack as being so 'ferocious that bits of [the victim] were literally flying off. The sound reminded me of a butcher's shop — the thud of cleaved meat, I'll never forget it.'[136] Even the Catholic Church, which was generally viewed as being pro-independence, was not safe. Several Catholic nuns, brothers and priests were murdered outside Baucau and in Suai.

Those Timorese who were not killed or did not flee were forcibly deported to West Timor by the militias. In all an estimated 280,000 people were forced over the border into Indonesian West Timor. There were strong Khmer Rouge-like, 'Year Zero' overtones to this. Or as a reporter from the Melbourne *Age* reported from Ermera during December 1999:

> Gleno, the provincial capital, was almost completely destroyed. All public buildings, including the court, schools and clinics, have been partially or completely destroyed, along with 90 per cent of private dwellings. Atsabe and Hatolia were similarly devastated. All electric power stations were vandalised and damaged … The [Gleno] communications centre, the only one outside Dili with a modern satellite facility, was completely destroyed.[137]

And yet by then the militias and Eurico Guterres were gone — vanished over the border. The red and white Indonesian flag they had murdered their fellow East Timorese to defend was lowered over Dili as their Indonesian paymasters packed up and went home. Eurico Guterres was later appointed to an important position within Megawati Sukarnoputri's party prior to her becoming President of Indonesia.

Despite attempts by Megawati, under pressure from the international community, to hold some of those guilty of the 1999 militia violence in East Timor accountable in Indonesian courts, there has been little progress towards real justice. Of the 116 suspects accused of human rights abuses in East Timor by the National Human Rights Commission, only twenty-three cases were prepared for prosecution. Of the eighteen soldiers and former militia members put on trial in Indonesia during 2002–03, less than half were convicted of any crime. One of the few found guilty was Eurico Guterres, who was finally sentenced to ten years in prison. The really 'big fish' however, swam free of the net. Although the United Nations claims he has a serious case to answer, General Wiranto, the overall commander of the Indonesian Army and the militia strategy in East Timor, was not charged with human rights abuses by the Indonesian government, although he did release a CD of love songs, *For You My Indonesia*, around the same time as the militia trials. He is currently running as a candidate for the Indonesian presidency in 2004.[138]

The historic failure of the Indonesian Army to crush the East Timorese resistance was more than a mere 'pebble in the shoe' for Indonesia, to use Foreign Minister Alatas' infamous phrase. In 1994 academic Adam Schwarz gave his assessment of how the East Timor issue was creating a crisis of confidence in the Indonesian military:

> The failure to pacify Timorese unrest has engendered in the army real doubts about the strength of Indonesian national unity and kindled fears that democracy could lead to the unravelling of the Indonesian archipelago.[139]

On Indonesian Independence Day in 1998 a leading Indonesian magazine published a poll that revealed that ninety per cent of surveyed Indonesians were worried the country was about to fall apart.[140] The intensification of secessionist struggles, sectarian conflict and ethnic violence after the collapse of the Suharto dictatorship during 1998 heightened these anxieties. Western academics began discussing the potential 'Balkanisation' of Indonesia and the resulting destabilisation of Southeast Asia. People who had only recently discovered that a place called East Timor existed were suddenly debating 'Timor-type scenarios' in West Kalimantan, Ambon and Aceh.[141]

In particular, the forgotten eastern Indonesian province of Irian Jaya (West Papua) seemed most worrying. West Papua is rich in nature and culture with the world's second largest tropical forest (after the Amazon) and hundreds of scarcely studied languages being spoken by its unique indigenous people. However, to its detriment, West Papua is also rich in minerals with the massive western-owned Freeport mine being the biggest known gold deposit in the world, as well as the planet's third-largest copper mine. Freeport, which began mining West Papua in the 1970s, became Indonesia's single largest taxpayer and Henry Kissinger sat on its board of directors. Located high above the clouds, Freeport's massive mine (four kilometres wide and 600 metres deep) was conservatively estimated to hold US$40 billion worth of minerals, and the company listed revenue of US$1.8 billion for the year 2000. Very little of this wealth has trickled back to the traditional owners. Instead, in 1997 the Indonesian press reported that an entire West Papuan village had been buried under mud and tailings pouring down from the mine.[142]

West Papua, whose people are Pacific Islanders rather than

Asians, was supposed to pass from Dutch colonial rule to independence under United Nations supervision. However, with the assistance of US President Kennedy it was handed over to Indonesia to 'administer' in 1963 as a prelude to an 'act of self-determination'. Indonesia simply annexed West Papua after a now discredited UN-sanctioned ballot held in 1969 (only one thousand hand-picked tribal elders out of a population of about one million were allowed to vote). Recently Chakravarthy Narasimhan, the former UN undersecretary who administered the passage of West Papua into Indonesian hands, commented that the vote was 'just a whitewash' and that the 'mood at the United Nations was to get rid of this problem as quickly as possible.'[143]

Rejecting the sham vote for integration, the Free Papua Movement (OPM) have maintained a long, bitter, armed resistance against Indonesian rule from the deeply jungled mountains. Although the Free Papua Movement does not currently have the international profile that East Timor's resistance managed to build, awareness of the West Papua situation is increasing. These days the OPM — who have fought the heavily armed Indonesian Army with axes, bows and arrows — even have their own website. The 'Liberation Army of the Free Papua Movement' homepage tells interested web surfers that:

> We are not terrorists!
> We do not want modern life!
> We refuse any kinds of developments:
> Religious groups, aid agencies, and governmental organisations
> Just Leave Us Alone, Please![144]

The website goes on to explain the 'Historical and Political Reasons for Fighting':

> We are misplaced by translocation/relocation, urbanisation and other social engineering activities carried out by the Indonesian government under the support of the World Bank and other international aid agencies ... We are regarded as [a] security disturbance force and terrorists even though we are fighting for our own environment, our own rights, and our own people ... Fighting back is important for the very survival of tribal people on this planet, not by lobbying, not by persuasion, not by diplomacy, not through democracy ... We will no longer be ignored.[145]

In this context, it is worth remembering that it had been Suharto who had commanded the 1962 Indonesian campaign to wrest West Papua from the Dutch and strangle the inchoate independence movement there. In this he was assisted by a young commando officer called Benny Murdani, who first won fame in Indonesia by leading a parachute mission in West Papua and later won international notoriety for his bloody role in East Timor. West Papua was the training ground for many of those who would construct Suharto's 'New Order' after 1965 and the experience of their violent 'pacification' campaigns there would influence the army's conduct during East Timor's occupation.[146]

Despite attempts by the Indonesian president, Megawati Sukarnoputri, to defuse the conflict in West Papua by offering semi-autonomy, during November 2001 a senior West Papuan independence leader, Theys Eluay, was murdered. Eluay's body was found in his car and it appeared he had been strangled to death. His killers had tried to push Eluay's mini-van into a ravine in order to make it appear like an accident, but its plunge had been stopped by a tree. Suspicion immediately fell on Kopassus, some members of which Eluay had met earlier in the evening. Eluay's death sparked off serious rioting and further rebellion in West Papua.[147]

The bloody situation in West Papua did not stop the Howard government from signing a post-September 11 'counter-terrorism agreement' with Jakarta which specifically recognised the 'territorial integrity' of Indonesia. The agreement was seen as a public rebuke of the separatist movements in Aceh and West Papua.

Many of the current leaders of the Indonesian military have built their careers fighting separatist struggles and eliminating 'disloyal' Indonesian civilians. Recent reports indicate that the Indonesian Army — which is already heavily implicated in violence around the Freeport Mine area — is attempting to replicate its East Timor militia strategy in West Papua and in Aceh.[148] In short, East Timor remains a litmus test for Indonesian democracy and human rights. Indonesia also remains Australia's greatest foreign policy challenge.

3

THE 'AXIS OF EVIL'

World Politics Beyond Good and Evil

States like these, and their terrorist allies, constitute an axis of evil, arming to threaten the peace of the world.

George W Bush

During his January 2002 State of the Union Address the President of the United States, George W Bush, denounced Iran, Iraq and North Korea as constituting an 'Axis of Evil'. Political analysts immediately began speculating as to why other countries had been excluded from the official evil club. Some obviously had their 'evilness' ignored because of political expediency (Saudi Arabia), others were too powerful to call evil in a public place (China), and some apparently just weren't important enough to register on President Bush's evil-detecting political radar (Burma). Joking emails started circulating regarding an 'Axis of Just as Evil' — made up of Libya, China and Syria — as well as an 'Axis of Somewhat Evil' which included Sudan. There was also a suggested 'Axis of Countries That Aren't the Worst But Certainly Won't Be Asked to Host the Olympics,' forgetting that even Nazi Germany got a chance to host the world games. The whole thing just seemed so ridiculous — an 'axis of evil' — as if the world could somehow be divided into groups of good guys and bad guys, with America and its 'Coalition of the Willing' waging a monumental war on an abstract noun — terrorism. Except that the president of the most powerful nation in world history was deadly serious, as 20 million Iraqis were soon to find out.

Quite how two mortal enemies and the world's most isolated state could constitute an 'axis' was never seriously challenged in mainstream media and politics. Nevertheless, the alleged existence of this 'axis of evil', when combined with the ongoing threat of terrorist attacks on the United States, provided justification for astronomical increases in United States military spending. Such increases were duly approved in the United States Congress despite the fact that in 1995, well before 9/11, the US already spent more than twice as much on its military as China, Russia, Iraq, Iran, North Korea, Syria, Libya, Cuba and all the other alleged 'evil-doers', axis members or not, combined.[1]

Or to look at the issue from another direction, why was a country like Uzbekistan left off President George Bush's 'evil' list? Perhaps part of the reason is because this Central Asian country was used as an airbase for US strikes against the Taliban in 2001. Not unlike Iraq in the 1980s, Uzbekistan is rich in gas and oil, and is a secular dictatorship in a region plagued by militant Islamic extremism. During 2003 Uzbekistan's government actually received US$86 million in funding from the US government, US$30 million of which went to Uzbekistan's police and security services. These are the same forces that, according to George Monbiot and based on data from Human Rights Watch, continue to hold more than 6000 political and religious prisoners:

Every year, some of them are tortured to death. Sometimes the policemen or intelligence agents simply break their fingers, their ribs and then their skulls with hammers, or stab them with screwdrivers, or rip off bits of skin and flesh with pliers, or drive needles under their fingernails, or leave them standing for a fortnight, up to their knees in freezing water. Sometimes they are a little more inventive. The body of one prisoner was delivered to his relatives last year, with a curious red tidemark around the middle of his torso. He had been boiled to death.[2]

It seems reasonable to assume that the reason Uzbekistan was not included on Bush's evil list was not because it is an unknown or unimportant country, but because Uzbekistan is currently an ally of the United States, Britain and Australia in the war on terror. Its sins are therefore ignored or forgiven, just as those of Saddam Hussein, General Suharto of Indonesia, Mobutu of Zaire, the Shah of Iran and numerous others were similarly ignored or forgiven by the United States, Britain and Australia during the Cold War.

Nevertheless, the current United States government, under President George W Bush, continues to promote the idea that the complex and complicated global political environment can somehow be explained by reference to biblical concepts of good and evil. On 11 October 2001, exactly one month after the 9/11 terrorist attacks, President Bush, speaking at a press conference, made the following remarks about the growth of hostility towards the United States government:

How do I respond when I see that in some Islamic countries there is vitriolic hatred for America? I'll tell you how I respond: I'm amazed. I'm amazed that there's such misunderstanding of what our country is about that people would hate us. I am — like most Americans, I just can't believe it because I know how good we are.[3]

Although it is axiomatic for Americans (and by extension British and Australians) that they are always on the side of 'good' in the current global war on terror, such views certainly aren't shared by everyone amongst the world's population. For example, the US State Department has allocated US$600 million to 'public diplomacy' — leaflets, seminars, broadcasts and other initiatives designed to convince the people of the world that the US occupation of Iraq and the ongoing war on terror is all in the interests of global peace, prosperity and security. It has not gone particularly well, especially in the Muslim world. As reported by the *New York Times*, US Congressman Jim Kolbe, reviewing the program in the House appropriations subcommittee, pointed out that polls revealed that 'only 15 per cent of Indonesians, 7 per cent of Saudis and 15 per cent of Turks have a favourable image of America — despite their governments' friendly relations with Washington.'[4] Even in major western nations like France, Canada or Germany a growing number of people see the United States as lurching dangerously towards continual military intervention and unilateralist foreign policy.

The politics of the 'axis of evil' and the war on terror seem to demand that we attack some heinous dictators and support others. The essays in this section reveal how such a course of action has failed in the past. History shows us that dictatorial regimes that receive funding, arms and political support from the West often beget even greater 'evil' when they finally collapse or are overthrown. This section of the book is about the United States' campaign against countries belonging to the so-called 'axis of evil' and about alternative methods of 'regime change'.

An Index of Acceptable Evil (abridged)

	Has WMDs	Has invaded neighbouring countries	Prohibits democracy	Tortures its citizens	Sponsors terrorism	Allied to USA
Saudi Arabia	X	X	√	√	√	√
Pakistan	√	√	√	√	√	√
Uzbekistan	X	X	√	√	X	√
Israel	√	√	X	√	X	√
Russia	√	√	X	√	X	N/A
Egypt	√	√	√	√	X	√
Indonesia	X	√	X	√	√	√
Turkey	X	√	X	√	X	√

(Sources: Human Rights Watch, Amnesty International,
US State Department Human Rights Report, 2003)

North Korea — Where the President is a Corpse and 'Dear Leader' Rules Supreme

I'm running out of villains. I'm down to Castro and Kim Il Sung.
US General Colin Powell,
at the end of the 1991 Gulf War [5]

North Korea is ruled by a corpse. The president of the Democratic People's Republic of Korea is still Kim Il Sung, a man who has been dead for ten years and whose mummified corpse is an object of national veneration. His son, Kim Jong Il, the effective ruler of North Korea, has not taken over his father's official title and Kim Il Sung is now referred to as 'President for Eternity' by North Koreans. There are 34,000 statues of Kim Il Sung in the country and his portrait is displayed in every building.[6] None of which changes the cold hard fact (excuse the pun) that the North Korean head of state is the President and the President is dead. Although his son is now the unquestioned communist dictator of the country, the austere ghost of President Kim Il Sung still haunts everything that North Koreans do, see or think.

George W Bush hates North Korea. In a private interview with veteran *Washington Post* journalist Bob Woodward, Bush exclaimed 'I loathe Kim Jong Il!' and waved his finger in the air. 'I've got a visceral reaction to this guy, because he is starving his own people.' In case he had missed the point the first time, Bush reminded Woodward that:

> It is visceral. Maybe it's my religion, maybe it's my — but I feel passionate about this.[7]

So visceral and passionate that he appeared prepared to risk war on the Korean peninsula for the second time in fifty years. At the beginning of 2002 Bush denounced North Korea's ruler, Kim Jong Il (who took over leadership in 1994 when his father died), as 'evil'. Condoleezza Rice, Bush's National Security Advisor,[8] explained to the media that this meant that North Korea (like Iraq) had been 'put on notice.' Soon afterwards Bush visited South Korea and stood behind bulletproof glass on the southern side of the Demilitarised Zone (DMZ) between the two Koreas. As Bush peered through binoculars into North Korea, a US soldier pointed out a 'peace museum' inside of which are allegedly axes used by two North Korean soldiers to kill two US soldiers in 1976 while they were working cutting trees in the DMZ. 'Did you hear that?' Bush asked the assembled media. 'No wonder I think they're evil.' Surveying the 248 kilometre barbed wire fence, guard towers and minefields which still divide the country almost a half-century after the Korean War ended, Bush proclaimed 'We're ready.'[9]

Ready for what? While Bush had said that the United States 'had no intention of attacking North Korea,' he had also spoken of the urgent need for 'regime change' there.[10] In his more warrior-like moments, Bush hinted that the winds of change (and war) which were about to overtake Saddam Hussein and Iraq might soon blow north along the Korean peninsula. Certainly the North Koreans interpreted Bush's inclusion of North Korea in the 'axis of evil' as, according to their foreign ministry, 'little short of a declaration of war.'[11] The problem was, from the North Korean perspective, that Saddam Hussein had tried to please the Americans and the United Nations, had allowed arms inspections and attempted to broker a deal, all to no avail. The UN imposed sanctions and the US dropped bombs. The North Koreans' conclusion (reached long before the March 2003 invasion of Iraq took place) was that the only thing that the Americans respect is armed force and the actual, as opposed to imagined, possession of weapons of mass destruction. And so in early October 2002, as Bush was preparing the political ground for an invasion of Iraq, North Korea announced that it was trying to build a nuclear bomb.

The Americans, jaws dropping, immediately quietened down the sabre rattling, emphasising that they were interested in dialogue with Kim Jong Il's government, not war. When questioned about why Iraq got sanctions and threats of invasion for its suspected development of WMDs, while North Korea got dialogue and debate for its actual admitted development of nuclear weapons, the US government replied that they treated each country, even evil axis ones, as separate cases requiring different approaches. Somewhere behind closed doors in North Korea, Kim Jong Il was smiling. When the US eventually invaded Iraq in March 2003, the North Korean government put out a statement saying that the attack proved that to prevent war 'it is necessary to have a powerful physical deterrent.'[12]

Perhaps President George W Bush should read a little more Korean history. If he did so he would discover that it is full of stories of Korean opposition, and unity, in the face of armed incursions into the peninsula by powerful foreigners. There is a unifying rage in Korea against the humiliations and injustices heaped upon its people by foreign armies of occupation in the past (the Chinese, Japanese, Soviets and Americans to name only the most recent). One story, particularly popular in North Korea, stands out. During the 1860s the United States government was seeking to open up foreign markets in North Asia via 'gunboat diplomacy'. In August 1866 a heavily armed American schooner, the *General Sherman,* sailed up the Taedong River in what is currently North Korea. The captain of the ship intended to sail to Pyongyang where he planned to petition the Korean monarchy to open up their markets and country to American influence. Ignoring constant Korean requests for the *General Sherman* to leave Korean waters, the American captain of the ship reportedly opened fire on Koreans protesting against the presence of the US ship from the banks of the river. Eventually the ship ran aground in shallow water. Angry Koreans then set fire to the *General Sherman* and killed its entire crew. Their corpses were mutilated and burnt.[13]

Although the *General Sherman* incident is not taught in American high schools and barely rates a mention even in university textbooks about US history, it still resonates in contemporary Korea. Similarly, many Koreans are aware that US Marines first invaded their country in 1871, forcibly opening Korea up to American trade via bayonets and bullets. About 350 Koreans and three Americans were killed in this little known armed conflict. And of course, during the twentieth century Korea suffered war and devastation on a grand scale.

First Korea endured the national humiliation of colonisation under the Japanese (1910–1945) followed by military occupation and partition by the Soviet Union and the United States at the end of the Second World War. Partition made absolutely no sense whatsoever to Koreans. Korea had been a single country and culture for millennia. Moreover, it was not a defeated protagonist in the Second World War, during which it had been an unwilling colony of Japan. (By comparison, no countries occupied or colonised by Nazi Germany between 1939 and 1945 — France or the Netherlands to mention just two — were similarly treated.) Partition made sense only within the distorted logic of the Cold War by which the Soviet Union and the United States divided the world into 'spheres of influence'.

In the contentious and disputed region of North Asia, the partition and joint occupation of Korea satisfied the needs of both superpowers for relative geopolitical parity. The Korean people were not consulted about what they thought of their country being cut in half. Indeed, the arbitrary border between North and South Korea at the thirty-eighth parallel was decided by two officials from the US State Department (one of whom was Dean Rusk, later US Secretary of State during the Vietnam War). The Russians accepted the proposal and Korea was divided, although officially partition was to be only temporary. Both superpowers then built client states inside their respective halves of Korea, a situation which dramatically increased political tension on the peninsula and led eventually to a disastrous civil war.

Between 1950 and 1953 communist North Korea (with Chinese support) fought capitalist South Korea and its American allies to a standstill. Armies swept up and down the peninsula devastating each other's territory. Control of Seoul, the capital of South Korea, changed four times, leaving the city in ruins. The civilian population suffered enormously, with bombing of civilians being common. The Korean dead and wounded from the war totalled 1.3 million in the South, and 1.5 million in the North — approximately 10 per cent of Korea's entire population. In addition, 33,000 Americans were killed and 900,000 Chinese became war casualties, including one of Mao Zedong's sons. When the killing ceased — and the Americans and Chinese withdrew — North Korea and South Korea remained frozen in hostility and staring at each other across the DMZ.

The country remained partitioned with 37,000 US soldiers stationed on the South Korean side of the DMZ. In the North, meanwhile, Kim Il Sung constructed a fiercely Stalinist state and a command economy out of the ruins of the war. North Korea has now been on a war footing for five decades. Its political leadership is dictatorial, insular, and thoroughly militarised. North Korea maintains an army that is one million strong and has an impressive array of 'conventional' weapons, including thousands of tanks, fifty surface-to-air missile sites, over ten thousand artillery pieces, as well as a reasonably well developed air force and navy.[14] In short, this is not a country that — were it invaded by the United States — would necessarily roll over and die. And North Korea knows that with nuclear weapons allegedly in its possession, the calculus of power has now been permanently altered.

North Korea is a fortress state. Kim Jong Il's government tolerates no internal dissent and forbids freedom of speech and association. There is no free press or independent trade unions. All demonstrations, except those organised by the state, are illegal. Those guilty of social or political crimes are severely punished. Although North Korea claims that there have been no public executions since 1992, Amnesty International's annual report suggests that during 2002:

> Public executions were reportedly carried out in places where large crowds gather, with advance notice given to schools, enterprises and farms. Some prisoners were reportedly executed in front of their families. Executions were by hanging or firing squad.[15]

A large and brutal 'gulag' system of punitive labour camps also exists for those accused of being disloyal to the North Korean regime. As many as 200,000 people, entire families in many cases, are estimated to be in these camps. At the same time Amnesty International reports that according to the North Korean government's own figures, 13 million of its own people are malnourished with 45 per cent of children under five being 'chronically malnourished'. The United Nations estimates that food production in North Korea is still 20 per cent short of the minimum requirements necessary to feed the country's hungry people. Others estimate that as many as two million people might have already starved to death over the past decade because of famine and economic stagnation.[16]

Politically, the 'cult of personality' that the North Korean state has built around Kim Jong Il is strange even by the measure of those previously dedicated to Joseph Stalin or Mao Zedong. There are stories in the North Korean media that when 'Dear Leader' appears somewhere snow melts. He is described as 'the greatest of great men produced by heaven.' He even has a flower named after him, the kimjongilia. In response to all of this, the western media has created an alternative mythology based upon the reports of North Korean defectors, CIA spooks, and leaked intelligence reports from South Korea. The result is an equal mixture of fact, slander and gossip. Accordingly, Kim Jong Il swills expensive cognac and is serviced by an elite team of sex workers called the 'Pleasure Squad', some of whom have been imported from Sweden. He either has four children from four wives, or three children from three wives, no-one is really sure. He watches Daffy Duck cartoons constantly (he allegedly owns the largest collection in the world) and is a connoisseur of western pornography.[17]

All of this is a distraction from the fact that North Korea is a country in terminal crisis. Its economy has failed, its people are hungry, its leadership deserves to be overthrown. More importantly, Kim Jong Il's regime lacks the means and vision to rescue North Korea from ruin. To the extent that North Korea survives at all it does so by shrouding its people in a mixture of fear, paranoia and ignorance of the outside world. Those who do not obey 'Dear Leader' are locked up, brutalised or disappeared. Still, as one historian has argued, North Korea's 'peculiar blend of terror, mobilisation and seclusion' is 'slowly losing its coherence.'[18]

In this context American threats and hostility are factors which actually help Kim Jong Il stay in power. North Korea has already survived one war in which nearly three million Koreans died and has been preparing for another one for the last fifty years. Moreover, Korean popular memory of the last war does not especially bathe America in moral glory. American forces used napalm for the first time during the Korean War, a hideous weapon which helped kill as many civilians as North Korean soldiers. Also, in the words of historian John Feffer:

> In June 1953, the United States bombed irrigation dams and the retaining wall of the Toksan reservoir, flooding cities and undercutting the capacity of North Koreans to grow food, acts considered war crimes when the Nazis did much the same to the Dutch.[19]

The fact that the US government debated dropping atomic bombs on Korea during the 1950–53 war is also a historical fact well known by Koreans, north and south of the artificial border that still divides the country. The mercurial General MacArthur, who commanded US forces in Korea, was enthusiastic about using atomic weapons during the war and was furious when his military advice was not heeded by the US government. Indeed, the Americans even took a practice run at dropping an atomic bomb on the North Korean capital of Pyongyang in 1951 — a reckless military stunt designed to instil terror in the minds of the people of North Korea at the height of the so-called Cold War. From 1957 the US kept nuclear weapons on the South Korean side of the DMZ. The US continued nuclear attack drills until as recently as 1998. The drills were always about intimidating North Korea and the message of the United States was — you may have a million soldiers, but we have the bomb. Not surprisingly, North Korea also concluded that the 'pre-emptive nuclear attack' proposed in the US National Security Strategy of September 2002 might be aimed at them.[20] In short, North Korea has lived under the threat of nuclear annihilation for fifty years. And it is this reality that has pushed Kim Jong Il's regime into their reckless pursuit of their very own weapons of mass destruction.

Back in 1993 when the United States originally discovered that North Korea was embarking upon a nuclear weapons program, the Pentagon dug out 'Operations Plan 5027' — its plan for an invasion of North Korea. It was estimated, according to one historian, that about one million people would die in Korea if the plan was put into effect, including about 100,000 US soldiers. The non-human cost of Operations Plan 5027 was calculated at $100 billion to the US government, and about $1 trillion in damage to Korea.[21] Facing such costs, and conscious of how badly the last Korean War had gone, the US opted for negotiation with North Korea instead. An accommodation was reached whereby North Korea promised not to develop nuclear weapons and the US promised to provide the communist government with shipments of fuel oil and aid. It was this reluctant deal which was subsequently broken by both sides and which leads us to George W Bush's talk of an 'axis of evil' and North Korea's admission that it was back in the workshop building a nuclear bomb. The CIA now believes that North Korea might already possess one or two nuclear weapons. Interestingly, it is the West's 'war on terror' Pakistani allies who are being blamed for providing the technology to North Korea necessary for the construction of a nuclear bomb.[22]

Meanwhile, under orders from US Secretary of Defence Donald Rumsfeld, in mid-2003 the Pentagon created a new Operational Plan — number 5030. Its purpose was the same as the previous version; an invasion of North Korea and the military overthrow of Kim Jong Il's government. The predicted casualties resulting from Operations Plan 5030 were revised to 52,000 US soldiers and 490,000 South Koreans within the first ninety days of a US-led invasion. The report was leaked to the press at a time of especially high tension between the United States and North Korea, making dialogue over the nuclear weapons issue extremely difficult.[23]

The Stalinist government of Kim Jong Il is unquestionably repressive. But its synchronised military parades and choreographed crowds hailing 'Dear Leader' are intended to conceal the fact that despite its military strength, the regime is rotten to the core. Specialists also point out that the North's military hardware is outdated even when compared to South Korea. The South Korean army spends approximately

US$163,000 arming, equipping and feeding each of its soldiers. North Korea spends US$1134. The entire national budget of the North Korean government is significantly smaller than South Korea's military budget. When compared to the United States this disparity is even greater. Kim Jong Il could not afford to buy a single US Stealth bomber with the US$1.4 billion in North Korea's annual military budget.[24] The level of threat posed by North Korea is therefore not quite as apocalyptic as some would have us think.

Current US policy towards North Korea is a case of, in the words of Korea specialist John Feffer, 'all sticks and no carrots.'[25] If the US and the rest of the world really want to assist the North Korean people, many Korea specialists argue that they should stop the threats of war and start looking at ways of opening up the DMZ. We should remember that the Berlin Wall fell not under the treads of US tanks, but because East German citizens saw their partitioned state for the lie it was. West German television (beamed in from the other side of Berlin), an insurgency of ideas and an internally generated popular movement against the government, toppled the Berlin Wall. When ordinary East Germans breached that artificial divide in November 1989, when they met and interacted with West Berliners, the whole world knew that the 'German Democratic Republic' (East Germany) was finished. Its bland communist rulers officially voted their state out of existence a few months later. The lessons of Berlin and all the Eastern European revolutions of 1989 are clear: neither barbed wire nor cruise missiles can change the way that people think.

There is an alternative. To the extent that South Korea is a vibrant democracy today this is because the South Korean students' and workers' movements have fought bloody (and often deadly) battles to strengthen civil society in the South. Only three countries in the world today (Israel, Egypt and Turkey) have received more US military aid over the years than South Korea. Moreover, most of this aid flowed at a time when South Korea was a dictatorship — albeit one with strong links to the major western democracies. The first authoritarian president of South Korea, Syngman Rhee, constructed a government made up mainly of wartime collaborators with the Japanese and he was overthrown after widespread student protests in 1960. After a brief interlude of civilian rule General Park Chung-hee took power, the first of three generals to rule South Korea between 1961 and 1993. In 1979 the head of the South Korean secret police (the KCIA) assassinated General Park at the dinner table and General Chun Doo-hwan took power. In 1980, under General Chun's leadership, the South Korean Army carried out a major massacre of civilians during an uprising against military rule in the city of Kwangju. Military rule had been seriously weakened by the democracy movement by the time of the Seoul Olympics in 1987 but the generals, with US support, still clung to power.

It was not until the 1990s that a genuinely reformist and democratic political order was established in South Korea. In 1995 popular pressure resulted in the country's two last military rulers, Generals Chun and Roh, being charged with corruption, mutiny and with responsibility for the Kwangju massacre. Interestingly, part of General Chun's defence was that when he launched his coup and ordered the army into Kwangju he was acting with US approval.[26] It is not surprising, therefore, that the politics of the democracy movement in South Korea remain neither pro-Pyongyang nor pro-Washington.

The South Korean workers' and students' movements have

already effected regime change in the South, and may yet turn out to be a decisive factor in causing regime change in the North. Indeed, in the midst of President Bush's talk about the possibility of a 'pre-emptive strike' against 'axis of evil' countries, during 2003 a public opinion poll found that 92 per cent of South Koreans were opposed to any potential war on the Korean peninsula.[27] Moreover, the impulse towards reunification in Korea is strong, with a majority of Koreans north and south of the DMZ raised in a shared national tradition that venerates resistance to foreign invasion. In short, regime change in North Korea is a task best left to the Korean people themselves.

'Regime Change' in Iran

I will never apologise for the United States. I don't care what the facts are.

So said George Bush the Elder in 1988 when asked to comment on the fact that an American warship, the USS *Vincennes,* had accidentally shot down an Iranian civilian airliner in the Persian Gulf. All 290 passengers on the Iranian plane (including sixty-six children) were killed but Bush, who was vice president at the time and was campaigning for the US presidency, knew that such patriotic comments, especially given that the dead civilians were Iranians rather than Australians or Swiss, would play well in the electorate. Americans have been trained to distrust and despise Iran, a country whose 1979 Islamic revolution was avowedly hostile to the United States, and with whom the US government had almost gone to war in the early 1980s. In the aftermath of the revolution, Iran's population had been variously portrayed as cowed and ignorant (the women) or violent and fanatical (the men) in the American media. Scenes of Iranians burning the US flag became commonplace on American television.

Three years prior to the *Vincennes* incident United States National Security Adviser Robert McFarlane drafted a top secret directive for the White House regarding 'US Policy Toward Iran'. The classified document attempted to summarise the current 'political environment' in the Islamic Republic.

> The clerical regime continues to believe that the US has not accepted the revolution and intends to reverse the course of events and install a puppet government. This perception has been reinforced by our restoration of diplomatic relations with Iraq, efforts to cut the flow of arms to Iran, and direct threats of military action in retaliation for Iranian-inspired anti-US terrorism.[28]

It therefore did not surprise American politicians when the Iranian government suggested in 1988 that the shooting down of the Iranian passenger jet by the USS *Vincennes* may have been deliberate. Such furious antics were regarded as typical of the Muslim extremists who now governed Iran. The country's religious rulers were considered incapable of seeing that American policy and its military presence in the Middle East were, unlike Iran's regime, logical, restrained and benign.

George Bush won the presidency in 1988 and after his son was (dubiously) elected president twelve years later, he too continued in the fine American tradition of denouncing and defaming Iran. Indeed, not long after Muslim extremists hijacked four American airliners on 11 September 2001, the Islamic Republic of Iran became, with North Korea and Iraq, the third partner in President Bush the Younger's infamous 'axis of evil'. Attempts by Iran's recently elected reformist government to point out that the country, whose Muslim population is overwhelmingly Shi'ite, was a long-term opponent of Al-Qaida were ignored in Washington. The fact that Iran had almost gone to war with the Taliban in 1998 (when Washington was still courting the Afghan regime) and had previously provided support to the current US-backed Afghan president, Hamid Karzai, were similarly ignored. What this pointed to, above all else, was a remarkable and continuing ignorance of Iran's entangled history with the western world.

Iran is the modern state built on lands that were once the core of the Persian Empire. Persia's history stretches back six centuries before the Christian era, with the first great Persian Empire expanding to encompass modern Egypt, Turkey and the eastern Mediterranean. Although this empire was eventually overthrown by Alexander the Great, Persia again rose to become a major power in the Middle East before falling to advancing Muslim armies in 637 AD. The religion of the Muslim Arab conquerors, Islam, spread throughout Persia at this time and the empire was dismembered.

By the sixteenth century Muslim Persia, under the Safavid dynasty, had re-emerged as an important power in the Middle East. Iran's modern borders generally follow the borders established at this time. Importantly for the future of Iranian history, Shi'ia Islam became the official religion in Persia under the Safavids. As a result, while Shi'ites are a minority within the Muslim world as a whole, they remain a majority in Iran.

The split between Sunnis and Shi'ites is often explained in western countries as being similar to the historic split between Catholics and Protestants within Christianity. The comparison, although relevant, is not especially useful. The schism within Islam has its origins in the struggle after the death of the prophet Mohammed as to who would be his successor. Mohammed was more than a prophet to Muslims. In his own lifetime he had revealed the word of God and established Muslim rule over Arabia. Islam has no priesthood, but Mohammed ruled as combined spiritual, civic and military governor in Muslim lands. Mohammed died in 632 AD. The caliph, or successor to Mohammed, was therefore the nominal religious and political ruler of all Muslims. The Shiat Ali, or Party of Ali, was based around the prophet Mohammed's son-in-law and was defeated in a military struggle to control the caliphate. The succession struggle ended when Ali's son, Hussein, was massacred with his followers at Karbala in Iraq in the year 680. Since then Shi'ites have generally perceived themselves as an oppositional Islamic current to the Sunnis who they consider to be usurpers. Outside Iran, Shi'ite Muslims generally continue to see themselves as a repressed minority within the Muslim world.

Despite palace coups and dynastic contests, Persia under a ruling shah (king) survived the various intrigues and wars of the ages. By the nineteenth century however, Russia (which shared an imperial border with Persia) and Britain began competing for commercial and geopolitical advantage in the region. In 1908 oil was discovered, dramatically increasing Iran's importance to the western powers. The British Navy converted to oil use in 1911, at a time when Persia was still nominally independent. The first major oil 'concession' was granted by the Shah to a New Zealander named William Knox D'Arcy, whose Anglo-Persian Oil Company exploited Iranian oil resources while paying royalties to the Shah. This model was replicated across the Middle East by various western (mainly British, French and American) companies as oil was discovered elsewhere. By the end of the First World War the British were manoeuvring themselves into a dominant position in Persia and throughout the Middle East.

Following the Russian Revolution of 1917 there was an

attempt to establish a Soviet Republic in northern Persia, although this was overthrown in 1921 by Colonel Reza Khan, commander of the Persian Cossack brigade. Two years later Khan became prime minister. Three years after that, after deposing the old shah, Reza Khan declared himself the ruler of Persia and became Reza Shah Pahlavi. As Imperial Russia disappeared from the regional political scene, a re-emergent Germany (under Hitler) became an important trading partner for Persia during the 1930s. In 1935 the Shah even changed the name of the country to Iran (meaning Aryan), allegedly in an attempt to draw Nazi Germany closer to his regime. In September 1941, during the Second World War, the Soviet Union and Britain, who were temporary allies, invaded Iran and the Shah abdicated in favour of his son, Mohammed Reza. The new Shah continued with his father's modernisation and westernisation program after the Second World War.

The above simple history is relatively uncontroversial and something similar still appears on the US Department of State's website. Their version of the post-1945 period, however, is truly remarkable.

> In 1951 Premier Mohammed Mossadeq, a militant nationalist, forced the parliament to nationalise the British-owned oil industry. Mossadeq was opposed by the Shah and was removed, but he quickly returned to power. The Shah fled Iran but returned when supporters staged a coup against Mossadeq in August 1953. Mossadeq was then arrested by pro-Shah army forces. In 1961, Iran initiated a series of economic, social, and administrative reforms that became known as the Shah's White Revolution.[29]

A negative impression is created of the 'militant nationalist' Mossadeq, who 'forced' the Iranian parliament against its will into nationalising Iranian oil. He is then replaced in a quick coup and the Shah embarks upon a large scale reform process. Except that history tells us the Iranian parliament actually unanimously supported oil nationalisation and that Mossadeq only became premier because he was closely associated with this demand. Mossadeq was widely popular in Iran (both inside the parliament and on the streets) precisely because he was seen as heading the movement to take back Iran's most precious economic resource from foreign exploiters. Iran had the third largest oil fields in the world and many Iranians were aware that the amount of money paid in royalties to Iran (actually, to the Shah) was less than the tax payments that the British government received from the Anglo-Iranian Oil Company (previously the Anglo-Persian Oil Company). The most glaring omission in the US State Department's account, however, is with regard to Mossadeq's removal and the pro-Shah coup. This was actually an American-made and American-funded affair.

Therefore, the reason Iran's post-1979 Islamic government continued to believe that the US intended to 'install a puppet government,' as mentioned in the White House's secret 1986 draft National Security Directive, was not because they were crazed Muslim conspiracy theorists at all, but because they knew something about Iranian history. They were acutely aware that such a course of action had been embarked upon before with disastrous results for the Iranian people.

It cost the US government about one million dollars to get rid of Mossadeq and buy 'regime change' in Iran in 1953. They berated the Shah until he agreed to dismiss Mossadeq, they orchestrated demonstrations, activated paid contacts inside the Iranian army, provided logistical support for the 'pro-Shah coup', bribed and manipulated the Iranian media, and helped re-install the Shah after Mossadeq's fall from power. This is no conspiracy theory fantasy. Indeed, in a moment of carefully calibrated diplomacy, in March 2000 the US Secretary of State, Madeleine Albright, spoke to a group of Iranian-American business people and admitted that:

> In 1953 the United States played a significant role in orchestrating the overthrow of Iran's popular prime minister, Mohammed Mossadeq. The Eisenhower Administration believed its actions were justified for strategic reasons; but the coup was clearly a setback for Iran's political development. And it is easy to see now why many Iranians continue to resent this intervention by America in their internal affairs.[30]

Less than a month after Albright's speech the *New York Times* published extensive details of the CIA's involvement in the coup. The journalist responsible for breaking the story, James Risen, wrote that 'the CIA, then just six years old and deeply committed to winning the Cold War, viewed its covert action in Iran as a blueprint for coup plots elsewhere around the world, and so commissioned a secret history to detail for future generations of CIA operatives how it had been done.' Drawing on the secret history, Risen wrote that the CIA 'had almost complete contempt for the man it was empowering, Shah Mohammed Reza Pahlavi, whom it derided as a vacillating coward.' The CIA's secret history revealed 'for the first time, the agency's tortured efforts to seduce and cajole the Shah into taking part in his own coup.' The CIA history gave seven reasons why the coup was necessary, with oil being paramount. James Risen then provides a summary of the CIA's activities during the overthrow of the Mossadeq government:

> The history says agency officers orchestrating the Iran coup worked directly with royalist Iranian military officers, handpicked the prime minister's replacement, sent a stream of envoys to bolster the Shah's courage, directed a campaign of bombings by Iranians posing as members of the Communist Party, and planted articles and editorial cartoons in the newspapers ... Two days after the coup, the history discloses, agency officials funnelled $5 million to Iran to help the government they had installed consolidate power.[31]

Ironically, one of the 'envoys' sent to convince the Shah that he should sign the decree dismissing Mossadeq (and thereby activate the coup) was General H Norman Schwarzkopf, the father of the commander of the US-led forces during the 1991 Gulf War. Schwarzkopf and others were appalled by the Shah's lack of confidence. The Shah believed that neither the army nor the Iranian people would support him against the popular Mossadeq. Paranoia gripped the Shah and during one meeting, according to the secret history, he 'led the general into the grand ballroom, pulled a small table to its exact centre' and climbed onto it. He insisted the general do the same. They conducted their meeting standing on the table because the Shah was convinced his palace was bugged by the British, Mossadeq, or his other enemies, both real and imagined. The Americans continued to encourage (and gently threaten) the Shah, with the CIA's main operative in Iran, the unusually named Kermit Roosevelt (a distant relation of two

US Presidents), telling the Shah 'that failure could lead only to a Communist Iran or to a second Korea.'

The first stage of the coup went very badly. Mossadeq refused to accept his dismissal and pro-Mossadeq demonstrations broke out. Statues of the Shah's father, overthrown by the British and Russians during the Second World War, were spontaneously torn down. The Shah went into exile and the CIA arranged for General Zahedi, whom they had chosen as Mossadeq's replacement, to be hidden in the US embassy along with other key Iranian agents so they could organise what the CIA history called a 'council of war'. Eventually, however, American money, intrigue, and a little bit of luck turned the political mood in the Shah's favour. Key pro-Shah elements in the army took control of the capital, Teheran, Mossadeq was arrested, pro-Shah demonstrations were organised, and the Shah returned from his temporary exile. According to the CIA's secret history, 'It was a day that should never have ended. For it carried with it such a sense of excitement, of satisfaction and of jubilation that it is doubtful whether any other can come up to it.'

The United States had put the Shah back in power. In return the Shah's brutal — but pro-western, modernising and secular — regime remained intimately tied to western capital, arms and diplomatic support. For the first time American oil companies were given significant access to Iran's oil fields. The Shah, however, retained an abiding fear and distrust of his own people. In the aftermath of the 1953 coup, the Shah surrounded himself with a formidable wall of spies, informers, torturers and jailers.

The Shah's secret police, SAVAK, was formed in 1957 and had strong links to the CIA. SAVAK operated its own prisons in Teheran, recruited informers and spies, and suppressed all opposition. There have been numerous allegations over the years that the CIA trained SAVAK operatives in the use of torture. Following the 1979 Islamic revolution the Iranians even claimed to have found a film made by the CIA for SAVAK which taught useful techniques for torturing women.[32] John Gerassi, who worked as an editor for *Time* and *Newsweek*, has also described a visit he made with former US Attorney General Ramsey Clark to Iran in 1980. While there he claims he saw videos of people, whom he believes were Americans, assisting SAVAK officers in torturing dissidents. According to Gerassi:

> I remember very vividly one horrifying case: a naked anti-Shah Iranian hanging six inches off the floor by a chain around his wrists, which were bleeding, in the middle of what appeared to be a cement bunker. Two Iranians in civilian clothes were having difficulty forcing a cattle prod, which was wired to an electric generator, into the man's rectum, because the body kept swinging to and fro. An officer, obviously an American, in uniform but sporting no insignia, pushed the Iranians to the side, grabbed the prod with his right hand, held the prisoner with his left, and rammed the prod as far as he could …[33]

Although it is exceedingly hard to prove the veracity of the evidence presented by Gerassi regarding alleged American involvement with SAVAK torturers, there have been some interesting admissions over the years. For example, in early 1979 the *New York Times* published a report based on interviews with Jesse Leaf, a former senior CIA analyst of Iran who resigned because, he said, American 'policy pretty much determines reporting rather than the other way around' — an interesting comment given the CIA's recent WMD failures in Iraq. Leaf claimed that, in the words of the *New York Times*, 'he and his colleagues knew of the torture of Iranian dissidents by SAVAK ... Furthermore, Mr Leaf said, a senior CIA official was involved in instructing officials in the SAVAK on torture techniques, although Mr Leaf said that to his knowledge no Americans did any of the torturing.' Leaf's revelations caused another *New York Times* journalist to comment that:

> We can read the accusations, even examine the evidence and find it irrefutable. But in our hearts, we cannot believe that Americans have gone abroad to spread the use of torture. We can believe that public officials with reputations for brilliance can be arrogant, blind or stupid. Anything but evil.[34]

Such views were not shared in Iran where years of western diplomatic intrigue, CIA entanglement with SAVAK, and the history of the Mossadeq coup caused most Iranians to believe that employees of the United States government were fully implicated in the repression and misery their country had endured since the CIA had placed the Shah back on his throne in 1953. In 1979, after the Islamic revolution, over sixty SAVAK officers were sentenced to death by the new regime. And in November 1979 radical Muslim students occupied the US embassy in Teheran, demanding the Shah's return from exile in the United States so that he could stand trial for what SAVAK had done to their people. Iranian and American relations settled into a pattern of determined hostility.

The US State Department's official background history of Iran now refers to SAVAK as Iran's 'hated internal security and intelligence service' without mentioning any of this unsavoury past. Nor does it mention that in 1976, at a time when Iran was one of the United States' staunchest allies in the Middle East, Amnesty International reported that the country had the 'highest rate of death penalties in the world, no valid system of civilian courts and a history of torture which is beyond belief.' In short, according to Amnesty International, 'No country in the world has a worse record in human rights than Iran.'[35]

By 1975 Iran was also the world's top arms importer. A few years earlier, in 1971, the Shah had invited the world's leaders to a lavish celebration of the longevity of Iranian civilisation out in the 2500-year-old ruins of Persepolis. At least nine foreign kings, a dozen presidents and other assorted dignitaries attended the festivities that cost Iran at least $100 million (some historians put the cost at three times that amount). Meanwhile, although the Shah's 'White Revolution' of social and economic reforms did help create a reasonably prosperous middle class in Iran's urban centres, poverty remained a major problem for millions of Iranians, particularly in rural areas. As part of his 'modernisation' campaign, the Shah also ordered the unveiling of Iranian women — a deliberate affront to traditional Islamic sensitivities. And so while US President Jimmy Carter continued to refer to Iran as an 'island of stability' in the Middle East, popular Islamic opposition to the Shah's rule grew. In particular, cassette recordings of the speeches of an exiled Muslim leader, Ayatollah Ruhollah Khomeini, illegally circulated throughout the country. No amount of repression by SAVAK could stop the growing popularity of the Ayatollah Khomeini's message that the Shah's regime was a foreign-dominated abomination to God.

The Shah's rule lasted until 1979 when he was finally overthrown in a popular revolution. During his last years in power the Shah had refused to travel around the capital, Teheran, in a car due to fears he would be attacked or assassinated by his own people. Apparently, when he was taken by helicopter across Teheran in late 1978 he saw mass demonstrations against his rule and was deeply disturbed by it. As in 1953, his confidence in his own rule withered. On 10 December 1978 an estimated one million people marched against the Shah and nearly two million protested again the following day. Widespread strikes and demonstrations continued, despite SAVAK. The whole country seemed to be rising in opposition and this time there was no Kermit Roosevelt or General Schwarzkopf to save the Shah. In mid-January 1979 the Shah fled the country for exile.

Shortly afterwards the Ayatollah Khomeini returned from his exile to unleash a further revolutionary upheaval which swept aside the government appointed by the Shah before he left Iran. A newly proclaimed Islamic Republic of Iran was implacably hostile to the Shah's program of westernisation and modernisation which Ayatollah Khomeini saw as being anti-Iranian and un-Islamic. The politics of the Ayatollah were reflected in one of his speeches shortly after returning from exile and not long before the overthrow of the Shah's appointees:

> I must tell you that Mohammed Reza Pahlavi, that evil traitor, has gone. He fled and plundered everything. He destroyed our country and filled our cemeteries ... Even the projects he carried out in the name of progress, push the country towards decadence. He suppressed our culture, annihilated people and destroyed all manpower resources ... I shall appoint my own government. I shall slap this government in the mouth. I shall determine the

government with the backing of this nation, because this nation accepts me.[36]

Other speeches of the Ayatollah Khomeini spoke of a new Islamic republic enjoying 'the backing of God' and he called on the Iranian army to 'abandon your foreign masters.' Iran's Islamic revolution passionately rejected both the 'East' (atheistic communism and the Soviet Union) and the 'West' (secular western democracy). Both, the Ayatollah claimed, had failed Iran and the world. Instead a revived and revitalised Islam — an Islam that rejected the ruling tyrants of the Middle East because they were puppets of foreign infidels — would sweep away the poverty, debauchery, misery and oppression of the region. The message had an appeal that went beyond Iran, beyond Shi'ites, and found a resonance amongst a segment of disenchanted Muslims throughout the Third World. That the Ayatollah Khomeini, an ageing, anti-western theocrat who wanted to turn Iran into a puritanical Islamic state, was able to emerge from the turmoil of revolutionary Iran to become the country's unquestioned leader is the most damning indictment of the historic failure of American 'diplomacy' and covert malfeasance in Iran.

Chalmers Johnson, whose 1999 book *Blowback* accurately predicted that 'World politics in the twenty-first century will in all likelihood be driven primarily by blowback from the second half of the twentieth century,' affords a special place to Iran in his view of current US foreign policy entanglements. Johnson argues:

Although the term 'blowback' has long been used in poison-gas warfare to refer to the likelihood of battlefield gasses blowing back on the forces that have released them, it first appeared in its political sense in the CIA's post-action report on the secret overthrow of the Iranian government in 1953 ... The attacks of September 11 are blowback in a direct line of descent from events in 1979, the year in which the consequences of the overthrow of the Iranian government in 1953 came due. In 1979, the Iranians took the entire staff of the American embassy in Teheran hostage and threw out the Pahlavi regime the US had installed. The succeeding Iranian revolution ushered in the fundamentalism of the Ayatollah Khomeini and the adventurism of the Reagan administration's Iran–Contra scandal. At that very moment in 1979, the United States was also deliberately provoking the former Soviet Union into invading Afghanistan.[37]

To compound matters, with the occupation of the US embassy in Teheran by Iranian students, the United States government began looking at ways to forcibly 'contain' Iran's Islamic revolution. For this reason, they covertly (and with time, more openly) supported Saddam Hussein's Iraqi dictatorship when it invaded Iran in 1980. To quote conservative historian Bernard Lewis:

The Iraq–Iran war had many different aspects. It could be and was portrayed in personal terms, as a confrontation between two charismatic leaders, [Ayatollah] Khomeini and Saddam Hussein; in ethnic terms, between Persians and Arabs; in ideological terms, between Islamic revivalism and secular modernism ... in sectarian terms, between Sunni and

Shi'a; in economic terms as a contest for control of the oil of the region; and even in old-fashioned power political terms as a quarrel over territory and a struggle for regional hegemony ... Impeded by neither domestic nor international pressures, nor yet — since both were oil exporters — by serious financial constraint, the two sides were able to pursue their mutually destructive war for eight years.[38]

War makes for strange political bedfellows. During the Iran–Iraq war it is claimed the Iranians got about 40 per cent of their imported weapons from North Korea — a fact which later provided evidence for President George W Bush and his supporters that the two countries were part of an 'axis of evil'.[39] If the Islamic Republic of Iran was, ironically, partly dependent upon atheistic communist North Korea for weaponry, this was because the United States had cut off the flow of arms to Iran after the overthrow of the Shah. Previously Iran had been the largest importer of weapons in the world, with the majority of these weapons being American made. Now America had switched its support to Saddam Hussein's Iraq, providing satellite intelligence of Iranian troop movements and even sending US ships into the Gulf to help 'police' the region. It was one of these ships, the USS *Vincennes*, which shot down an Iranian airliner in 1988 after mistaking it for an Iranian (American-made) F-14 fighter jet. Although the US government later paid US$61 million compensation to the families of the victims, the Iranian government never did get an apology from George Bush.

It is now twenty-five years since Iran's Islamic revolution began. A whole generation of Iranians have come of age who have no direct experience of the Shah's brutal regime. A third of Iran's population of 65 million people are between fifteen and thirty years old. Many amongst this younger generation resent the theocratic rule of the Ayatollahs and the religious vigilantes who police public morality. In major cities like Teheran there is a large underground youth culture based around the trade in secret copies of forbidden western music, videos and so forth. In the streets of Teheran and elsewhere, tens of thousands of Iranians (particularly university students) have marched in support of democratic change and social reform over the last few years. A formal representation of this bubbling discontent was the electoral victory of the Iranian reform movement led by Mohammed Khatemi, who got 69 per cent of the vote in the May 1997 elections and 77 per cent in June 2001.

Iran's constrained democracy — under the 'guidance' and 'protection' of a twelve member Guardian Council dominated by religious conservatives — is bursting at the seams as it attempts to deal with the aspirations of the younger generation. At the start of 2004 the Guardian Council refused to approve more than 2000 of the 8200 prospective candidates for Iran's upcoming elections. Those denied the right to run for election included 87 sitting members of the 290-seat parliament who were associated with the reform movement. At the start of February more than one-third of Iran's parliament resigned in protest. The resignations (123 in all) coincided with the twenty-fifth anniversary of the return from exile of the now deceased Ayatollah Ruhollah Khomeini whose leadership had inspired Iran's Islamic revolution in 1979. Although the elections held in late February 2004 were claimed as a victory by religious conservatives, it was a hollow one.[40] The Ayatollahs are increasingly out of touch with their own people. They may be able to manipulate an electoral outcome but a growing segment of

Iranian society, especially amongst the young, has lost faith in the ability of Iran's theocratic political system to reform itself. For a country with such a long history of popular revolt, such a loss of faith could potentially have massive ramifications.

In late 2003 the Nobel Peace Prize was presented to Shirin Ebadi, an Iranian lawyer and human rights activist. The choice (a female human rights activist) was a deliberate attempt by the Nobel committee to foster the democratic movement for change in Iran. In the face of the mounting political crisis in Iran, Shirin Ebadi had a clear message to the President of the United States, George W Bush: 'The US should show its good will and good intentions. Calling Iran the axis of evil is no way to do that.'[41] Shirin Ebadi and, even more importantly, this new young Iranian generation, want something better than the kind of Iran that more than two decades of theocratic rule have delivered. Iran, once again, appears to be struggling with its relationship with the West, and the meaning of Iranian democracy.

Cuba: America's Last Great Anti-Communist Crusade

We must continue to stand with the brave people of Cuba, who for nearly half a century have endured tyrannies and repression.

US President George W Bush, 12 January 2004

In May 2002, four months after President George W Bush's famous State of the Union address, the US Undersecretary of State, John Bolton, gave another signal speech entitled 'Beyond the Axis of Evil'. Bolton added three more nations to the list of 'rogue states' Bush had identified in January. The new additions to the exclusive evil club were Cuba, Libya and Syria. The Caribbean island of Cuba, with its population of ten million people, had been a focus of obsessive American hostility for over forty years. In the post-9/11 world, the United States, with its nearly 300 million people and its unprecedented armed might, appeared determined to bring the regime of President Fidel Castro to its knees. The US Undersecretary of State even went so far as to say that his own government (which had sponsored a failed invasion of Cuba in 1961, had tried to assassinate Castro a dozen times, and had rigorously enforced a severe trade embargo of the island for four decades) had often 'underplayed' the threat that Cuba posed to the United States. He accused Cuba of harbouring terrorists and developing 'dual use' biotechnology that could be used to manufacture chemical weapons.[42]

A short time later Jimmy Carter became the first former US President to visit Cuba since the 1959 revolution. While on the island he called for the lifting of the US trade embargo and visited the biotechnology research facility that had been accused of developing the potential chemical weapons mentioned by Undersecretary Bolton. Carter revealed that before entering Cuba he had specifically asked the US State Department and the White House whether they had any specific evidence of Cuba sharing biotechnology with 'terrorists', or of any attempts by the Castro regime to produce weapons of mass destruction. The answer, according to Carter, was a plain and simple 'no.' Embarrassed by the publicity surrounding Carter's comments, Secretary of State Colin Powell commented, 'We didn't say it [Cuba] actually had such weapons, but it has the capacity and capability to conduct such research.'[43] Such schoolyard legal tricks failed to convince Team Bush's critics who accused Washington of pandering to the political prejudices of Florida's sizeable Cuban-American community:

> Appeasing your base of supporters is one thing, but fabricating evidence and shoveling it out for the world to see is brazenly reckless, particularly in a world made fragile by lunatics, fanatics, and lies.[44]

The great irony here, missed in most of the mainstream press, was that Cuba's sophisticated and successful biotechnology industry was not only unique given that Cuba is a Third World country, but is an industry Cuba was forced to develop because of the US trade embargo which prohibited US medicines being sold to the country. As a result Cuba is now a world research leader in the area of tropical medicine. Despite Carter's praise, the research facility he visited remains a potential target for a US cruise missile.

America's forty-five year political obsession with Cuba has been truly bizarre. For example, during August 1994 Academy Award-winning documentary film-maker Mike Moore's first television show, 'TV Nation', aired an interesting segment called 'Health Care Olympics'. Using professional sports broadcasters, 'TV Nation' pitted the government-subsidised health care system of Canada against the health systems of communist Cuba (where all health care is free) and the United States of America, where medical technology is as fantastically efficient as it is astronomically expensive. The competing health centres were Sunnybrook in Toronto, Broward General in Florida and Colesto General in Cuba. Each health centre was given a patient to admit with a broken limb. Their treatment was then compared by the sportscasters as if it was a live gladiatorial sporting event. Colesto General in Cuba won the Health Care Olympics but no American television viewer was ever allowed to know that. In the words of Mike Moore:

> For the first and only time on TV Nation, NBC censors made us change the ending of a segment. The truth is, by applying the standards of competition fairly to each country, Cuba won. It provided the best care in the fastest time and for absolutely no fee to the

patient. The censor told us that politically there was no way we could show Cuba winning on primetime television. We were told to make Canada the winner. We argued right up to show time that this was both dishonest and also pretty silly. Did NBC think a new missile crisis would erupt if we showed the commies winning? Did they fear a new set of Boat People — but this time with hundreds of Americans sailing to Cuba for decent, affordable health care?[45]

Forty million Americans have no health insurance and Cuba remains the unforgivable revolution. So unforgivable in fact that President George W Bush can't even countenance the idea that people might travel to Cuba and make their minds up for themselves about the country. During October 2003 President Bush announced that his administration would, according to the *Guardian Weekly*, 'work harder to punish Americans who visit Cuba.' Strangely, visiting the country for purposes of tourism is prohibited under US law, although no such restrictions apply to the Stalinist dictatorship of North Korea,[46] which has been on the US list of states which sponsor international terrorism since 1988 and which currently holds 200,000 of its own citizens in slave labour camps. Bush is actually seeking to tighten restrictions which have already led to a Texan businessman being charged with 'Trading with the Enemy' after he led a fishing trip to Cuba in 1987.[47]

In October 2003 President Bush also announced the establishment of a government committee to plan for 'Cuba's transition from Stalinist rule to a free and open society.'[48] One of the co-chairs of the committee is US Secretary of State Colin Powell. One wonders how the United States would react if a well-armed communist country with which it had a forty-year history of animosity, like China or North Korea, publicly announced it was establishing a similar committee openly dedicated to the overthrow of the US government? The whole dangerous scenario got me thinking about my own time in Castro's 'terrorist haven'.

It was a wonderful thing to be young and ignorant and to travel to exciting places. I spent the summer of my twentieth year in Cuba, working on a bean commune during the hot days and sleeping in a cool wooden barracks at night. It was 1988 and the last days of communism and no-one knew it yet. Especially not me and certainly not the communists. The Berlin Wall had one year's life left in it. It was twelve months before Nicolae Ceausescu would be videotaped shot to pieces in a bad suit, looking confused by death, lying stiff beside a cold wall in Romania. Vaclav Havel was still a little-known Czech poet. Even the tanks of Tiananmen Square were still far off. All this was unwritten and yet it was clear to everyone, and to no-one in particular, that the communist monolith was decaying. Not crumbling, but slowly rotting, like old fruit.

I was twenty and knew very little of communism or Marxism-Leninism or Stalinism and all the other isms except that I was always for the poor and weak against the rich and powerful. And that was a basis for a belief in something. I had been offered a trip to Cuba for 'training' because I was a young apprentice carpenter and active in the Building Workers Industrial Union. In 1988 Cuba had captured my imagination because of its romantic association with pirates and slave rebellions. I also knew a little about Che Guevara and so when I was offered the chance to visit the island, I seized it wholeheartedly. From December 1988 until February 1989 I worked in Cuba. There were shortages of everything while I was there — meat, petrol, brassieres, pencils, batteries, socks and medicines of all sorts. But there was a wealth of conversation, poetry, music, beans, sugar cane and hard work.

Long-suffering Cuba, originally invaded by Christopher Columbus and then by slave traders, movie stars and mobsters, had been destroyed by Spanish conquistadors and Yankee hustlers. It was the last Spanish colony in Latin America to gain its independence, only winning its freedom in 1898 after a war against Spain that lasted three years. However, Cuba Libre immediately found itself entangled with the United States. The last two decades of the nineteenth century were a time of expansion for the US, which sought to project and consolidate its power (economic, political and military) in Latin America and the Caribbean. Just before America went to war with Spain, mainly over the issue of Cuba's independence, the *Washington Post* tried to describe the new popular mood in the country.

> A new consciousness seems to have come upon us — the consciousness of strength — and with it a new appetite, the yearning to show our strength ... Ambition, interest, land hunger, pride, the mere joy of fighting, whatever it may be, we are animated by the new sensation. We are face to face with a strange destiny. The taste of Empire is in the mouth ... [49]

By the first decade of the new century American interests dominated the Cuban national bank, controlled the police force, openly manipulated the government, and had even demanded the insertion into Cuba's constitution of a clause (referred to as the Platt Amendment) which explicitly gave the United States the right to intervene in Cuba at any time if the US government felt that the interests of its citizens were threatened. It subsequently did so four times between 1900 and 1933. While Cuba did not become an outright colony of the United States, it became the next best thing — a subservient and servile protectorate with its economy dominated by United States capital, and its political leadership completely beholden to Washington in order to stay in power.

By the 1950s, under the dictator Fulgencio Batista, the country was impoverished beyond hope — it was little more than a playground for Miami millionaires and the mafia who ran the Havana casinos. Although the United States repealed the Platt Amendment, it still insisted on keeping a substantial naval base at Guantanamo Bay on the eastern edge of Cuba. American dominance continued. According to historian Howard Zinn, 'American companies controlled 80 to 100 per cent of Cuba's utilities, mines, cattle ranches, and oil refineries, 40 per cent of the sugar industry, and 50 per cent of the public railways.'[50]

Then came Fidel Castro. Following a two-year insurgency the two beards (Fidel Castro and Che Guevara) and their rough guerilla army toppled the Batista dictatorship on 1 January 1959. Their popular 'regime change' took Cuba on a path to national regeneration and that that path also led into the arms of stodgy Soviet bureaucrats tells us little other than the fact that there was a Cold War on and that toppling a US-puppet when you are only 150 kilometres off the Florida coast is a risky business. Especially when you start challenging the stranglehold foreign companies (in this case American) had on your economy. The rest, including the missile crisis and the United States' failed 'Bay of Pigs' invasion, is history. Cuba's revolution remained clouded in mystery and Cold War malfeasance.

It was not until the fall of the Berlin Wall in 1989 and the collapse of Cuba's economy after losing all its Eastern bloc trading partners that Castro was forced to reopen the place to western money. It was only then that Cuba was rediscovered as a tourist destination for rich Europeans and Canadians in search of a suntan. Suddenly it seemed like you couldn't open a glossy magazine without reading about some movie star lying on Varadero beach sipping rum from a coconut and admiring the natives. Che t-shirts appeared in fashion boutiques. Cuba became chic again. It was forgotten that the rumba had originally been a dance of Cuban slaves, a powerful and erotic dance, before it was taken to New York in the 1920s and turned into the diluted chachacha so that it could be taught to 1950s American suburbanites in polyester slacks. The conga line, without which no geriatric retirement cruise around the Caribbean would be complete, was also a slave dance, the steps deliberately short for those in shackles. All this had been forgotten, reinvented, and now had to be forgotten all over again. Cuba was back. Or as Robin Blackburn commented:

> In the West, most people's image of Havana today comes from Wenders's *Buena Vista Social Club* — a wash of leprous surfaces and deliquescent pastels, a city of melancholy ruins.[51]

When I went to Cuba in 1988 the US blockade was still strong and Australia had only just established diplomatic relations. It was illegal to travel from the United States to the island. We had to remove our Cuban visas from our passports and our work brigade was investigated by the Australian Security Intelligence Organisation (ASIO) when we returned. We arrived in Havana during the thirtieth anniversary of the Cuban revolution. Dignitaries from various Eastern bloc countries were also arriving for the celebrations and we would bump into them from time to time. In less than a year they would all be crushed under the Berlin Wall and the weight of their own terrible history.

I spent part of my time in Cuba working on a collective farm about a hundred kilometres from Havana. After work picking beans in the fields one day we drove back to camp. In the barracks there was an envelope sitting on my bunk. Inside was a brown piece of printed cardboard:

INVITACION
El Comité Central del Partido Comunista de Cuba
le invita al Acto Central,
en conmemoración del XXX Aniversario del Triunfo
de la Revolución y la Inauguración de 'EXPOCUBA.'
Lugar: EXPOCUBA
Fecha: 4 de Enero de 1989

And so I went, as invited, to see Fidel. I was one of twenty-five members of the work brigade chosen to join a group of about 100,000 Cubans to celebrate the *triunfo de la revolución*. We were right up near the front and the heads of the crowd went far beyond where we could see, back to where the massive palm trees looked like matchsticks. Fidel wore his army greens, still had fire in him and cracked jokes with the multitude.

'I don't know how the acoustics are here. It's not such a big gathering, but there are many people seated and the place extends way back. I don't know whether those over there at the back can hear well. I think they said they can, right?'[52] One hundred thousand people chuckled like he was the warm-up act in a nightclub.

Castro mentioned that 'no child or teenager on their birthday is criticised for any defect; instead their virtues are emphasised,' and then launched into a three-hour speech about how far Cuba had come in the last thirty years. In 1953, before the revolution, there was about 60 per cent illiteracy, now it was about 1.5 per cent. Before the revolution there were sixty deaths for every one thousand live births, now there were twelve. Fidel pointed out that this rate was virtually unequalled elsewhere in the Third World and was on a similar level with infant mortality in the United States, the richest nation on earth. Before the revolution, twelve out of every 10,000 mothers died in childbirth. Now, only 2.6 did, one of the lowest maternal mortality rates on the planet. Before there were 6000 doctors in the whole country. Now there were 31,000 and all health care was free. Life expectancy had gone from about fifty-five years to over seventy. In every one of the key indices regarding health and education, tiny Cuba was unquestionably a world leader (a fact acknowledged by the United Nations and the World Health Organization). Commenting wryly on the fact that some children still left before finishing high school, Fidel joked that 'Socialism has not yet found the formula for preventing teenage marriages.'

There was much applause and Fidel spoke for several more hours, but I decided to walk around instead. I met some young Cuban children who wanted to talk about Australia and kangaroos. By the time I returned to my seat Fidel was winding up, and he commented sarcastically on the advice that was offered in the editorial columns of Miami's newspapers regarding Cuba's political future. 'We really don't want to give anybody sleepless nights and we don't understand why we're such a source of concern to so many people.' Laughter rippled through the massive crowd and I wondered what the newspapers in Miami would make of it. Regardless, Fidel thanked everyone for turning up and ended with his customary, *'Patria o muerte!'* — the homeland or death — to which one hundred thousand people shouted back, *'Venceremos!'* — we will win.

A few days later I got to see Fidel speak again. We were driven in buses to Ciudad Libertad, Liberty City, an old Batista-era army base on the outskirts of Havana that had been transformed into an education complex after the revolution. Out front was the most bizarre monument — a towering syringe in memory of Carlos Juan Finlay, who in 1881 discovered the cause of yellow fever. That day was the thirtieth anniversary of Fidel's entrance into Havana after Batista fled into exile and the revolution first triumphed. As we waited for Fidel the massive crowd of young *pioneros* (schoolchildren) grew restless. There was bedlam amongst the pioneros when Fidel finally arrived and he spoke for a long time, and with much passion, to the assembled youth about the state of the world and the revolution. It was January 1989 and Fidel had time, Gorbachev, and all the problems of the Soviet bloc on his mind. 'The imperialists openly proclaim that when this revolutionary generation leaves the scene, when the generation of the people who made the war and carried out the revolution is no longer present, their task will be easier.'[53]

Fidel mentioned the 'imperialist euphoria' regarding the 'reforms and self-criticism taking place in various socialist countries,' a reference to the developing crisis in the Soviet bloc. He hoped that 'the current generation will understand the enormous task on its shoulders. In a way, it is an even greater task than the one we had, for at the time of the victory of the revolution socialism was prospering and united, without difficulties and with growing prestige.' He urged the Cuban youth to continue to develop its ties with Africa, where Cuban soldiers had helped defeat the racist apartheid army's intervention in Angola. He was thrilled that 18,000 international students, including SWAPO guerillas from Namibia, studied on the Isla de Juventud. Fidel went on and despite the passing of several hours most of the youth were still listening. He appeared to be almost on the verge of tears when he ended his speech.

> There is a lot I could say but I think that is enough. Perhaps I might add that our generation, called the Generation of the Centennial because it began its struggle at the time of the centennial of Martí's birth; the generation of the revolution of January 1, 1959, believes in you, has faith in you, the generation of the thirtieth anniversary ... And on behalf of the party and all the revolutionary fighters of my generation — older or younger — I express our absolute faith in you, our absolute confidence that you will know how to deal with the great challenges of the future ... Allow me to express my complete certainty that no generation in the history of our country has ever had the privilege of seeing young people like this come up after it!

There was much applause then, followed as always, by 'Patria o muerte!' and 'Venceremos!' as the pioneros appeared very happy with themselves.

In 1989 I saw Cuba through the eyes of someone who was a guest of the Cuban government. I undoubtedly got a distorted view. But I also worked in the fields on a bean commune, on construction sites building low-cost housing in the countryside, and made friends beyond our officially designated guides. Outside of the camp where I lived, I walked where I wanted and talked to whom I wanted. I attended mass at an old Catholic Church in Havana. I spoke to Cubans who approached me, illegally, to see if I could help them get US dollars so that they could buy western goods. I got drunk with young people my age and like all twenty year olds, we made confessions to one another, swore undying friendship, and sat up listening to music all night.

None of my Cuban friends agreed with *everything* the Cuban Communist Party did. All were unhappy and openly critical of the rationing and bureaucracy they often had to endure, although most blamed the rationing on the US embargo. One of my Cuban friends was gay and he felt he was forced to live a secret life. He feared he would lose his job if he was 'out'. But in this regard he was not that different from gay friends of mine in Australia, who similarly feared social ostracisation. When I criticised the Castro government's handling of AIDS, we debated the issue back and forth for days. Another Cuban, with whom I was romantically involved, felt the Young Communist League was nothing more than a vehicle for career advancement. Her harshest criticism of it though, was that the Young Communist meetings were 'boring'. She would join it anyway, she said, because she wanted to work as a government translator (she spoke perfect English) and being a Young Communist would help you get a better job.

Most of my young Cuban friends were worried about what would happen when Fidel died. Few trusted that the other members of the Cuban government possessed minds as sharp as Fidel's. One told me he did not like Raul Castro, Fidel's brother and the head of the Cuban Army. 'Why?' I asked. 'I just don't think he is a good leader,' he said. This conversation took place at dinner and was overheard by several Party members who ran the barracks where I was staying. Some laughed, one challenged him, others paid the conversation little attention. Nothing happened to my friend. Not then. Not since. He did not disappear into a gulag, he was not tortured, he did not lose his job or his free place at Havana University.

All my Cuban friends were opposed to any attempt by the US to overthrow the Cuban revolution. None wanted the Miami Cubans to return and take over the government of the country. All supported free health care, education and 'international solidarity' with Africa. Far from being 'brainwashed', all the Cuban friends I made could discuss politics, literature and life on a level far beyond the average university tutorial in Australia. They passionately disagreed with each other as often as they agreed or disagreed with me. There was no 'Party line' or coerced conformity evident in their discussions. Indeed, none of my friends were members of the Cuban Communist Party. All wrote poetry and drank beer. We debated democracy, socialism, Gorbachev's reforms, punk music, sex and the morality of war. No topic was off limits. The young women complained about Cuban bras and said Cuban men were still too caught up in their own *machismo*. The young Cuban men wanted to listen to my Metallica tape, thought Ernest Hemingway was over-rated as a writer, and were fiercely patriotic.

Cuba has achieved monumental successes in social welfare over the past forty-five years. For example, from having almost no public health infrastructure at the time of the revolution in 1959, Cuba now sends doctors to other Third World countries. According to the World Health Organization the number of doctors per 100,000 of population in Cuba is 530, as compared to 240 in Australia and 279 in the United States. Cuba is not a socialist paradise, but its people are not cowed robots living under Stalinist tyranny either. Cuba may be part of some fanciful 'axis of evil' for those who lie awake in their beds at night as the ghosts of previous presidents stalk the Cold War hallways of their mind. But to me it is simply a Third World country grappling with its colonial past, its Cold War inheritance, and its own shortcomings.

Cuba was crushed by the collapse of the Berlin Wall in November 1989. With the demise of the Soviet bloc at least a third of Cuba's GDP was wiped out. Cuba lost about 70 per cent of its export market and 75 per cent of its cheap imports. The CIA estimated that between 1989 and 1992 Cuba's export earnings fell from US$5 billion to US$1.6 billion. The financial constraints and the end of the Cold War had other consequences as well. In May 1998 the head of the US Southern Command, Marine General Charles Wilhelm, estimated that the size of Cuba's armed forces had been reduced by almost 50 per cent since 1991. As a result, Wilhelm reported, Cuba had 'no capability whatsoever to project itself beyond the borders of Cuba, so it's no threat to anyone around it.'[54]

Nevertheless, the US government continued to portray Cuba as an aggressive regional threat and during the 1990s, as Cuba's economy was collapsing, the US intensified pressure on the country. Federal laws passed in 1992 and 1996 banned the foreign subsidiaries of US companies from conducting business with Cuba and threatened to seize the US assets of any foreign company that traded with the country. Any ship that entered a Cuban port was banned from entering a US harbour for the following six months. US 'subsidiary trade' with Cuba fell from US$700 million in value during 1991, to a 'minuscule' amount of $1.6 million in 1993 due to these new punitive laws.[55] While

President Clinton was sending truckloads of desperate illegal Mexican immigrants back across the border, his government was still encouraging Cubans to defect to the United States.

Therefore, when President George W Bush's government denounced Cuba as belonging to an axis of evil it did so within an American political tradition that has now spanned four decades and nine US presidential administrations. But there was an additional factor. George W Bush has not forgotten that many of the 800,000 Cuban-Americans in Miami-Dade County in Florida are registered Republicans. They voted for Bush in 2000 and the votes of Florida were decisive to the outcome of the presidential election. Meanwhile Bush's brother Jeb is not only the Governor of Florida, but is also closely linked to the Cuban American National Foundation (CANF). The CANF is dedicated to the overthrow of the Castro regime and between 1982 and 1992 it provided more than US$670,000 in donations and campaign contributions to members of the US Congress (Republican and Democrat) deemed to be sufficiently friendly to the CANF's platform.[56]

In August 2003 little brother Jeb criticised big brother George for not taking a hard enough line on Cuba. Brother Jeb goes back a long way with the Miami Cubans. In 1984 he was chairman of the Dade County Republican party while Camilo Padreda, a former intelligence officer during the Batista dictatorship, was finance chairman. Padreda later pleaded guilty to defrauding millions of dollars from the government's housing department. An earlier indictment on a $500,000 embezzlement charge was allegedly dropped after the CIA spoke in favour of Padreda's Miami Cuban co-accused. During the 1980s Jeb was also employed by Miguel Recarey, another shady Cuban character with links to the CIA who had been implicated in an attempt to assassinate Fidel Castro. Jeb Bush was also campaign manager for Ileana Ros-Lehtinen, who in 1988 became the first Cuban-American to win election to the US House of Representatives. So when Big Brother Bush appeared in Florida alongside Little Brother Bush in 2002 and attacked Castro's government, he did so with votes in mind and the love and support (financial and otherwise) of Jeb's special Cuban friends.[57]

The United States position on Cuba, and its cruel trade embargo, is completely at odds with global political opinion. Even Pope John Paul II, whose historic role in opposing and undermining Eastern European communism is widely applauded in conservative circles, described the US embargo as 'unjust and unethical' during a January 1998 visit to Cuba. Every single year during the 1990s the United States lost a vote in the United Nations General Assembly regarding its blockade against Cuba. In 2002 there were 173 votes in favour of ending the US embargo, four abstentions, and only three votes in favour of retaining it — the United States, Israel and the Marshall Islands. The US, as always, ignored the motion. That same year an interesting book was published, *Cuba Confidential: Love and Vengeance in Miami and Havana,* by Ann Louise Bardach, an award-winning journalist. Bardach and other reporters investigated Cuba's links to international terrorism. What they found was truly disturbing.

One case included a Cuban called Orlando Bosch who has been implicated in at least thirty terrorist acts since the late 1960s. These acts included firing a rocket at a Polish ship and blowing up a passenger plane in 1976. When the plane exploded seventy-three civilians on board were killed, including the crew and all the members of a sporting team. The problem is that all of the terrorist acts Bosch was implicated in were directed *against* the Castro regime. Convicted in a US court of the attack on the ship, Bosch was released from prison by President George Bush Sr. Interestingly, responsibility for bombing the Cuban airliner in 1976 was admitted by a Cuban exile group Bosch led which had strong links to the CIA. George Bush Sr was head of the CIA at the time. Following his release from prison Bosch was granted US residency and now lives in Miami where he is still active in anti-Castro activities.[58]

Bosch has become something of a hero within the Miami Cuban community. Raoul Cantero, a grandson of the former Cuban dictator Batista, represented Bosch in court and described him on radio as a 'great Cuban patriot'. Far from being censored for encouraging terrorism, in July 2002 Jeb Bush nominated Cantero for a position on the Florida Supreme Court. Similarly, when President George W Bush spoke in Miami in May 2002, Orlando Bosch was initially invited to sit on the platform with the president, although when advisers became nervous about possible negative publicity the seating was rearranged and Bosch ended up in the audience.[59] It seems all terrorists are not created equal.

Indeed, the CANF (which the entire Bush political dynasty, but especially Jeb, have close links to), has publicly supported acts of terrorism against Castro's regime. For example, in mid-1997 three Havana hotels catering for Cuba's fledgeling tourist industry were bombed. The CANF 'unconditionally' supported the bombings and a later investigation by two *New York Times* journalists linked CANF to the actual bombers. In 1998 the US Justice Department also arrested seven Cuban-Americans for planning to assassinate Fidel Castro. Several of those indicted were CANF officials.[60]

None of this excuses the failings of the Castro regime, including its April 2003 crackdown on dissidents. About seventy-five journalists and pro-democracy activists were arrested for allegedly receiving money from a foreign power (the US) among other charges. Most got harsh prison sentences. As cruel and unnecessary as this crackdown was, the abuse of power involved was not nearly as extreme as what was happening at the other end of the island. At Guantanamo Bay — a massive US military base on the Cuban mainland that is occupied by the US against Cuba's will — the Americans built 'Camp X-Ray'. Inside the camp are an estimated 600 suspected 'terrorists', many of whom have been held in a foreign country without access to a lawyer or the benefit of a trial since late 2001.

Seumas Milne, writing in the British *Guardian*, argued that Cuba's failings need to be placed in hemispheric context.

> ... what has long been obvious: that US hostility to Cuba does not stem from the regime's human rights failings, but its social and political successes and the challenge its unyielding independence offers to other US and western satellite states. Saddled with a siege economy and wartime political culture for more than 40 years, Cuba has achieved first world health and education standards in a third world country, its infant mortality and literacy rates now rivalling or outstripping those of the US ... while next door, in the US-backed 'democracy' of Haiti, half the population is unable to read and infant morality is over 10 times higher. Those, too, are human rights, recognised by the UN declaration and European convention.[61]

Finally, one of President George W Bush's strongest criticisms of Cuba is that the government of Fidel Castro is unelected and illegitimate — Bush says Castro has not won government in a free and fair election where voters were given a real choice between candidates and where the votes of all people were counted regardless of who they voted for. He says Cuba's presidential elections suffer manipulated outcomes where the personal loyalties of leading state officials (like regional governors and judges perhaps?) to Castro make a mockery of democracy. He says that Fidel and his brother Raul Castro run communist Cuba as a family business, as if the national presidency is a matter of family inheritance. What's that old saying about glass houses and stones, or the one about American pots calling Cuban kettles black?

With Friends Like These Who Needs Enemies? — Saudi Arabia, Pakistan and Other Great Allies in the War on Terror

In his famous State of the Union Address of January 2002 — where he named North Korea, Iran and Iraq as an 'Axis of Evil' — US President George W Bush read a few words from the teleprompter that deserved greater media attention.

> All fathers and mothers, in all societies, want their children to be educated, and live free from poverty and violence. No people on Earth yearn to be oppressed, or aspire to servitude, or eagerly await the midnight knock of the secret police.

Bush neglected to mention that this was as true of people in Saudi Arabia, Pakistan and other oppressive states currently allied to the United States, as it was of those regimes officially targeted in the 'War on Terror'.

Almost twenty years ago in 1986 it was CIA chief William Casey who dramatically expanded US financial support for the

Afghan Mujaheddin, sending more money, as well as Stinger anti-aircraft missiles and US advisers, to help the Muslim rebels in their guerilla war against Soviet occupation. So connected did the CIA feel to the Mujaheddin's anti-Russian jihad that Casey backed a Pakistani idea to recruit Muslims from around the world to join an 'Islamic international brigade' — the forerunner to Osama bin Laden's Al-Qaida network. In the ten years leading up to 1992 an estimated 35,000 Muslim extremists from over forty countries came to Afghanistan to fight with the Mujaheddin. Not all appreciated the extent to which their jihad was funded mainly by Saudi princes, Pakistani ISI (Inter-Services Intelligence) spooks and the 'Great Satan' itself — the government of the United States of America.[62]

Zbigniew Brzezinski, one of Washington's premier Cold Warriors, had stated that he wanted to bleed the Soviets white in Afghanistan. It would be their Vietnam, he would tell people while he was US National Security Adviser.[63] Meanwhile, on the barren mountains of Afghanistan young men were praying on dusty prayer mats before going off to fight heavily armed Russian soldiers encased in tanks and helicopter gunships. A million Afghans died. In Brzezinski's judgement, however, it was all worth it:

> What was more important in the world view of history? The Taliban or the fall of the Soviet Empire? A few stirred-up Muslims or the liberation of Central Europe and the end of the Cold War?[64]

Along the way the Americans inadvertently helped a few exceptional Muslim extremists carve out careers for themselves. One such individual was the lanky son of a Yemeni construction millionaire from Saudi Arabia, Osama bin Laden, who in the mid-1980s allegedly helped build the CIA-funded Khost tunnel complex deep in Mujaheddin-controlled mountains near the Pakistan border. It was allegedly from this same camp in 1998 that Osama bin Laden's Al-Qaida network issued its manifesto for an 'International Islamic Front for Jihad against Jews and Crusaders' and declared that to kill Americans — 'civilians and military' — was an 'individual duty for every Muslim who can do it in any country in which it is possible to.'[65] By 1998 the Russians were long gone and the feuding Mujaheddin had proved a disappointment to Islamic extremists like Osama. He had already formed a strategic alliance with the Taliban and was now directing his rage at his former American allies.

We actually have Saudi Arabia and Pakistan — the United States and Australia's allies in the current war on terror — to thank for the Taliban. Having bankrolled the jihad of the Mujaheddin during the 1980s the Americans lost all interest in Afghanistan following the Soviet withdrawal in 1989 and the end of the Cold War. Not so the Pakistanis and Saudis. In July 1996 the Saudi intelligence chief Prince Turki al Faisal visited Taliban-held territory in Afghanistan to discuss increased funding. The Taliban military offensive in the north of the country in 1998 was supplied by US$5 million from the Pakistani ISI and 400 new pick-up trucks from the Saudis.[66]

With the military coup in Pakistan in October 1999, Islamabad increased its support for the Taliban. Support for the Taliban was already so entrenched in the Pakistani state bureaucracy that in mid-1998 the Pakistani Finance Ministry paid US$6 million in salaries to Taliban officials in Kabul. In all, Pakistan provided the Taliban with an estimated $30 million in food, equipment and arms during the 1997/98 financial year alone. Taliban-controlled Afghanistan, technically a foreign country, was even integrated into Pakistan's domestic telephone system. It is also estimated that 80,000 Pakistanis crossed into Afghanistan to fight alongside the Taliban between 1994 and 2001.[67] The Pakistani government viewed this movement of Islamic fundamentalists as being a useful safety valve. It was better to allow such people to fight and die for the Taliban in Afghanistan than have them sit, unemployed and angry, at home in Pakistan.

Although most western governments condemned the October 1999 coup in Pakistan, it was especially noticeable that in the aftermath of September 11 'General Musharraf' very quickly became 'President Musharraf' as Britain and the US moved to secure his support for a war against the Taliban — an organisation his own military had helped create! The lesson for Third World dictators elsewhere was obvious. The West's professed support for Pakistani democracy was negotiable as soon as landing strips and air-space to conduct bombing raids were needed. Although an official ally in the war on terrorism and in defence of 'civilisation', Pakistani police tortured twenty-six people to death during 2002 according to Amnesty International.[68] Such is life, democracy and human rights under 'President' Musharraf.

Along similar lines, it is interesting to contemplate why the countries of Iraq, Iran and North Korea were declared members of an exclusive 'axis of evil' by President Bush, but that Saudi Arabia scarcely received a rude letter from the US government over the events of September 11.[69] After all, fifteen of the nineteen hijackers on September 11 were Saudis and 'two-thirds' of the 'Islamic terrorists' incarcerated by the Americans at Camp X-Ray in Cuba were Saudi nationals.[70] The answer lies not only in the US reliance on Saudi Arabian oil, but in the ultra-conservative (and ultra-rich) Saudi royal family's long-term structural engagement with the American economy, as well as their support for pro-western foreign policy in the Middle East. During the 1950s and 60s the Saudis could be relied upon as a buttress against the rise of militant Arab nationalists (Nasser in Egypt for example) who were perceived as a threat to western interests. In the 1980s they could be relied upon as a buttress against the anti-western Islamic fundamentalism of the Iranian revolution (the Saudis were more than happy to do this as the Iranians were Shi'ites). The Saudis also provided much of the money required to fund America's proxy war against the Soviet Union in Afghanistan.

Saudi Arabia remains one of the most sectarian and fanatical dictatorships in the entire world, as well as being a major sponsor of global terrorism. As with the Taliban, subjugation of women in Saudi Arabia (where they are not even allowed to drive a car) is encoded in law. There are no real elections and no real parliament. Slavery was only abolished in 1963 and free trade unions are still illegal. Amputation of limbs and death by beheading are accepted punishments for violation of the country's extremist Islamic laws — during 2000 there were over one hundred punitive beheadings. And yet President Bush, a born-again Christian, seems content to have close diplomatic ties with a government whose police were reported to have tortured dozens of Filipino Christians who were arrested in late 2000 after they were caught secretly practising their faith.[71]

Amnesty International's 2002 report on human rights in Saudi Arabia provides some frightening reading. A woman was sentenced to sixty-five lashes after she accused her sister's husband of raping her. The accused rapist was sentenced to 4700 lashes and six years in prison — not for rape, but for 'adultery'. Seven people had their right hand amputated for stealing. At least forty-eight people were executed during the year, three of whom were given death sentences for being homosexual. According to the *San Francisco Chronicle*, based on Saudi sources, the three men were 'convicted of sodomy and marrying each other' and were beheaded. Amnesty International also reported that 'torture and ill-treatment' of prisoners were systemic in Saudi jails.[72]

In August 2003 the Saudi Arabian government released from jail six British men who were arrested three years previously after a series of bomb attacks in Riyadh. The Saudi police, scornful of suggestions that dissident Islamicists within the kingdom may have been responsible, claimed the bombings were the work of a renegade group of illegal alcohol smugglers from the West. Upon returning to Britain after being released, one of the men, forty-four year old Sandy Mitchell from Scotland, claimed he had been tortured and systematically deprived of sleep by the Saudi police in order to get a confession out of him. He was kept in solitary confinement for over a year. Detailing the methodology of the Saudi police, Mitchell told of how:

> I was kept awake for nine days, chained to the door of my cell so I could not sleep or sit down … The beatings started with punching, kicking, spitting, and eventually progressed to hitting me with sticks. They had this axe handle and I was beaten on the soles of my feet.[73]

Not surprisingly, when subjected to such conditions Sandy Mitchell eventually confessed to a crime he did not commit. Although intervention by the British government got him and the other British men released after three years, the Saudi government still claims the men were guilty.

On the issue of supporting terrorism, the Saudi Arabian

government (not counting various private Saudi jihad support networks) gave US$4 billion to the Mujaheddin in Afghanistan between 1980 and 1990. In March 1990 the Saudis gave US$100 million to help back a failed coup attempt by ex-Mujaheddin warlord Hikmetyar to overthrow the pro-Soviet Najibullah government. Tens of millions more in funds flowed into Taliban coffers after 1994. The largesse only ended when Mullah Omar personally insulted Prince Turki and Osama bin Laden continued his much-publicised tirade against the heresy and treachery of the House of Saud from his bases in Afghanistan.[74]

More recently the *New York Times* claimed that its reporters in Saudi Arabia had seen documents (given to them by Israeli Intelligence it seems) relating to an October 2002 meeting between Khalid Mishaal, a senior member of Hamas, the extremist Islamic Palestinian group which has carried out many of the suicide bombings of the last three years, and Crown Prince Abdullah, 'the de facto Saudi ruler'.[75] Khalid Mishaal, who is based in Syria, is currently on the US Treasury Department's list of 'terrorist financiers'. American and Israeli intelligence claim that about half of Hamas' annual budget of US$10 million comes from Saudi individuals and charities and that Hamas divides the money, roughly, between its charitable work (including running health clinics and schools) and its armed wing (which carries out the suicide bombings).

Allegedly the documents, which are Hamas' summary of the meeting, involve Khalid Mishaal thanking the Saudis for continuing 'to send aid to the people through the civilian and popular channels, despite all the American pressures exerted on them.' While the Saudis have disputed the contents of the documents and others have suggested that they might be an invention of Israeli intelligence, no-one has denied that the meeting between Khalid Mishaal and Crown Prince Abdullah actually took place. Interestingly, the meeting occurred while Mishaal was in Saudi Arabia attending the World Assembly of Muslim Youth, a Saudi charity whose American branch was established in 1992 by Abdullah bin Laden, one of Osama's relatives. If nothing else, the two per cent of their annual income which most wealthy Saudis donate to charity continues to flow in some dangerous directions.

Then there is the question of our 'Northern Alliance' allies inside Afghanistan — mainly ex-Mujaheddin forces who the US State Department described in 1995 as having gone on a 'rampage' in Kabul, 'systematically looting whole streets and raping women.' When the feuding Northern Alliance retreated from Kabul in 1996, they left 50,000 dead civilians behind them. In October 2001 Human Rights Watch described the Northern Alliance's army as being guilty of 'widespread and systematic' crimes against humanity. Respected journalist and Middle East specialist Robert Fisk (incidentally, one of the few western journalists to interview Osama bin Laden) described the Northern Alliance as a 'confederacy of warlords, patriots, rapists and torturers.'[76] While the establishment of a post-Taliban government is to be applauded, we should be under no illusions regarding the credentials of those involved.

General Abdul Rashid Dostum is a case in point. He is a huge man in every sense. Over six feet tall, Dostum is an ethnic Uzbek and has fought on every side of Afghanistan's bloody wars. He has changed sides nine times according to those bothering to count. Since 1978 Dostum has fought 'for the Soviets, the Soviet puppets, the Mujaheddin, the Taliban, and now the Northern Alliance.' At the height of his power, Dostum managed to run six northern provinces of Afghanistan during the civil war. Pakistani journalist Ahmed Rashid recorded an encounter with the General at his headquarters in Mazar-e-Sharif:

> The first time I arrived at the fort to meet Dostum there were bloodstains and pieces of flesh in the muddy courtyard. I innocently asked the guards if a goat had been slaughtered. They told me that an hour earlier Dostum had punished a soldier for stealing. The man had been tied to the tracks of a Russian-made tank, which then drove around the courtyard crushing his body into mincemeat, as the garrison and Dostum watched.[77]

At the time of the US bombing campaign in Afghanistan in late 2001, the US military command considered Dostum to be, in the words of General Tommy Franks, 'the best we've got.' Dostum's troops were later implicated in an incident in the Shibarghan desert where hundreds of Taliban prisoners were placed in sealed containers and suffocated to death. In post-Taliban Afghanistan, General Dostum managed to secure a post for himself as Deputy-Minister of Defence and regional army commander. As a columnist at the *Boston Globe* wrote in response to his appointment, 'Whoever said irony died on Sept. 11 should report to re-education camp immediately.'[78]

However, the greatest irony of all in the tragedy that is modern Afghan history has been the role of the United States. Following the 9/11 terrorist attacks CIA operatives were dispatched to Afghanistan with US$10 million in cash to buy friends and rent allies. Bob Woodward, in his 'inside' history of the Bush administration's war against the Taliban, details a meeting between CIA team leader 'Gary' and General Mohammed Fahim, the military commander of the Northern Alliance, which took place on 27 September 2001. Gary put one million dollars in cash on the table in front of Fahim and told him 'this is the world stage.' Fahim responded by saying, 'We welcome you guys. We'll do whatever we can.'[79] And thus, America's anti-Taliban democratic alliance was purchased. The Americans were back (with a few Australians behind them), arriving with bulging wallets and the belief that if they couldn't find the kind of allies they desired, at least they could still buy the result they needed. History should have already taught them otherwise.

4

WHERE THE PAST IS NOT DEAD

Living in the Shadow of One Another

It's a political cliche that knowledge is power. In our age of 'dumbed down' broadcasting and 'infotainment', the nightly news usually offers only thirty-second soundbites and scripted platitudes to explain all the troubles of our world. It becomes increasingly difficult for people to find out the reasons, explanations and alternatives to the disturbing and disconnected images. And so while the average television news watcher will have seen images of violence in Northern Ireland, Bosnia, Kosovo or Rwanda, or heard many times about the UN Security Council, World Bank and IMF, how many of us actually know anything about these places or about how these institutions really operate in the world?

The International Monetary Fund (IMF), for example, is essentially an appendage of the US government. When the financial crisis of 1997 ravaged the 'Asian tiger' economies of Thailand, Indonesia and South Korea, most of the mainstream media simplistically reported that the IMF had come to the rescue. The IMF offered $US57 billion to South Korea, $40 billion to Indonesia and $17 billion to Thailand to save them from total economic collapse. In return these countries had to open their economies up to IMF-imposed 'austerity measures', budget cuts, and IMF control of macro-economic policy. Officially, severe IMF controls eventually stemmed the economic haemorrhaging. But as Chalmers Johnson has detailed:

> By the time the IMF was finished with Indonesia, over a thousand shopkeepers were dead (most of them Chinese), 20 percent of the population was unemployed, and a hundred million people — half the population — were living on less than one dollar a day.[1]

Reviewing the overall impact of the IMF on Third World debt, in 1999 Jeff Faux wrote in *The Nation* that:

> For two decades the International Monetary Fund and its major client, the US Treasury, have made privatisation, austere social budgets and market deregulation conditions of loans to the world's poorest nations. The goal has been to turn these economies into models of American-style capitalism, which among other benefits would generate the growth to enable them to pay back the money. Instead, per capita growth has slowed, debts have piled up, and today these countries are trapped in a downward spiral of poverty and social disintegration.[2]

Faux pointed out that by 1999 several nations in sub-Saharan Africa were spending more on their foreign debt repayments than on education and health combined. In Zimbabwe over the 1990s real income declined by nearly 40 per cent for ordinary people while 25 per cent of national income was directed towards servicing the country's mounting foreign debt.[3] In other African nations the country's foreign debt situation was often the result of irresponsible economic management under previous dictatorial regimes. In the Congo, for example, foreign debt accumulated under President Mobutu's corrupt dictatorship (sometimes described as a 'kleptocracy' by journalists). Although Mobutu was overthrown in 1997, he fled into exile with money he had stolen from the Congolese people and the Democratic Republic of Congo was left with the economic aftermath of three decades of institutional corruption. In 2003 the IMF and the World Bank agreed to write off US$10 billion in debt owed by the Congo, but the remaining $2 billion was still an extraordinary burden for the war-ravaged country to carry.

International non-governmental organisations and prominent individuals — from the Quakers to Nelson Mandela and the musician Bono — pointed out that Africa's debt crisis was at odds with the way the western powers, IMF and the World Bank acted elsewhere. For example, after capturing Cuba from the Spanish in 1898, the US encouraged Cuba to repudiate its debts to its former colonial master, Spain, on the grounds that previous Spanish loans had been unjust. There have been recent suggestions from the United States that Iraq's US$90 billion in foreign debts, accumulated under Saddam Hussein's regime, should be similarly wiped away. Anti-debt campaigners also point out that in places like the Congo the IMF contributed significantly to the economic mess the country is now in. In 1978, under the Mobutu regime, the IMF appointed a German banker to run Congo's central bank. Two years later the banker resigned after writing a highly critical report on Congo's economic management. Nevertheless, IMF loans continued and were often little more than bribes to Mobutu to keep him in the western camp during the Cold War. Congo's debt doubled from

US$5 billion to $10 billion over the decade of the 1980s.[4]

Africa's foreign debt is about US$300 billion. Africa transfers US$15 billion a year in debt repayments (mainly to western banks) and receives about $13 billion in aid (mainly from western governments). Anti-debt activists claim that this vicious cycle of 'odious debt', IMF exploitation and charity dependence (not to mention the AIDS catastrophe) is an 'evil'. However, President Bush, Prime Minister Blair and John Howard certainly don't give AIDS and Africa's 'odious debt' the emphasis that they give to the danger posed to international security by the alleged 'axis of evil' and the threat of terrorism. But a statistical comparison is interesting in this regard. According to the US State Department's 2003 report *Patterns of Global Terrorism* there were 355 'international terrorist attacks' during 2001, 198 in 2002 and 190 in 2003. These attacks resulted, globally, in 5431 casualties in 2001, 2738 in 2002 and 1900 in 2003. There were four terrorist attacks in the USA in 2001 (including 9/11) and none in 2002 or 2003. Twenty-six US citizens were killed in international terrorist attacks in 2002, and thirty-five were killed in 2003.[5]

By comparison, over two million people died of AIDS in sub-Saharan Africa during 2003. In all, fifteen million people have died of AIDS in Africa since the 1980s. According to the United Nations an estimated 1.5 million Africans also die of tuberculosis or malaria annually. The fight against AIDS in Africa is also a war against terror — the terror of disease, poverty and social disintegration. Or if we limit our concerns purely to those of a martial nature, 3.5 million people have been killed in Congo's civil war since 1998; many more people, I dare venture, than will ever be killed by Osama bin Laden's terrorist assassins or Saddam Hussein's still undiscovered weapons of mass destruction.

What then are the underlying causes of the wars, poverty and political crises in disparate corners of the globe that flicker on our television screens at night? Why are two million people dying of AIDS in Africa each year? How did past policies of western governments foster civil war and genocide in Central Africa, and contribute to the descent into 'ethnic cleansing' in the former Yugoslavia? Why do people kill each other over religion in Northern Ireland? Why can't the United Nations stop war and ethnic violence from breaking out in places like Bosnia or Kosovo? And what are the historical connections between these seemingly unrelated events and issues?

There is a saying in Gaelic, *Ar scath a chéile a mhaireann na daoine* (Human beings live in the shadow of each other).[6] In June 2000 I flew into Northern Ireland and was immediately struck by what a different town Belfast is in summer during a 'peace process'. For one thing, you could see the sky, buildings and people. There were colours and kids everywhere playing in the streets. Mums in tracksuit pants talking over fences. Men standing outside betting shops discussing the form. Most importantly of all, there were no British soldiers on the streets. It made me realise that all my previous Belfast experiences had been through the grim prism of winter and war.

Later I left my cousin's house in West Belfast and went for a stroll up the Glen Road in the sun. I thought of how much of my book *Exit Wounds* and the tragedies within it had been played out on the troubled streets that intersect with the Glen Road. With a warm and vivid Black Mountain above me I walked past St Teresa's (where Catholic families burnt out of their homes had sheltered during August 1969), Rosnareen Avenue (where the IRA had engaged in gun battles with British soldiers), the Bass Brewery (where my Aunt Jean worked) and the Travellers' camp where several young girls were sunning themselves against a wall beside one of the caravans. Then I walked on past the Shaws Road and up to the exact spot by the Oliver Plunkett School where a bullet came for Aunt Jean twenty-eight years and eleven days before.

Twenty-eight years, eleven days, and the exit wounds she left in the lives of those who loved her were as real as ever. I stood there for a while with the sun on my neck and the sound of a bumble bee, pestering a nearby bush, reverberating in my ears. Cars passed up and down the Glen Road. A British Army helicopter buzzed high above me, momentarily drowning out the bee and then disappeared. Skinny teenage girls with white spaghetti arms walked past eating ice-creams. But there was no sign, evidence, or trembling hint of that awful moment and terrible act of violence that robbed our family of Jean and Jean of her life. Nothing at all. Just me, the bumble bee and a nondescript patch of pavement where a young mother lost her life on 8 June 1972. Jean Veronica Campbell. Shot dead by the IRA in 'a case of mistaken identity'. Just one of 3637 people — and counting — killed over the last thirty years of 'the Troubles' in Northern Ireland. Those left behind live in the shadow of each and every one of them.

There is no doubt that Irish history is a complicated business, defying the determination of tabloid commentators throughout the world to reduce the conflict to palatable simplicities, including the alleged peculiar penchant of the Irish for tribal lunacy. Since 1969 Ulster's resurgent violence has been routinely condemned, but seldom explained adequately, contributing to a perception that Northern Ireland is a bombed-out industrial wasteland populated by bloodthirsty religious bigots. Few struggled to rise above the comfort of stereotypes. Liam de Paor, a lecturer in history at University College Dublin, set out in 1970 to illuminate the complexities of the Ulster situation to a non-Irish readership bewildered by the return of 'the Irish question':

> In Northern Ireland Catholics are Blacks who happen to have white skins. This is not a truth. It is an oversimplification and too facile an analogy. But it is a better oversimplification than that which sees the struggle and conflict in Northern Ireland in terms of religion ... There is no burning urge on either side to convert the other to the one true faith, nor does a member of one side strike a member of the other on the head with a club in the hope that he will thereby be purged of his theological errors and become a better candidate for heaven. The Northern Ireland problem is a colonial problem, and the 'racial' distinction (and it is actually imagined as racial) between the colonists and the natives is expressed in terms of religion.[7]

Despite the passage of more than thirty years of violence in Northern Ireland, de Paor's comments remain relevant to understanding the resilience of the Irish 'Troubles' today.

A year after visiting my family in Belfast during mid-2000 I was in the Kimberley region of Western Australia on a field trip with American students studying at the University of Notre Dame. We had just spent five days in the outback staying at the remote Aboriginal community of Mudnunn. Returning to Broome I switched on my mobile phone to discover several frantic messages from ABC Radio. It was urgent. There was a big news story in Northern Ireland and they wanted to know if I could go on the radio to provide some comment and analysis at

2.15 pm 'sharp'. I checked my watch, the first time I had had to do so in a week. It was 2.07 pm. I phoned the producer at ABC. 'Simon!' she exclaimed, 'we've been trying to reach you all day!' I explained that I hadn't seen a newspaper, radio or television in a week. I asked what was going on.

'Oh, some Protestants are protesting (the pun was not intentional on her behalf) against Catholic schoolchildren in Belfast. They've been abusing the girls and their parents, and throwing bottles and stones at them.'

My heart froze. I asked what the name of the school was.

'Ummm,' I could hear her shuffling through her notes, 'Holy Cross in North Belfast, why?'

When I mentioned that my father came from Ardoyne in North Belfast and that I had a little cousin and the daughters of friends at the Holy Cross Girls School the producer was positively ecstatic. 'That's great. It'll add to the story.'

A few minutes later I was on hold listening to a report by the ABC's British correspondent and the screams of little girls as they and their parents ran a gauntlet of abuse from Protestant loyalists who objected to the presence of a Catholic school in their area. I became emotional. It was just too horrible and gut-wrenchingly personal. The screams were anonymous, belonging to several unidentified girls from Holy Cross, but in my own mind it could easily have been the terrified shrieks of my cousin Kathleen's daughter, or young Róisín, the curly-haired daughter of a friend of mine.[8]

Róisín's family had already suffered so much. Before she was born one of her relatives had been shot dead by the IRA when he was falsely accused of being an informer. Then a few years later an elderly relative of hers was killed by Protestant loyalist paramilitaries in front of his wife. His crime? He was Protestant by birth but had married a Catholic woman and moved across the sectarian residential divide to live with her in Ardoyne. He was murdered inside his own home on Alliance Avenue, just around the corner from my grandparents' house. I had written about his death in my book *Exit Wounds*.

Somehow I managed to disassociate myself from the screams and from my thoughts of family and friends. I did the political commentator thing for ABC Radio and then they, and 'the story', moved on. It was not as easy for Róisín to move on. When I spoke to her family some months later they mentioned that Róisín had developed a psychologically induced skin complaint and had started wetting her bed. Each day her mother would lead her by the hand up to Holy Cross. She was spat on and called all manner of vile names. Every single morning was a ritual of tears, humiliation and sectarian abuse. And now, most nights they had to experience Róisín crying as they changed her wet bedsheets.

A few days after the radio interview I was phoned by another journalist who nonchalantly commented, while interviewing me, that 'both sides are as bad as each other, really.' Perhaps I'm just a sensitive soul, but I took immediate offence to this, inquiring if the journalist truly believed that the adults hurling glass bottles at girls as young as five years old, and the little girls upon whom the bottles were falling, were somehow equal in terms of guilt and innocence. 'No,' he said, 'but you know what I mean.' Indeed I did and I disagreed. What was difficult for the world's media to understand was that specific historical conditions gave rise to the Holy Cross protest. It was not the result of some innate Irish predisposition for violent barbarism.

I would have thought that it went without saying that the rights of innocent children to attend school without being threatened, abused and reduced to tears, should not depend upon their religion or race. I also wondered if the journalist I had spoken to would dare advance such a line of argument if the Holy Cross girls had been black and the people abusing them were white, or vice versa? But because the victims and perpetrators were all white, and because the complex ethnic issues and the history of sectarianism in Northern Ireland are, well, complex, it was just safer to write it off as the insane antics of the fighting Irish. (Incidentally, Ulster Protestants have never appreciated the extent to which, despite their professed British identity, they are still seen as irredeemably Irish by those outside of Northern Ireland.)

It also occurred to me that this callous sense of superiority regarding the alleged tribal backwardness of peoples and societies still mired in religious and ethnic conflict is not confined to newspaper journalists in Western Australia reporting on Northern Ireland. There exists in the western world a substantial body of opinion that regards the victims of civil war and ethnic cleansing in Rwanda, Kosovo and elsewhere to be, essentially, victims of their own ignorance and of circumstances for which they themselves are largely to blame. Such a position is as morally repugnant as it is historically inaccurate.

So Why Do Catholics and Protestants Kill Each Other Anyway? (Or, Explaining Four Centuries of Conflict in Northern Ireland from the Price of Rat Meat in 1689 to the IRA's 1994 Ceasefire)

The past is not dead. It's not even past.

William Faulkner

John Hume, with echoes of Bob Dylan, said it best: 'Times have changed in Northern Ireland and the Assembly members know that.'⁹ He was speaking after the re-establishment of a power-sharing government in Northern Ireland in June 2000. It was yet another important moment in a momentous week of this monumentally significant and agonisingly slow thing we call the 'peace process'. Almost six years had passed since the IRA's August 1994 ceasefire, which opened up a whole new phase in the Northern Ireland conflict.

From about the twelfth century until 1920 Ireland had been,

in whole or part, England's colony. Colonisation intensified from the 1600s onwards when England had assiduously 'planted' the northern part of Ireland (Ulster), with settlers loyal to the Crown. Many of these settlers were Scots Presbyterians and their relationship with the Irish Catholic natives was acrimonious to say the least. The loyalist plantation of Ulster created, through violence and dispossession, a majority settler population in the north-east corner of Ireland with a vested interest in maintaining British rule. Despite the passage of centuries and despite being born, raised and eventually buried in Irish soil, these Protestant loyalists continued to reject the Irish as alien and subversive. They constructed a fierce localised ethnic identity based around loyalty to the Crown and Ulster Protestantism.

For instance, in the rural village of Coleraine a debate erupted a few years ago over what to do with an interesting historical relic — the 'Curfew Bell'. The Curfew Bell was apparently sounded in Coleraine at nine o'clock every evening since 1616 in order to warn Catholics to get out of town. The *Irish News* reported that it last rang out its sectarian chimes in 1954 when a caretaker working for the local council refused to ring it any longer, not out of solidarity with his Catholic countrymen, but because he had been denied a wage increase. The bell was removed and then lingered in moral limbo at the Coleraine cattle mart until a local history group suggested it be rescued from obscurity and put on public display. The proposal was accepted by Coleraine council, although one representative warned that 'some of the backwoods men around Coleraine' might still view the Curfew Bell 'as a symbol of their own retarded aspirations.'[10]

Traditionally it was the Orange Order that gave voice and structure to Protestant loyalist aspirations. The Order was established in 1795 following a nasty little sectarian affray near the northern village of Loughgall. A member of the Orange Order must swear that he is 'not, nor ever was, a Roman Catholic or Papist' and pledge undying allegiance to the British Crown. Since 1795 the Orange Order has been dedicated to upholding the 'immortal memory' of King William of Orange and celebrating the anniversary of the 1690 Battle of Boyne each July. It is commonly viewed as a historic victory which secured Protestant settler ascendancy and Catholic native dispossession. No matter that the battle actually took place on 1 July 1690, not the 'Glorious Twelfth' as it is now celebrated. No matter either that documents discovered in the Vatican archives reveal that the loyalist hero — William of Orange, better known as 'King Billy' — was actually on the Pope's payroll.

Indeed, in 2001 two Italian historians uncovered evidence that Pope Innocent XI made considerable financial donations to the military campaign of William of Orange in the hope that by doing so he could secure an ally in the Protestant camp while simultaneously lessening the Europe-wide influence of Catholic King Louis XIV of France, who was an ally of James II (William's Ulster battleground foe). According to our scholarly Italian friends, Pope Innocent XI actually gave William of Orange the modern equivalent of about ten million dollars.[11] In this way, ironically, the Pope not only helped bankroll the consolidation of the Protestant Church in England, but also hastened the decline of Catholic Ireland. William of Orange's victory at the Boyne was even celebrated with prayers and blessings by the Pope. Such complications are unlikely to be explained on the gable walls of contemporary East Belfast, however, where King Billy might still be viewed sitting astride his white horse near rough graffiti that reads, 'No Pope Here!'

Which is not to say that Ulster's Protestant community has not suffered their own deprivations. Central to loyalist history, for instance, is the 'siege of Londonderry' in 1689 where a brave collection of Protestant settlers inside the fortified city walls held off the besieging army of James II for 105 days — the last great siege in Irish and British military history. The situation inside the city (which Irish nationalists call by its original name of Derry) was desperate, with starvation rife. One leading citizen provided a price list of saleable meat inside the town during the siege:

> Horse-flesh 1/8d a lb; quarter of a dog 5/6 (fattened by eating the bodies of the slain Irish); a dog's head 2/6; a cat 4/6; a rat 1/10; a mouse 6d; a small flook taken in the river; not to be bought for money ... [12]

When the siege of Londonderry was eventually lifted, stories of its heroes (the Apprentice Boys who shut the gates) and its villains (Governor Lundy, who was accused of treachery and is still burnt in effigy each year) would echo down through Ulster loyalist history. 'No surrender!' had been the rallying call of the Londonderry defenders, accompanied by a generous chorus of shot and ball, as they rejected James II's entreaties for them to capitulate. Dumbstruck and out of lethal range, James II apparently sat on his horse in the pouring rain pondering what to do with these recalcitrant Protestant settlers. He eventually rode off for Dublin, leaving his besieging forces behind, before making his own date with destiny one year later at the Battle of Boyne. 'No surrender!' remains the rallying cry of Ulster loyalists today.

It was the Orange Order and the descendants of the loyalist Protestant 'plantation' who campaigned most vigorously against the proposed introduction of Irish Home Rule in the late nineteenth and early twentieth century on the grounds that

'Home Rule is Rome Rule!' Their threats of civil war and their cries of 'Ulster Says No!' delayed the introduction of what might have been a reasonably peaceful decolonisation process in Ireland. Instead, Ulster's intransigence helped precipitate Ireland's relapse into armed insurrection. During Easter 1916 Irish nationalists launched a failed uprising against British rule in Dublin. Infamously, fifteen of the surrendered leaders were shot by a British firing squad, including the wounded James Connolly, who had to be strapped into a chair. Three years later the Irish Republican Army's guerilla war was under way and all Ireland was torn asunder. Although the IRA succeeded in fighting the British Army to a standstill, the price paid by the Irish people was tremendous. It was a time of death and ruin.

The Anglo–Irish War, as it is called, resulted in partial independence for Ireland. While the southern twenty-six counties were eventually given their own government, six of the north-eastern counties of Ulster (where Protestants were concentrated) remained under British rule. 'Northern Ireland', therefore, was born of war and partition. And as the Northern Ireland statelet was constructed by Protestant loyalist politicians during the 1920s, they ensured that it was built on policies of religious apartheid. The Catholic minority (who formed one-third of the population) were treated with contempt — various loyalist politicians referred to them as disloyal and backward. All of Northern Ireland's major political leaders between 1920 and 1972 were members of the loyal Orange Order. All remained dedicated to the memory of 1690, to the inheritance the plantation had secured, and to maintaining their small sectarian statelet under British rule.

It was this state of affairs which produced the Northern Ireland civil rights movement of the 1960s. Catholic radicals and middle-class liberals (including the young John Hume, the future Nobel Peace Prize winner) were drawn into civil disobedience. However, the marches of the civil rights movement provoked violent reprisals from Orange loyalists and from the militarised Northern Ireland police, the Royal Ulster Constabulary (RUC). Several innocent people were beaten to death. Riots followed. In August 1969 houses were burned in Belfast and the largest movement of refugees (mainly Catholics) in Western Europe since the Second World War took place. Displaced Catholic families generally moved back into the long-established 'Catholic ghetto' of West Belfast, leading to significant overcrowding in the area. Desperate Catholics screamed for someone to protect them. While the British Army arrived to restore British 'law and order', the IRA re-emerged as the armed defenders of Catholic neighbourhoods. An ancient conflict suddenly resurfaced with all the fury of 1960s youth.

The resulting 'Troubles' dominated the politics of Northern Ireland from 1969 to 1994. In loyalist areas, paramilitary groups were formed to ensure that 'the Brits' did not waver in the face of the IRA's increasingly bloody armed struggle against British rule. It was a time of tragedy and little hope. Over three thousand people were killed in the tiny backstreets of Belfast and Derry, or out in the border villages and farms. And not until the IRA's ceasefire of 1994 did it seem like it might ever end. Despite the subsequent temporary breakdown of both loyalist and republican ceasefires, long months of tense negotiations between all of Northern Ireland's political strands finally resulted in the Good Friday Agreement of 1998. When that agreement was ratified by 86 per cent of Ireland's people — Protestant and Catholic, both north and south of the 1920 partition border — it seemed as though things were finally moving towards resolution of a conflict which had cost more than 3500 lives over the preceding thirty years.

However, the truth is that no-one knows how the 'peace process' is going to end. A few years ago I had the opportunity to speak to Derry journalist Eamonn McCann, one of the leaders of the 1960s civil rights movement and a man who has dedicated a good part of his professional life to intricately analysing the political minutiae of the Northern Ireland conflict. I asked him if he thought the peace process would survive and how it would develop.

'I haven't a clue,' replied Eamonn.

'You must have some inkling?'

'Nothing. I have no idea whatsoever.'

Eamonn returned to his pint for solace. I asked Sinn Féin President Gerry Adams the same question in February 1999. He looked at me like I was not in full possession of my faculties.

Irish history certainly has a way of challenging your expectations. If it has taught us anything it is not to hastily declare victory. One is reminded of the Jacobite general, the Marquis de Saint-Ruth, who on 12 July 1691, after watching enemy forces loyal to William of Orange get stuck in the heavy bog in front of his lines, presumptuously declared 'They are beaten, *mes enfants!*' Seconds later a cannonball tore off his head. The Williamite Army won the day and it is this victory, celebrated by bonfires in Belfast, that was commemorated on the 'Glorious Twelfth' each year until it was fused in popular memory with the more famous victory of William at the Boyne eleven days and one year earlier. In short, never presume anything in Irish history.

With the beginning of the new millennium the certainties of the past seemed to be slowly crumbling in Northern Ireland. Although everyone emphasised that the divisions were still enormous, there was a feeling that nothing would ever be the same again. For instance, during 2000 the City Council in Derry (or Londonderry) elected a Sinn Féin member as Lord Mayor.

Cathal Crumley was the first Sinn Féin lord mayor to be elected in Ireland since Terence MacSwiney in Cork in 1920 (MacSwiney later died on hunger strike). A former IRA member, Crumley was sentenced to 300 years in Long Kesh prison before having his conviction quashed and being released in 1986.

Crumley was the first ever Sinn Féin mayor of Derry, a town whose sectarian gerrymandering of local government meant that for fifty years a minority of Loyalist Protestants ruled over a majority of Catholic Nationalists. Derry symbolised everything that was wrong with the old Orange-tinged partitionist Northern Ireland government. Some of the very first civil rights marches were held there. Derry's 'Battle of the Bogside' in 1969 arguably signalled the opening phase of the modern 'Troubles' and 'Bloody Sunday' in Derry during 1972 (when British paratroopers killed fourteen civilians) marked the degeneration of Northern Ireland into a seemingly intractable bloody little conflict.

That Crumley could be elected mayor by twenty-one of Derry council's thirty members — who came from both traditions and all sides of politics — gave many people hope, regardless of their political sympathies. The importance of the moment was obviously not lost on Crumley himself, who in his acceptance speech assured the packed Derry Guildhall that, 'The failed politics of exclusion end tonight … I offer the hand of friendship to the unionist community and trust they will have the maturity to react in a reciprocal fashion for the betterment of this city.'

But what did all of this mean for the future of Northern Ireland and the 'Troubles' at the start of the new millennium? That other famous Derry republican, Sinn Féin's Martin McGuinness, once compared the peace process to his grandson's first attempts to walk. Apparently he was up on his feet, but every time he looked set to walk he faltered and clutched at the chair, holding on for dear life. It was not an especially academic analogy, but it fitted. For every slow faltering step towards peace in Ireland, there continued to be terrifying moments of insecurity and collapse.

During the second week of September 2003 I was reading the *Belfast Telegraph* and noticed that the Holy Cross case had finally come up for judicial review in the High Court in Belfast. The mother of one of the Holy Cross girls was arguing that the British Secretary of State and the Chief Constable of the Royal Ulster Constabulary failed to provide adequate protection for the parents and children at Holy Cross between June and November 2001 when loyalist protests against Catholic schoolchildren were at their height. The woman — who was identified only as 'E' in order to protect her safety — had taken on the services of a lawyer, Seamus Treacy QC, who argued that the 'security forces' in Northern Ireland failed to protect the basic human rights of children who were guilty of nothing more sinister than attending a Catholic school in a Protestant area. One of the witnesses at the High Court hearing, the headmaster at Holy Cross Boys School, compared the treatment that the girls had received as being 'akin to the treatment of American blacks in Alabama in the 1960s.'[13]

Certainly the Holy Cross protest revealed the lingering bitter historical divisions of Northern Ireland at their very worst. Over several months the girls had been subjected to sectarian abuse on a daily basis, as well as a generous barrage of loyalist spittle, beer bottles, bricks and even a pipe bomb on at least one occasion. One account of what the families were subjected to was published in the book *Ardoyne: The Untold Truth* where two mothers, Philomena and Isobel, recounted their experiences. Philomena recalled that the day the attacks on Holy Cross began in 2001 the police blocked off Ardoyne and stopped desperate parents from getting to the school as loyalists went on the rampage.

> We could see men and women in the loyalist crowd. Some of them were masked and many of them were holding sticks, hammers, knives, everything. In the middle of all that were some of our children who had already come out of the school and who were trying to make their way down the road.[14]

Philomena was eventually reunited with her terrified daughter, who had literally wet herself in fear. However, as soon as she got home she heard more 'squealing coming from up the road.'

> I ran out and there was a group of kids crying. They were really badly shaken up and clinging to a woman for their dear lives. I brought them all into my home … There was a complete state of distress. My wee girl is seven, a timid, fragile child. Since all of this happened she has reverted to acting like a baby again. Her whole character has changed and her behaviour has become very difficult to cope with. She says she never wants to put a Holy Cross uniform on her back again because she feels like she is a target when she wears it.[15]

Isobel's daughter was similarly affected by the situation at Holy Cross.

> The next morning at about 7.30 am I came into the living room to find my seven year old watching the

news. I asked her what she was doing and she said that she was looking to see if her school had been burnt down because she never wanted to go back to it or walk up that road again. I had to try to explain to her, a seven year old who did not even know what a Catholic or Protestant was, why we had to try and go back up that road.

The people who led the protests against the Holy Cross girls considered themselves to be Ulster Protestants by birth, by religion and by political conviction. From their point of view, since the signing of the Good Friday Agreement in 1998 their precious statelet, Northern Ireland, was slowly being whittled away. The attempted peace agreement — which opinion polls during 2003 revealed a majority of Northern Protestants now rejected — undeniably has a political dynamic which both the British and Irish governments hope will lead to a united Ireland. A watered down united Ireland achieved by consent (rather than IRA bombs), but a united Ireland nevertheless. Similarly, while the Catholic population of Northern Ireland has grown relentlessly in size and political confidence over the last few decades, the Protestant population is in decline in terms of demographic and political importance. Arguably, it is in North Belfast where the new political and residential realities have been felt the sharpest.

During my father's childhood North Belfast was 'mixed' (as they would say) but predominantly Protestant. Moreover, although both communities were gripped with poverty, there was a sense in the 'loyalist heartlands' that they had the jobs and political security within the United Kingdom, and that their 'Protestant state for a Protestant people' was unconquerable. However, thirty years of the 'Troubles' combined with the higher birth rate amongst the Catholic population has changed all that. During the 1990s Protestant schools, churches and community centres closed in North Belfast at the same time as their Catholic counterparts expanded. These days it's the Catholic residents of Ardoyne who host an international festival each summer, and who have their own newspaper and vibrant community organisations.

In Glenbryn, where Holy Cross Girls School is located, only about one thousand Protestants remain in an area separated from the seven thousand Catholic residents of Ardoyne by concrete 'peace walls'. In response to the burgeoning political confidence and thriving sense of community in Ardoyne, loyalist Glenbryn now perceives itself as a frontier outpost holding out against the disloyal Irish hordes. In reality it is simply a working-class housing estate which Tony Blair will never visit because, at the end of the day, he doesn't care all that much about the people who live there, or their diminished sense of national identity.

North Belfast's stark concrete walls, or 'peace lines', still divide Protestant and Catholic communities. In the 1991 official census of Northern Ireland, conducted prior to the peace process, approximately 63 per cent of people lived in areas in which the ethnic mix was more than 90 per cent Protestant (British) or 90 per cent Catholic (Irish). A decade later, after tortuous years of peace processing, 66 per cent of people now live in communities overwhelmingly dominated by one or other of the two major ethnic groups.[16] In short, the painful crawl towards a better future in Northern Ireland has seen an increase in residential segregation, not a reduction. Similarly, in January 2002 the *Guardian Weekly* published details of a survey of 4800 households in twelve neighbouring housing estates in Northern Ireland. The study revealed that there is now less 'integration' between

Protestants and Catholics than before the peace process started. The report on the survey revealed that 68 per cent of respondents had 'never had a meaningful conversation' with someone from the other side of the peace wall.[17] As the attacks on Catholic schoolgirls at Holy Cross revealed, communication and dialogue are at an all-time low in North Belfast.

So what does the future hold for Northern Ireland and the girls of Holy Cross? Well, the jury is still out … literally. The Belfast High Court has not ruled yet on whether the police should have used greater force to suppress the loyalist protests against the Holy Cross children. And there is still much to be pessimistic about. In response to the beginning of the High Court hearing during September 2003, loyalist paramilitaries placed a deadly pipe bomb at the front gates of Holy Cross to welcome the girls back on the first day of the new school year. Thankfully, no-one was hurt.

But there are glimmers of hope too. My cousin Kathleen took her daughter out of Holy Cross during the protests.[18] And then she did the one thing that is even more offensive to the worldview of the loyalist paramilitaries than Catholic Girls Schools, the Good Friday Agreement and the possibility of peace. My cousin sent her daughter to a small, but growing, cross-community, non-denominational school. These days, some of her best friends are Protestant. The girls play and learn together beyond the ethnic labels and historic divisions others would impose upon them. And together they might actually build a future where there is no room for balaclavas, pipe bombs and sectarian hate.

Genocide and Civil War in Central Africa

How does a blue [United Nations] armband vaccinate against
the racism and paternalism of people whose only vision of
Africa is lion hunting, slave markets and colonial conquest?
                        P Lumumba, prime minister of the Congo,
                                        assassinated in 1961

In 1906 an African 'Pygmy' from the Congo by the name of Ota
Benga was caged in the monkey house at the Bronx Zoo in New
York. He had been brought to America by a white missionary-
explorer from South Carolina called Samuel Verner who first
'exhibited' him at the World's Fair in Saint Louis in 1904. Two
years later Ota Benga became the star attraction at the Bronx Zoo
and crowds would throng around his cage, with bones scattered
across the floor as props, to view this African 'wild savage' with
his sharpened teeth. He was displayed in an enclosure he shared
with an orang-utan near other cages with chimpanzees and a
gorilla called Dinah — emphasising his role in the chain of
evolution from apes to Africans. Contemporary journals, like the
respectable *Scientific American*, described 'Congo pygmies' as

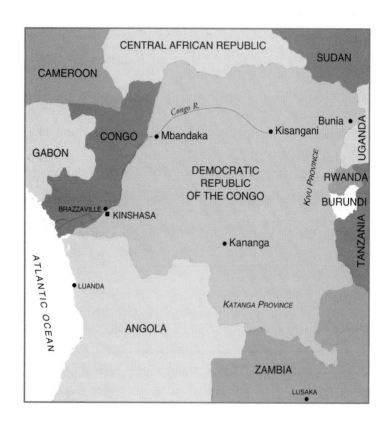

Central Africa

'small, apelike, elfish creatures, furtive and mischievous, they closely parallel the brownies and goblins of our fairy tales.' Such creatures normally lived 'in the dense tangled forests in absolute savagery,' so what better place to house one than in a zoo?[19]

Ota Benga was displayed in the monkey house with the expressed support of the Bronx Zoo's Director, Mr Hornaday, who was quoted in the *New York Times* of 11 September 1906 as saying he believed that apes and Africans were closely related. As many as 40,000 visitors a day came to the Bronx Zoo to see the 'wild man from Africa'. A number of black Americans, particularly ministers of religion, protested. In the words of Reverend Gordon, also quoted in the *New York Times*, 'our race … is depressed enough without exhibiting one of us with the apes. We think we are worthy of being considered human beings, with souls.'

Due to protests from black Americans, as well as some by anti-evolutionists (!), Ota Benga was released from his cage in the monkey house and allowed to wander around the grounds of the Bronx Zoo dressed in a white suit. He was followed everywhere by crowds of curious white Americans who found the spectacle of a four-foot eleven-inch African in a suit almost as fascinating as the notion of a black monkey-man imprisoned in a cage. Director Hornaday wrote to his friend Sam Verner, who was responsible for dumping Ota Benga at the Bronx Zoo in the first place, to let him know what his 'wild man' was up to:

> Of course we have not exhibited him in the cage since the trouble began. Since dictating the above, we have had a great time with Ota Benga. He procured a carving knife from the feeding room of the Monkey House, and went around the Park flourishing it in a most alarming manner, and for a long time refused to

give it up. Eventually it was taken from him. Shortly after that he went to the soda fountain near the Bird House, to get some soda, and because he was refused the soda he got into a great rage ... This led to a great fracas. He fought like a tiger, and it took three men to get him back to the Monkey House. He has struck a number of visitors, and has 'raised Cain' generally.[20]

At night Ota Benga continued to sleep in the monkey house and dreamt of Africa. He became more agitated and desperate with his daily situation of humiliation and harassment. At one point he made himself a rudimentary bow and arrow and started shooting it at zoo patrons. He was eventually released from the zoo and placed in the Howard Colored Orphan Asylum in Brooklyn. He was later moved to Virginia where he learnt English, worked in a tobacco factory and was looked after by the black community there. He taught local African-American children to hunt in the nearby woods and he told people that what he wanted most of all was to return home to the Congo. In March 1916, ten years after his ordeal in the Bronx Zoo began and realising that he would never be able to afford the steamship fare back to Africa, Ota Benga committed suicide.

Ota Benga remains a lesson to us of the ways in which the West has historically misunderstood, misrepresented and abused its relationship with Africa and Africans.

The Democratic Republic of the Congo (called Zaire from 1971 until 1997) is an enormous country of 55 million people that runs from the west coast of Africa along the Congo River and into the very heart of the continent. Before colonisation the Congo had been a major region for the collection of slaves for the

American market. It is estimated that nearly a million African slaves were taken from the Congo and Angola to Brazil during the nineteenth century. As the slave trade slowly ended the Congo was then colonised by agents of the Belgian king as the Congo Free State and became a Belgian colony in 1908. Its colonisation was particularly brutal with European traders enslaving or murdering entire villages in their desperate pursuit of rubber, ivory and other riches. The colonial powers (principally the Belgians) manipulated tribal divisions as they took control of the area. By some estimates more than a quarter of the population was exterminated. It was not just that the Congo was conquered by force; this happened in Australia and many other places, but rather, that for several generations the entire political economy of the Belgian Congo was based upon open violence and coercion.[21]

Despite this history the enormous crisis which has engulfed the Congo since late 1996 has seemed to most people to be simply another of Africa's confusing and seemingly undecipherable conflicts. The western news media has consistently divorced politics and historical context from the equation, continually portraying the earlier civil war in neighboring Rwanda and Burundi as a senseless and barbaric tribal conflict. Images of terrified refugees fleeing for their lives before the advance of machete-wielding mobs does make, after all, fairly compelling television.

However, news coverage is often as significant for what it leaves out as for what it shows. So, for instance, we know that about 800,000 ethnic Tutsis and moderate Hutus were slaughtered by Hutu extremists in Rwanda during 1994 over a period of about one hundred days and that this conflict spilled into neighbouring Burundi. Yet, what is often not mentioned is that the regime that carried out the killing in Rwanda, and was eventually toppled, had previously been supported by several western powers, particularly France. Indeed, it was French troops who intervened and occupied portions of western Rwanda under the auspices of the United Nations, helping the Hutu extremists who had carried out the genocide flee into Zaire when the military balance of power finally turned against them. In the words of a leading African political analyst, Professor Nzongola-Ntalaja:

> Having supported the [Rwandan] Habyarimana regime and trained its genocidal machine, including the extremist Hutu Interahamwe militia, the French were relieved to have in Kinshasa [Zaire's capital] a regime that would let them permit the Rwandan killers to cross into Zaire with all their weapons. The fact that these killers were now free to use Zairean territory to launch raids into Rwanda, and to slaughter Tutsi citizens and residents of Zaire, is the immediate cause of the current fighting in eastern Zaire.[22]

Yet, to emphasise the complicity of a major western power in Africa's 'tribal violence' would perhaps undermine a widely held belief that Africa's problems spring from an inherent backwardness, rather than from history. Indeed, it is only through understanding the history of western intervention in Central Africa that one can really understand the crisis that engulfed the entire region at the end of the 1990s.

The two small pre-colonial kingdoms of Rwanda and Burundi, which border the Congo, were able to survive western occupation relatively unscathed until the twentieth century. Ethnic Hutus and Tutsis have lived in both kingdoms since pre-colonial times and other ethnic Tutsis (including the Banyamulenge) settled in portions of the Congo during the seventeenth century. Belgium took over 'trusteeship' of Rwanda and Burundi in 1920 with the blessing of the League of Nations and continued to rule the Congo, Rwanda and Burundi thereafter.

In Rwanda the tensions between Hutu and Tutsi are largely a product of this European colonial rule. In the words of historian Stephen Shalom:

> In pre-colonial Rwanda, the categories 'Tutsi' and 'Hutu' were somewhere between castes and ethnic groups. The boundaries between the two groups were permeable, with movement permitted between them. Some members of each group were local chiefs and there was not systematic Tutsi–Hutu violence. The brief period of German colonial rule brought European racial theories to Rwanda: the more European-featured Tutsi were deemed to be the natural-born local rulers and the Hutu destined to serve them. These theories were put into practice by the Belgians who took over from the Germans after World War One. They replaced existing Hutu chiefs with Tutsis and issued identity cards indicating each person's ethnic group, thus eliminating some of the social mobility of the old system.[23]

From this European imposed colonial 'caste' system grew deadly ethnic, social and political tensions. In other words, it was not ancient African barbarism that produced the Rwandan genocide, but ideas about race and ethnicity that had their intellectual origins in Europe. The European mental universe which created the gas chambers of Auschwitz also made possible Rwanda's 100 bloody days.

It was not until the post-1945 period that national liberation movements began to seriously challenge colonial regimes throughout Africa. Indeed, seventeen African colonies achieved independence in 1960 alone via an eclectic mixture of armed struggle, popular mobilisation and foreign diplomacy. In Central Africa, as elsewhere, while the colonial authority ceded formal independence (Congo in 1960, Burundi and Rwanda in 1962) European powers tried to maintain informal 'spheres of influence' and cultivate potential rulers whom they found amenable to their interests. In particular the political momentum of the Cold War between the United States and the Soviet Union spiralled into real war in Africa as western governments did their best to divide or repress national liberation movements that were perceived as being too left wing.

For example, as the resource-rich Portuguese colony of Angola (to Congo's south) approached independence in early 1975 both the Americans and Soviets sought out supporters amongst the various armed factions vying for power. With superpower meddling (and a supply of arms and money) a low-level civil conflict escalated into an all-out civil war, eventually drawing in the South Africans, who invaded in late 1975. The United States was willing to tacitly support this invasion by white troops from apartheid South Africa if it prevented the nominally Marxist MPLA from consolidating power in Angola. When the South African invasion was repulsed by the MPLA (with the notable assistance of 30,000 soldiers from Cuba) the Americans increased funding to rebel movements (mostly organised along ethnic lines) opposed to the Angolan (MPLA) government. Ten years later Lucio Lara from the MPLA accurately described the ongoing civil war in his country as a lingering 'cancer of imperialism'. The civil war continued until the end of the Cold War in the 1990s and did not truly halt until the death of the recalcitrant warlord Jonas Savimbi in 2002. By the 1990s Savimbi's unwillingness to be part of any peace deal had caused him to become estranged from his supporters in Washington. In 1986 however, during the Cold War, Savimbi had actually been welcomed to the White House by President Reagan who had described him as a freedom fighter against communism.[24]

In Rwanda, meanwhile, it had been the 'elite' Tutsis who were disproportionately represented in the leadership of the anti-colonial movement. As a result, after 1960 the Belgians played the ethnic card, replacing Tutsi chiefs with Hutus and encouraging the growing tensions between representatives of the two groups. The new Hutu elite encouraged the idea that Tutsis were a historically privileged and 'alien' minority in Rwanda. After independence a wave of anti-Tutsi violence in 1963–64 drove 300,000 Tutsi refugees from Rwanda.[25] The situation in neighbouring Burundi, which had a similar colonial history and ethnic development under the Belgians, mirrored the violence of Rwanda — with one major difference. In Burundi the Tutsi elite was able to hold on to power after the departure of the Belgians and the Tutsi-dominated state embarked upon massacres of Hutus after a failed Hutu uprising in 1972. At least 80,000 Hutus were killed in a country with a population of less than four million people.[26]

To the west in the newly independent Congo the popular and charismatic left-wing leader of the post-colonial government, Patrice Lumumba, was murdered in 1961. It had been Lumumba who stood before the assembled Belgian dignitaries, including the king and prime minister, on Congo's independence day in June

1960 and lambasted them for Belgium's past colonial cruelties:

> We have known sarcasm and insults, endured blows
> morning, noon and night because we were 'niggers' …
> We have seen our lands despoiled under the terms of
> what was supposedly the law of the land but which
> only recognised the right of the strongest.[27]

Such words won him popularity throughout Africa and the Third World, but created powerful enemies beyond Belgium. Britain had mining interests in Katanga province and the United States was concerned by Lumumba's contacts with the Soviet Union. Recently declassified documents and new historical research reveal that US President Dwight Eisenhower discussed the Congo with the British foreign secretary, Lord Home, in September 1960. According to the US account of this meeting, 'The president expressed his wish that Lumumba would fall into a river full of crocodiles.' In response Lord Home, 'said regretfully that we have lost many of the techniques of old-fashioned diplomacy.' A few months later Lumumba, who was supposed to be under UN protection, was arrested and handed over to his political enemies in breakaway Katanga province. He was beaten, tortured and finally executed. A Belgian commanded the firing squad.[28]

In 1975 a US Senate Committee revealed that the American CIA had conspired in Lumumba's murder and had funded and armed his right-wing political opponents. It was one of these opponents, Joseph Désiré Mobutu, an army officer who had played an important role in Lumumba's isolation and murder, who profited most from the turmoil, eventually emerging with strong western support in 1965 as the anti-communist military ruler of a country he renamed Zaire. Over the following thirty years Mobutu ruled Zaire (Congo) with an iron fist. Political opponents were murdered and he plundered the country of its natural resources, reportedly becoming the richest man in Africa in the process. Moreover, despite the fact that Mobutu's military regime was fundamentally undemocratic, completely corrupt and unquestionably brutal, he was able to do all of this with the tacit approval of successive US, Belgian and French governments. Indeed, crucial US military and 'humanitarian' aid to Mobutu's government was decisive in keeping him in power.

The reason for this consistent western support lay in the geo-political dictates of the Cold War. In particular, Mobutu allowed south-western Zaire to be used as a staging ground for military incursions by US-backed Angolan guerillas fighting to topple the 'Marxist-Leninist' MPLA regime in neighbouring Angola. It was the seismic political shift of 1989, which saw the much-celebrated 'death of communism' in Eastern Europe, that facilitated Mobutu's downfall. One result of the collapse of the Soviet Union and the new post-1989 realpolitik was mounting international pressure for negotiated settlements to a number of longstanding African conflicts. Partly as a result, after 1990 the civil wars in Angola and Mozambique (by right-wing guerillas against left-wing governments) slowly ground to a halt, while in South Africa there was a successful transition from apartheid to a conventional non-racial democracy. Quite simply, Mobutu outlived his usefulness to western powers as a regional anti-communist strongman. After supporting Mobutu's dictatorship for thirty years, from 1993 onwards the United States started publicly calling for a transfer to democracy in Zaire.

The end of the Cold War undoubtedly made life more precarious for Africa's dictators. This factor, when combined with the ravages of International Monetary Fund structural adjustment programs, endemic poverty, malnutrition and the AIDS epidemic made Central Africa an entirely unpleasant place to live for the vast bulk of the population. One symptom of this multifaceted crisis in the early 1990s was the attempt by various regimes in the region to whip up ethnic hostilities in order to deflect popular discontent. Specifically, in Rwanda it was the convergence of these factors that led the French-backed Habyarimana regime to increase its racist anti-Tutsi rhetoric. The Interahamwe, an extremist Hutu militia backed by the government and partly trained by the French, started killing Tutsis. Then during October 1993 the Hutu president of Burundi was assassinated by Tutsi army officers in an attempted coup and widespread ethnic violence broke out. Finally, in April 1994 Habyarimana was himself assassinated and the Interahamwe militia were set loose. The net result was the Rwandan genocide of 1994. Over half a million Tutsis and tens of thousands of moderate Hutus were murdered.

When the perpetrators of these crimes, extremist Hutu militias and the Hutu-dominated Rwandan Army, were granted sanctuary in Zaire they were also given control over the hundreds of thousands of Rwandan refugees who fled in the wake of the collapse of the Habyarimana regime. From Zaire Hutu extremists continued to launch murderous incursions into Rwanda and Burundi and were involved in attacks on local Tutsis in Zaire — the Banyamulenge. Local Zairean authorities, facing their own share of increased problems in the aftermath of the Cold War, saw their opportunity to similarly scapegoat ethnic minorities. During September 1996 the Deputy-Governor of South Kivu province in Zaire stated that if all Tutsis (both local Bunyamulenge and Rwandan refugees) did not leave the province within a week they would be put into camps or exterminated.

However, the morally and politically bankrupt Zairean regime seriously miscalculated. Local Tutsis not only defended themselves, they actually defeated the Zairean army, forced the mass migration of about 400,000 Hutu refugees back into Rwanda and broke the back of the extremist Hutu militias in Zaire. In the process they welded themselves into a multi-ethnic rebel army that (with crucial support from the new Rwandan Tutsi-dominated army, formerly the Rwandan Patriotic Front) displaced the Mobutu regime from most of south-eastern Zaire, including the important gold-mining region of Bunia. By early 1997 the rebels had joined with the forces of ageing anti-Mobutu guerilla leader Laurent Kabila and controlled nearly a quarter of the country. Eventually, Kabila's forces overthrew the Mobutu regime and the cancerous old dictator hobbled off into exile with his millions of dollars stolen from the Zairean treasury.

It was not just Zaire that was at stake here. The whole of Central Africa, including Uganda, the Central African Republic and Tanzania, was in crisis. Poverty, AIDS and social discontent created a climate of permanent instability. To Zaire's south-east, in Zimbabwe, October 1996 saw the most widespread and important labour unrest in the country since independence in 1980. As the social crisis in Zimbabwe intensified over the following years the president, Robert Mugabe, desperately attempted to deflect criticism of his own undemocratic rule by encouraging supporters of his party to attack white farmers. Rather than solve the political crisis in Zimbabwe, such an approach merely deepened it. Diplomatically, Zimbabwe was constantly criticised by western powers (including Australia) and facing sanctions and mass unemployment, its economy neared the point of collapse. The inflation rate hit 500 per cent. By early

2004 the United Nations reported that an estimated 7.5 million Zimbabweans (close to two-thirds of the population) urgently required food aid.[29] Anti-Mugabe protests, food riots, and general political instability continued.

Indeed, the years since 1997 have brought little reprieve for the bureaucratic thieves and dictators who rule most of the countries in Central Africa. During 1997 there was a general strike in Swaziland and even Kenya, until then regarded as the most stable country in Africa, experienced major anti-government rioting. Although these events were easily as politically important as what was occurring in Zaire, they received almost no coverage in the Australian, European or American press. Zaire, whose crisis confirmed western preconceptions of Africa's violent instability, was the African story of 1997 and its descent into chaos was photographed, documented and then promptly forgotten.

Post-Mobutu Zaire was renamed Congo but Laurent Kabila's rebel army proved incapable of delivering peace, democracy and social change to the people of the country. Eventually Kabila fell out with his military and political backers — particularly the government of post-genocide Rwanda — and by 1998 Uganda and Rwanda were supporting a new armed rebellion against Kabila's post-Mobutu regime. Desperate to stay in power, Kabila turned to Zimbabwe, Angola and Namibia for help and armed intervention. The fighting in the renewed civil war was heaviest on the eastern border areas where thousands of civilians were displaced or killed. Then during January 2001 Kabila was assassinated by one of his bodyguards and his son, Joseph, became the new un-elected president of the Congo. The democratic elections which had been promised by all three dictators (Mobutu, Kabila and now his son) are still to be held. It seems the long-suffering Congolese will have to wait before they have any hope of a genuinely free life — safe from warlords, violence and dictatorship.

During these years of civil war and political collapse Washington seemed to maintain a 'hands off' attitude. The US government had dithered during the Rwandan genocide and it had done almost nothing to support democracy in Zaire during the thirty years of Mobutu's dictatorship. Washington has done very little since. It has simply absolved itself, or so it seems, of responsibility and left the competing warlords in the region to get on with killing the Congolese people and plundering the country's natural resources. While the Congo is rich in gold, cobalt, copper, tantalite, uranium and diamonds, most people survive on about US25 cents a day.[30]

It is estimated that 3.5 million people have died in the civil war in the Congo since 1998 — this makes it the most costly war on this planet since the end of the Second World War. Hundreds of thousands of Congolese have been killed in fighting, or have died because of its consequences — disease, starvation and displacement. You could argue that for once the United States was allowing a region to sort things out for itself and that there were no 'good guys' in power worth supporting, only a series of competing 'bad guys'. However, this neglects the fact that the mess in the Congo, Rwanda, Burundi, Angola, and throughout sub-Saharan Africa, is a mess that European colonialism and then American and Soviet foreign policy during the Cold War helped create.

It is true that now the Cold War is finished few people in the West want to listen to Africa's problems. And so the area is left to fester and rot in endemic war, poverty and disease until something forces the hand of the world, or material self-interest rears its ugly head once again. Interestingly, it is estimated that by

2015 the United States will be importing 25 per cent of its oil from Africa, prompting one US congressman to comment that, 'African oil should be treated as a priority for US post-September eleventh security.'[31] One of the principal providers of this oil will be Angola, another country, like the Congo, destroyed by Cold War malfeasance and nearly thirty years of civil war. In Angola's enormously destructive civil war the United States, with apartheid South Africa, backed Jonas Savimbi's UNITA rebels fighting against the leftist MPLA government. Mobutu also provided support and bases inside Zaire for right-wing Angolan rebels.

With Mobutu gone, the Cold War over and Angola's civil war finally finished, the US is now building a US$40 million new fortified embassy in the capital, Luanda, and an estimated 60 per cent of Angola's precious oil is pumped by US company ChevronTexaco. The profits go into American pockets, or those of corrupt local government bureaucrats, with the IMF confirming that up to US$1.7 billion a year in oil money was stolen from state accounts in Angola between 1997 and 2001.[32] Such practices continue while the majority of Angolans — including the tens of thousands who were crippled, wounded or widowed by the war — will never see any tangible benefits from the wealth their country creates. And so the cycle continues.

Prior to his murder in 1961, the Congo's Patrice Lumumba contemplated the tragic legacy of colonialism and of Africa's engagement with Europe. He wrote that, 'One day history will have its say ... Africa will write its own history, and it will be one of glory and dignity.'[33] That day is yet to come and that history is yet to be written.

Africa's Holocaust — AIDS

Africa remains the most marginalised and most misunderstood continent on earth. For the major western powers and global financial institutions, Africa is a perennial disaster area. For the international press corps Africa's tragedies seem to be an incidental reminder that this is a part of the world that may provide the occasional photo opportunity, but which is otherwise brutal, backward and best ignored. The tragedy of genocide in Rwanda, famine and war in Somalia and Ethiopia — all of these events simply reinforced a popular western perception of Africa as a mysterious, dark and violent land. Still, we live in an interconnected world and in July 2003 US President George W Bush visited Africa in order to support African states which backed his war on terror (Africa had borne the brunt of Osama bin Laden's 1998 attacks on United States embassies), and to show that he was genuinely concerned by the great plague of our times — AIDS.

Interestingly, according to a report of the American IRS, the 400 richest Americans had a combined income of US$69 billion in the year 2000. That was more than the combined incomes of the 166 million people who live in four African countries which President Bush visited in 2003 — Nigeria, Senegal, Uganda and

Botswana. At the time that Bush visited Africa the average life expectancy in the United States was seventy-seven years. The average life expectancy in Africa was less than fifty. And in some AIDS-ravaged countries it is less than forty.[34]

The situation for those who are sick and poor in Africa is desperate beyond comprehension. During September 2003 the United Nations and the World Health Organization revealed that an estimated 15 million Africans have already died of AIDS and at least another 25 million are HIV-positive. In Botswana, which President Bush visited during 2003, about 39 per cent of adults are either HIV positive or have AIDS. Of those people infected with the deadly virus, only an estimated 50,000 Africans currently have access to cheap anti-retroviral drugs. Indeed, access to medicines continues to be a life or death issue in poverty stricken Africa.[35]

On a continent with vast structural unemployment where those in paid work generally support a much larger network of relatives unable to find jobs, the burden of paying for basic medicines is crippling. For those estimated five to six million Africans south of the Sahara with AIDS the cost of drugs that might seriously prolong life is simply beyond reach. It is for this reason that African governments have been petitioning western governments and drug companies to allow cheaper 'generic' anti-AIDS drugs to be sold in Africa. For example, the prices of 'branded' zidovudine capsules and generic ones are $198 and $24 respectively. For stavudine capsules the prices are $129 and $5. For lamivudine, $143 and $14. In total, HIV/AIDS medicines that currently cost about $10,000 a year can easily be made available, generically, at a cost of about $250–350 for a year's supply. While the major international drug companies and African governments continue to fight over just how affordable and accessible these drugs will be to a dying 'market' of African AIDS sufferers, millions of people continue to go without medicines.[36] Or as Stephen Lewis, the United Nations special envoy for AIDS in Africa, commented during September 2003:

> What's happening to the continent makes me extremely angry ... I'm enraged by the behaviour of the rich powers. This is a full-blown emergency; in every emergency there is a division of labour. Africa is struggling to hold up its end; the West is not.[37]

In addition to Africa's AIDS catastrophe, about 1.5 million Africans die each year from tuberculosis and malaria. In response to this, in 2001 the World Health Organization made a desperate suggestion. It said that if the richest nations on earth contributed around US$25 billion a year to the Third World (mainly in terms of mosquito nets and basic drugs) they could save about eight million lives annually. This would be part of a WHO-run 'Global Fund to Fight AIDS, Malaria and Tuberculosis'. The WHO suggested that the United States' share of this requested $25 billion (based on the size of its economy) would be $8 billion per year.

The United States' current contribution to Third World aid programs (despite funding increases resulting from Bush's AIDS in Africa initiative) amounts to about US$2.1 billion for 2004. Of this money, only about $200 million will be directly funnelled through the UN Global Fund. Meanwhile, the Bush administration has cut taxes for the richest segment of US society. In 1995 the top 400 income earners in the United States paid almost 30 per cent income tax. After the Bush tax cuts they were paying around 18 per cent. The resulting savings (i.e., the tax money this richest 400 no longer have to pay) amounts to about US$7 billion a year. In other words, the $7 billion from the richest 400 Americans, plus the $2 billion the US government has already allocated, easily equals the $8 billion the WHO has asked for from the US for its Global Fund. Jeffrey Sachs, from the World Health Organization, wrote an article on this very issue in the *New York Times* where he argued that:

> Of course, it's strange to rely on only the goodwill of a few hundred super-rich people to save the lives of millions of the poor … Yet given the huge tax cuts that have gone to the wealthiest Americans, the moral and practical obligations facing them are greater than ever.[38]

While in Africa in July 2003, President Bush spoke about the trans-Atlantic slave trade, describing it as 'one of the greatest crimes of history.' Bush visited a port (now a museum) off the West African coast where slaves were imprisoned and sold before transportation to the Americas. Bush commented that the historical injustice of the trans-Atlantic slave trade had bound the history and peoples of Africa and America together. He is correct. And many people, especially in Africa, believe it is now incumbent upon his country, which is the richest nation on earth partly because of the tremendous wealth which African slaves produced, to help contemporary Africa out of the poverty trap that slavery, colonialism, AIDS and the Cold War helped create.

There are now between 25 and 28 million HIV-positive people in sub-Saharan Africa. Three million people died of AIDS throughout the world during 2003, with at least 2.2 million of those deaths occurring in sub-Saharan Africa. Eleven million African children have already lost a parent to AIDS and it is estimated that by 2010 there will be 20 million African AIDS orphans. Predictions are that the economies of several struggling sub-Saharan countries may completely collapse under the resulting social and economic strain. For example, in Zambia an estimated three thousand schoolteachers died of AIDS between 1996 and 1999, wiping out an entire layer of trained educators who cannot be easily replaced. In Zambia's largest hospital eight out of every ten beds are already occupied by AIDS patients and the health system is at breaking point. For these countries and people, the future is bleak.[39]

Exasperated with the failure of western governments to appreciate the magnitude of the health, welfare, social and economic catastrophe which is confronting Africa, during September 2003 the United Nations special envoy for HIV/AIDS in Africa denounced the 'grotesque obscenity' of western governments who allowed millions to face death without affordable AIDS medicines in Africa while they 'can find over $200 billion to fight a war on terrorism.' The UN Secretary General, Kofi Annan, estimated that an extra US$3 billion was needed to help save three million lives in Africa by 2005.[40] Nicholas Kristof, reporting from Africa for the *New York Times*, commented that:

> In America, we think of AIDS simply as an epidemic.
> In fact, like the Holocaust, it is a moral challenge to
> the world, one we are failing.[41]

Frustrated to the point of rage and despair by the lack of decisive action on the part of western nations, Stephen Lewis, the United Nations special envoy, described Africa's AIDS pandemic as 'mass murder by complacency.'[42]

The response of the Bush administration to all of this has

been, at best, mixed. Bush seemed to give with one hand and take away with the other. For instance, during his African tour President Bush committed himself, and his country, to the fight against AIDS in Africa. Then during September 2003, shortly after Bush had asked for an extra US$87 billion from the US Congress to maintain the occupation of Iraq, it was reported that the US government's earlier decision to deprive funding for any overseas aid organisation that promoted abortion as a potential option for pregnant women in the developing world had cut off financial aid to dozens of organisations that work with AIDS sufferers. Moreover, the funds which the Bush administration had allocated to help fight AIDS in Africa came with the stipulation that a third of the money must be spent on programs which promote sexual abstinence and discourage condom use as a means of protection. In the words of the *New York Times*:

> While every good AIDS prevention program includes messages about postponing sex or reducing the number of sexual partners, the blanket advocacy of abstinence until marriage is a proven failure at protecting people from disease. The message has no meaning for gay men or for women who are forced by poverty into prostitution. In much of Africa, teenage girls — many of them AIDS orphans themselves — are coerced into sex by older, wealthier men. Knowing how to negotiate condom use could save their lives.[43]

Nicholas Kristof, reporting from Kenya, also criticised Bush's 'ideological war' against health charities, like Marie Stopes International, which don't subscribe to his 'pro-life' Christian worldview.

Mr Bush probably sees his policy in terms of abortion or sex, or as a matter of placating his political base. But here in the shantytowns of Africa, the policy calculation seems simpler: women and girls will die.[44]

BBC News detailed the case of 'Asmara', a twenty-two year old prostitute who had previously received free condoms (an essential protective against HIV infection) from a Marie Stopes International Clinic. The clinic closed when the United States government cut off its funding. Asmara got pregnant and died of blood loss, probably from a DIY abortion. The BBC also reported that a recent study at Addis Ababa hospital had found that half of female deaths were caused by unsafe backstreet abortions. A spokesman from the Ethiopian Family Guidance Association told the BBC that if unwilling local mothers 'are forced to give birth they throw the children into latrines or abandon them for the hyenas to eat them.' He accused the US government of 'driving women into the hands of backstreet abortionists.'[45]

There is no doubt that ideology, economic interests and theology have distorted the Bush administration's response to Africa's disasters. In this regard, perhaps most telling of all was Bush's choice of the person to be the United States 'Global AIDS Coordinator'. Bush appointed Randall Tobias, a former CEO of the major pharmaceutical corporation Eli Lilly, a company that has opposed several attempts to get cheap generic drugs onto the world market and into the hands of AIDS sufferers.

AIDS has already killed more people than the Black Death in mediaeval Europe. Back in the late 1980s, when Africa's AIDS catastrophe was still developing, United States intelligence agencies undertook a review of the implications (military, economic and social) of Africa's crisis. Kenneth Brown, who helped write one of the major intelligence reports, found his colleagues on the National Intelligence Council to be less than empathetic. One colleague's 'penetrating analysis was, "Oh, it will be good, because Africa is overpopulated anyway."' Another opined that if AIDS started killing officers in various African armies, 'That boosts morale, because there's more room for advancement.' In June 1992 the World Bank's population and human resources department similarly speculated that like the Black Death in fourteenth century Europe, AIDS might even have a positive affect on Africa's economy, increasing per capita income while decreasing the total population.[46] While such views may now seem harrowingly callous in their disregard for human life, they still seem to linger in the attitudes of many western governments who continue to see AIDS as an issue of sexual morality, or who endlessly debate the economics of discount pharmaceuticals and foreign aid budgets as Africa confronts its holocaust.

AIDS versus Terrorism

- Number of international terrorist attacks in North America 2000–2003 = 4

- Number of international terrorist attacks in Africa and Asia 2000–2003 = 434

- Estimated number of people who died in 11 September 2001 terrorist attacks = 2948

- Total number of people killed in international terrorist attacks throughout the world in 2003 = 307

- Total number of people in the world who died of AIDS in 2003 = 3,000,000

- Number of people who died of AIDS in sub-Saharan Africa in 2003 = 2,300,000

- Number of people who died of AIDS in Asia and the Pacific in 2003 = 500,000

- Total number of US citizens killed in international terrorist attacks in 2003 = 35

- Total number of US citizens who died of AIDS in 2003 = 16,000

(Sources: US State Department *Patterns of Global Terrorism Report*, 2002, 2003; *UNAIDS Report* 2002, 2003)

The Balkans

Whither Krajina?
War and 'Ethnic Cleansing' in the Balkans

9/11 remains the biggest news story of our frail new century. On 11 September 2003 the 'civilised world' mourned the second anniversary of the terrorist attacks with live television coverage of the commemoration service at the remains of the World Trade Center. Children who lost loved ones movingly read a list of the names of every person killed that day. Tears and cameras rolled. That week it seemed like every journalist in the free world wrote a piece about what we all now call '9/11', respectfully conforming with American calendar preferences. In the newspapers thick black column inches ran viscous with the hyperbole of remembrance. Radio airwaves chattered and televisions flickered to the same symphony of mournful regret.

On the second anniversary I was at work in Fremantle where I had an interesting conversation with a Serbian student I teach. Her name is Olja and she is a refugee from Croatia. Her relatives were 'ethnically cleansed' (to use the atrocious parlance of the Balkans War) from Krajina when the Croatian army invaded during August 1995. The invasion of Krajina resulted in an estimated 200,000 refugees. Photographs from the time show long pathetic lines of Krajina Serbs fleeing with whatever meagre possessions they could load onto a tractor, horse-drawn cart or car. Many people just walked and no-one knows for sure how many died or were killed along the way by the invading Croatian Army. Robert Fisk, reporting from the region for the London *Independent*, was one of the few western journalists to write compassionately about the tragedy of the Krajina Serbs:

> Many of them had to be carried on to the buses, clinging on to their crutches, their shawls, their pathetic plastic bags. We quickly lost count of the old women among the 1340 Serbs from Krajina, weeping — most of them — or coughing in the near freezing breeze that swept down from the plains of Vojvodina. One mumbled about murder, or a neighbour bayoneted on a tractor, or six others gunned down by a Croatian soldier wearing a black headband on a mountain road.[47]

Olja told me that what bothered her was how little concern there had been for the victims of this hideous 'ethnic cleansing' in most of the western media. Unlike the general sympathy for the Bosnian Muslims and other earlier civilian victims of the Balkans conflict, few wept for the Krajina Serbs as their homes were burned, farms looted and the population displaced. Most reporting of this situation contrasted with the legitimate revulsion voiced in the western media when Serbs overran the UN 'safe haven' of Srebrenica and started killing or deporting people. Many respected mainstream newspapers like the *Independent* were too caught up in celebrating Serbia's defeat to notice Krajina's civilian tragedy:

> It is tempting to feel euphoric about this weekend's Serbian defeat at the hands of the Croats. At last, the Serbs have been taught an overdue lesson, given a dose of the medicine that they have so freely administered in recent weeks to Bosnia's Muslims.[48]

Later, during the NATO bombing of Serbia, tabloids in the United States and Britain would take such views to their logical extreme, with headlines such as 'Clobba Slobba' and 'Serbs them Right'.[49]

The truth, which the media in the West generally chose to ignore, was that most of the Krajina Serbs were innocent victims too and that all the main armies and militias fighting in the Balkan conflict — Serbian, Croatian and Bosnian Muslim — had the blood of innocents on their hands. The problem was not 'the Serbs' or 'the Muslims' or any other single group of otherwise ordinary people. The problem was the intense social crisis and economic decay of the former Yugoslavia at the end of the 1980s. In attempting to soothe the popular anger of ordinary people in the midst of intense political and economic turmoil, many former communist rulers simply reinvented themselves as arch-nationalist bigots. After the implosion of the Yugoslav Federation in 1991, the presidents of Serbia and Croatia were Slobodan Milosevic and Franjo Tudjman. In many ways they were simply mirror images of one another. Both had strong connections to the old crumbling Yugoslav communist state, both relied on extremist ethnic nationalism to win popular support, and both were vicious warmongers.

To truly understand the descent into 'ethnic cleansing' in the Balkans one has to understand the complicated history of Yugoslavia. The entire Balkan region has long been an area where rival empires have rubbed against one another. The area is home to more than a dozen distinct ethnicities. The two main ethnic groups, the Serbs and the Croats, share a heritage as descendants of seventh-century Slavic tribes who settled in the northern region of the Balkans. Although they speak a common language, Serbo-Croat, Serbs and Croats use different alphabets and have, historically speaking, generally followed different faiths (Serbs are Orthodox Christians. Croats are Catholic). For more than five hundred years prior to the outbreak of the First World War most Serbs were absorbed into the western reaches of the Turkish Ottoman Empire, while Croats lived under the Habsburg (Austro-Hungarian) Empire. Both empires, weak in relation to the growing power of Russia, Britain and France, allowed separatist nationalist currents to develop in their Balkan possessions.

Serbia officially gained independence in 1878. Thirty years later the Austro-Hungarian Empire annexed Bosnia-Herzegovina, the region between Croatia and Serbia. To complicate matters, Bosnia was home not only to large local Serb and Croat populations, but also to a considerable number of Muslims. These Muslims also speak Serbo-Croat, but are considered an entirely distinct ethnic group (Bosnian Muslim) from their Serb and Croat neighbours. Bosnian Muslims are, essentially, Slavs who converted to Islam during the fifteenth century when the area was under Ottoman rule. They have since developed a distinctive cultural identity.

Two Balkans wars were fought in 1912 and 1913 with considerable meddling by the great powers. A year later the volatile competing ethnic nationalisms of the Balkans region were, of course, the spark that ignited the First World War. Britain, France, Russia and Germany, all of which were tied in support or opposition to one another as well as to some local

Balkan nationalism, found themselves at war over the actions of a Bosnian Serb assassin in Sarajevo. At the end of the resulting international slaughter (which we call the First World War) the demise of the Ottoman and Austro-Hungarian empires led to the formation of the Kingdom of Serbs, Croats and Slovenes. In 1929 the kingdom was renamed Yugoslavia.

Ten years later the region was again plunged into crisis by the start of the Second World War. The German Army marched into Yugoslavia in 1941. Nazi Germany and the other Axis powers (notably Italy, Hungary and Bulgaria) then set up right-wing puppet regimes amongst one or other of the competing regional ethnicities. By far the most notorious of these was in Croatia where the Nazis found political fellow travellers amongst the Croatian fascists, the Ustashe. The Ustashe not only repressed and murdered Serbs, they also willingly collaborated with the Nazis in the transportation and extermination of Yugoslavia's Jewish population.

Unlike the rest of Eastern Europe, Yugoslavia was freed from the Nazis without the help of the Soviet Red Army. The Yugoslav resistance movement, led by the charismatic Josip Broz (a half-Croat, half-Slovene communist better known as Tito), had fought the fascists of the Croatian Ustashe as well as the mighty German Army. They did so, in part, with arms and support from Britain. Repeating the entanglements of the First World War, British Prime Minister Winston Churchill's attitude to the Balkans at this time is revealing in that he was concerned with the region only to the extent that it impacted on Britain's war against Nazi Germany. He told one of his top military advisers, Sir Fitzroy Maclean, to 'find out who is killing the most Germans in Yugoslavia, and how we can help them to kill more.'[50] Tito got Britain's support on this basis.

Most importantly, Tito's guerilla movement was genuinely multi-ethnic and by the end of the war it had built much popular support across large areas of the Balkans. After the war Tito set about constructing a Stalinist state on the Soviet model. It was to be multi-ethnic and federalist, uniting Serbs, Croats, Bosnian Muslims, Albanians, Slovenes and all of the Balkans' other diverse ethnic minorities under a single Yugoslav communist banner. However, a strong independent streak and the knowledge that, unlike the other Eastern European communists, his power and popularity did not depend upon Soviet tanks, meant Tito was unwilling for Yugoslavia to become a servile Soviet satellite like East Germany or Poland. In 1948 Tito publicly broke with Stalin and for the following forty years Yugoslavia officially remained an independent, non-aligned, 'socialist federation'.

The Yugoslav economy achieved impressive growth in the post-war period. Gross National Product grew by an annual average of almost 10 per cent between 1952 and 1960, and still averaged over 6 per cent during the following decade. When economic downturn first started to seriously affect Yugoslavia during the 1970s, Tito's solution was to try to dismantle the over-centralised economy by encouraging regional self-management. One inadvertent consequence of this was growing economic independence, and competition, between the various republics which made up the Yugoslav Federation. The central government also borrowed heavily from western banks and governments which were keen to support Yugoslavia in the hopes that its economic success and political example might infect the Soviet satellite states of Eastern Europe, encouraging them to similarly break with the Soviet Union. By the early 1980s, however, an enormous portion of the Yugoslav economy was being directed towards debt repayment. Inflation and unemployment grew.

When Tito died in 1980 Yugoslavia was already mired in intractable economic crisis and internecine regional bickering. Economic decentralisation exacerbated economic decline which, in turn, further encouraged regional separatism. Disastrously, the real value of wages continued to fall. But what was truly remarkable was the way that those who inflicted this misery upon the Yugoslav people in the first place — leading Communist Party bureaucrats in the various republics — were then able to exploit the crisis they had created. A leading Serbian Communist Party bureaucrat, Slobodan Milosevic, was a particular case in point. By 1987 he was leading huge rallies of Serbs where he invoked the ghosts of mediaeval Serbian struggles against foreigners. Milosevic, who had dedicated his life to working within Tito's crumbling Communist state, now became a born-again ethnic nationalist dedicated to returning Serbia to mythical historic greatness.

An essential part of this project was blaming Serbia's ethnic rivals for the woes, economic and otherwise, that Serbia and Yugoslavia were experiencing. Encouraging strong communal ethnic affiliations was a particularly attractive modus operandi as it deflected attention from the people who had really caused Yugoslavia's problems — the communist bureaucrats of various ethnic backgrounds who had administered the Yugoslav state for the past forty years. And of all the minorities in Yugoslavia to choose to persecute, Milosevic focused on the weakest — the ethnic Albanians of Kosovo.

When the nation of Albania was created early in the twentieth century, the major powers left a significant number of ethnic Albanians (and their lands) officially outside the borders of the new country. The predominantly Albanian region of Kosovo was given instead to Serbia to administer. Serbia ruled Kosovo much like a colonial province, even granting Serbian migrants free land there. In general, however, the Serbs neglected to develop the region. As a result, even during the best years of Yugoslavia's 'socialist federation' Kosovo still remained the poorest area of the country. In 1987 Kosovo was declared bankrupt. From 1987 onwards Slobodan Milosevic and his chauvinistic Serbian nationalist supporters stigmatised and victimised Kosovo's ethnic Albanians — seeing them as a drain on resources, and viewing Kosovars as violent and alien ethnic outsiders. This long-term campaign would result, ultimately, in war in Kosovo in the late 1990s during the final stage of the Balkans conflict.

More immediate, however, was the question of what to do with Slovenia and Croatia. As Yugoslavia's economic crisis peaked in 1988 and 1989 the leaders of the various Yugoslav republics became more desperate in their attempts to deflect popular discontent. Weimar Republic style hyper-inflation reduced the value of Yugoslav currency to almost nothing. In response there were major strikes in various parts of Yugoslavia, especially Serbia, against the leaders of the old crumbling system. Milosevic's attempts to blame Serbia's woes on everybody but the old Serbian communist regime he had served found an audience amongst bitter, demoralised and desperate Serbs who had seen their livelihoods destroyed by Yugoslavia's economic crisis. Milosevic's strategy was replicated elsewhere. In particular, Franjo Tudjman of Croatia relied on right-wing nostalgia for the wartime Ustashe to blame Croatia's problems on the Serbs who many Croatians believed dominated the old Yugoslav federation. In Slovenia another former communist leader, Milan Kucan, advocated secession from the Yugoslavia Federation as a solution to the republic's problems. By 1991 Yugoslavia's economy had basically collapsed and these political tensions boiled over into open war.

In June 1991 both Slovenia and Croatia declared their independence from Yugoslavia. The Yugoslav Federal Army (which had become, essentially, the army of Serbia) invaded Slovenia and fought a brief war with the breakaway republic. Slovenia seceded from Yugoslavia. Then Serbia and Croatia went to war with one another with Serbia taking control of about one-third of Croatia. By the start of 1992 thousands of people had already been killed. Bosnia was then dragged into the war.

In 1992 Bosnia's population of about 4.5 million people was mainly Muslim (about 44 per cent), Serb (30 per cent) and Croat (17 per cent). With Serbia and Croatia at war, and with Slovenia forcibly removing itself from the Yugoslav Federation, Bosnia became a battleground for contending local ethnic militias. Both Serbia and Croatia invaded Bosnia in order to expand their territories and incorporate local Serb or Croat communities (and local ethnic militias) into a 'Greater Serbia' or 'Greater Croatia'. Bosnian Muslims fought to defend the Bosnian government and their communities from attack. Yugoslavia then added one final awful phrase to the lexicon of twentieth century war and cruelty — 'ethnic cleansing' — as each side sought to 'purify' the territory it held of rival ethnic groups. Mass executions, rape, looting and the burning down of entire villages were widespread. By 1993 it was estimated that half the population of Bosnia had become refugees.

Bosnia's agony continued for three bitter years until the 1995 peace treaty between Muslims and Croats decisively shifted the balance of power against the Serbs. By mid-1995 the United States was under increasing pressure to do something to stem the flow of blood in the former Yugoslavia. With the world engrossed by seemingly unending Serb atrocities in Bosnia, few appreciated the magnitude of the horror inflicted upon Serbian Krajina.

Krajina means 'frontier' and the Serbs who formed the ethnic majority in the region for the three hundred years prior to 1995 had traditionally been a buffer between Serbia and Croatia. When Croatia declared independence in June 1991 the Krajina Serbs wanted to remain part of Yugoslavia. A Republic of Krajina was declared by local Serbs as the Balkans degenerated into four years of war, rapine and horror. Milosevic saw Krajina as an expression of the Serbian nationalist dream of a 'Greater Serbia' and Tudjman saw Krajina as an insult to the idea of an independent Croatia. The people of Krajina were crushed between the competing interests of these two ethnic warlords.

The 1995 Croatian invasion of Krajina came soon after the establishment of a military alliance between the Croatian and Bosnian governments which was brokered by the US Ambassador to Croatia, Peter Galbraith. Moreover, the Croatian offensive was supported by NATO air strikes against the Bosnian Serbs. The air strikes seriously weakened the Serb militias as Bosnian Muslim and Croat forces moved to retake most of Bosnia. The Croat offensives in Bosnia and nearby Krajina were therefore part of a coordinated military effort to roll back Serbian gains from earlier in the war. Retired US military personnel, with the encouragement of the US government, had actually helped train the Bosnian and Croatian troops prior to the 1995 offensive. Why? Because the United States government, which had been under increasing public pressure at home to 'do something' about the terrible situation in the Balkans, had simply chosen sides. It was with the Croatian and Bosnian ethnic cleansers and against the Serbian ethnic cleansers. It could just as easily have been the other way round. And so while Milosevic was later indicted for war crimes, Tudjman (who once declared, 'Thank God my wife is not a Jew or a Serb') was not.[51]

Presumably the moral justification for all of this was that with the defeat of the Bosnian Serbs and the expulsion of the Serbian population of Krajina, the United States was much better placed to impose its will, and a peace plan, on the region. Or as US Defence Secretary William Perry put it, 'a window of opportunity' had been opened.[52] The strongest military power in the Balkans conflict, Serbia, had been dramatically weakened while the position of the Croats and Bosnian Muslims had been strengthened. Croatia, in particular, had been bought off with US military support and by the world consenting to their invasion of Krajina. The net result was to essentially validate the process of ethnic cleansing by officially re-partitioning the region along ethnic lines. From the point of view of US foreign policy, the expulsion of the Krajina Serbs might have been viewed as a necessary evil. From the point of view of the civilian victims, like Olja's family, it was just an evil. And herein lies one of the enduring lessons of world politics.

The United Nations

In June 2001 Dili, the capital of East Timor, still felt a little like the Portuguese colonial port it once was, only mixed in with an ex-Indonesian occupation architectural style as well. It was a sleepy seaside town with a terrifying history. Driving around Dili for the first time I saw a Che Guevara portrait painted on the wall of a building torched by the pro-Indonesian militias in late 1999. There were entire streets of burnt out shops and gutted buildings. The ruins also of what I was told was the old Indonesian Army 'interrogation centre' where soldiers had tortured independence activists. All of that was in the past.

White United Nations vehicles were now everywhere in Dili, crawling like giant beetles over the city. UN choppers and UN ships and containers too: all painted white and with those stark, unmistakable two-letter black 'UN' stencils. The head of UNTAET, the UN administration in East Timor, was Brazilian diplomat Sergio Vieira de Mello. He had told western journalists that there was 'no precedent that matches the scope of the challenge facing the UN in East Timor,' where the pro-Indonesian militias had destroyed the entire water, electrical and telephone systems, and almost every significant building had been burned down.[53]

On my first day in Dili we drove through a burnt-out Dili suburb where Indonesian officials and army officers used to live. The United Nations was trying to renovate some of the large homes for UN staff. At the same time, dirt-poor Timorese had started camping under UNHCR tarpaulins in the blackened ruins of some of the homes. Plastic sheets hung from the charred walls of former Indonesian mansions. Meanwhile UN staff were visible all over Dili, sitting in the bars and cafes which spilled out onto the dirty sidewalks, or clogging up the aisles of Dili's only western-style supermarket, 'Hello Mister'. The supermarket was later burned down by rioting East Timorese frustrated with the slow pace of change.

While in Dili I had an interesting discussion with an Australian policeman working for the UN police in East Timor, CIVPOL. Andrew complained about all the waste, useless bureaucracy and madness of the United Nations and how frustrating it was. He also mentioned that when he arrived in East Timor he had to attend an introduction session run by CIVPOL at which a Nigerian cop asked them to remember that while torture of suspects was acceptable in his own country, people should remember that it was not allowed in CIVPOL! Another CIVPOL from Jordan told me about his time with the UN in Bosnia and how the East Timorese were nicer to work with than the Serbs who apparently vandalised your vehicles and told you, 'Fuck off, I kill you.'

In those UNTAET days Dili appeared to be two cities. One was East Timorese: broken down, impoverished and improvised. The Dili of the East Timorese was hungry, tropical and sweaty, living on the promise of independence and better days. The other Dili was the city of the United Nations. It was air-conditioned, whitewashed and freshly painted, with bottled drinking water and imported flush toilets. The two Dilis regarded each other with admiration and suspicion in equal measure. Never before in my life had I seen the First World and the Third World in such stark cohabitation.

In this context it is worth remembering that the UN mission to East Timor, to assist in its transition from illegal Indonesian occupation to independence, is generally regarded as a success story in the organisation's history. It was certainly long overdue. José Ramos Horta had been sent overseas three days before the Indonesian invasion of his country in December 1975 in order to take the East Timorese cause to the international community and the world's media. At only twenty-five years of age he was the youngest foreign minister in the world. José went to New York to lobby the United Nations. He later wrote that:

> I was shy, intimidated, excited, euphoric and fearful. As the exiled representative of an extinguished government, I was allowed to address the UN Security Council: the youngest ever ... I had never addressed any formal forum apart from the mass meetings in my beloved island and a few meetings with students and labour unions in Australia.[54]

José would not set foot in his homeland for another twenty-four years. Western governments chose not to enforce United Nations Security Council Resolutions 384 and 389 that called on Indonesia to immediately withdraw its troops from East Timor. The diplomatic resolutions spoke of the fact that the UN Security Council was 'gravely concerned' about East Timor and that they had unanimously resolved 'to remain seized of the situation.' Reflecting on his involvement with the UN, in 1987 José wrote that as he left East Timor in 1975 his sister had written to his aunt expressing her opinion that:

> 'José will get the United Nations to help us. He is going to talk to big powers. That is our only hope.' My sister's hope was the hope of everybody else. Her fears were the fears of an entire nation ... The Portuguese had left with neither honour nor dignity, abandoning the country to the mercy of a ruthless neighbour. I had my own hopes and illusions about the United Nations. Ten years after the invasion, and as many General Assembly and Security Council resolutions later, Indonesian forces are still entrenched in East Timor. The killing, torture and rape continue. And my illusions are gone.[55]

The East Timorese joined the long list of oppressed nationalities whose representatives regarded the United Nations as a bureaucratic behemoth that, despite its lofty rhetoric about peace and the brotherhood of nations, was an institution where the rich and powerful nations of the world regulated the conduct of the poor and weak. Within this schema, 'UN diplomacy' was viewed as little more than a cynical exercise in power politics.

There is certainly a great deal of bad history to support such cynicism. For example, when Iraq invaded Kuwait in August 1990 the United Nations Security Council passed resolutions condemning the Iraqi government. Iraq was then attacked in January 1991 by a US-led force in order to defend a small country (Kuwait) from its larger, more powerful and aggressive neighbour (Iraq). Kuwait was freed from Iraqi occupation and the rules of international law were protected. East Timorese, enduring their sixteenth year under Indonesian occupation after a similarly unlawful and much more violent occupation of their country — an invasion which had also been condemned in various UN Security Council resolutions — must have wondered why no United Nations force had been sent to liberate them. A decade later the United States again began lobbying the United Nations to support another invasion of Iraq because of its alleged non-compliance with UN orders to dispose of its weapons of mass destruction. In *The Nation*, a well known American magazine, Steven Zunes wrote about the United States' and the United Nations' 'double standards':

> A survey of the nearly 1500 resolutions passed by the Security Council, the fifteen-member enforcement arm of the UN in which the United States and the four other permanent members wield veto power, reveals more than ninety resolutions currently violated by countries other than Iraq. The vast majority of these violations are by governments closely allied to the United States. Not only have the Bush Administration and its Congressional allies not suggested invading these countries; the United States has blocked sanctions and other means of enforcing them, and even provides the military and economic aid that helps make ongoing violations possible.[56]

Zunes provided the example of Indonesia's annexation of East Timor in 1975 and quoted the then US ambassador to the United Nations, Daniel Patrick Moynihan, who was responsible for making sure that the UN's condemnation of Indonesia did not result in any effective course of action to free East Timor.

Moynihan later bragged that the US 'Department of State desired that the United Nations prove utterly ineffective in whatever measures it undertook. The task was given to me, and I carried it forward with no inconsiderable success.'[57]

Nor is Indonesia's twenty-four year illegal occupation of East Timor the only case that springs to mind. For more than thirty years Turkey, a crucial American ally in the Muslim world, has illegally occupied northern Cyprus in defiance of UN Security Council Resolution 353. Most glaring of all, however, is the case of Israel, the largest recipient of United States aid in the world. Israel has defied UN Security Council resolutions 242, 252, 267, 271, 298, 446, 452, 465, 471, 484, 497, 592, 605, 607, 608, 694, 799, 904 and 1402. These nineteen resolutions, passed between 1967 and 2002, deal with the illegal seizure of land by armed force, violations of the Fourth Geneva Convention, attacks on and deportations of civilians, and various other violations of both human rights and international law. Israel's continual defiance of the United Nations is reflected in the fact that many of these UN Security Council resolutions simply reiterate earlier demands to withdraw from annexed territory, cease illegal deportations, etcetera. The list is not exhaustive — there are at least six other resolutions prior to 1967. None of the resolutions has been enforced by means of UN invasion or sanctions and many of the issues involved are still not resolved.

To some people such double standards seem perplexing. Most people think of the United Nations as a positive force in the world — its job is peacekeeping, assisting refugees, facilitating a dialogue between nations, and it should therefore be above manipulation by the world's great powers. Such belief is, however, at odds with the UN's history since its inception.

The United Nations was the successor to the failed League of Nations set up in 1919 after the First World War. The punitive Treaty of Versailles, which dismembered the defeated German, Ottoman and Austro-Hungarian empires and divided the spoils amongst the war's victors, had been signed shortly beforehand. Behind its diplomatic ideals, the League's essential purpose was to police the agreed upon post-war distribution of power and territories, avoiding conflicts of interest where possible. None of the major powers to emerge from the First World War — Britain, France and the United States in particular — wanted a repeat of the imperial rivalries and complex alliances which had dragged Europe into a disastrous conflict in 1914.

Outside of Europe the western powers were given 'mandated territories' to administer and supposedly help towards national self-determination. In reality, the League's mandate system became a form of de facto (or sometimes direct) colonialism as the great powers sought to compensate themselves for losses of prestige and wealth suffered during the First World War. Britain, for example, was given control of most of the Middle East just as the region's oil was becoming increasingly important to the world economy. The League of Nations fundamentally failed in its stated aim of avoiding a repeat of the First World War and defending the rights of small nations. The League collapsed with the outbreak of the Second World War.

The United Nations, formed in 1945, evolved from the wartime alliance between the Soviet Union, Britain and the United States. These three powers realised that with the impending defeat of Nazi Germany and Imperial Japan there would once again be a need for an international institution to reflect the new equilibrium of power. The new United Nations was big on democratic rhetoric, but light on democratic content.

While it capitalised on the desire of ordinary people around the world for a future free from war, it was a product of the great power politics that had caused the two world wars in the first place. For example, although the United Nations was constructed with a General Assembly where all the nations of the world could debate global issues, real power resided in the Security Council where five permanent members (the US, USSR, France, China and Britain) would be able to veto any decisions of the Council. Other countries were elected to sit temporarily on the Council, but none of them had veto rights. What this meant was that in practice no meaningful action by the Security Council (to defend a country from invasion for example) could be taken without the consent of all the Security Council's permanent members.

Indeed, in the fifty-nine years of the UN's existence there has only been one occasion when the Security Council has taken military action which was clearly detrimental to the interests of one of its permanent members. This occurred in 1950 when the UN endorsed a US-led force to repel Communist North Korea's invasion of South Korea. This was only able to occur because the Soviet Union, which was allied to the North Korean regime, was boycotting the UN at the time because of the world body's refusal to recognise Communist China as the legitimate government of the Chinese people (mainland China's seat was still held by the deposed Chinese government who had fled to Taiwan). In short, the purpose of the Security Council remains twofold — it constrains any single great power from acting beyond the agreed boundaries of global power and influence, and it provides these same great powers (France, Britain, China, the US and Russia) with an institution that can be used, in the name of world peace, to enforce their will upon any lesser nation that threatens their collective interests and the international balance of power.

In contrast to the Security Council, the UN General Assembly (which has grown from 51 to 184 members) is little more than a glorified debating chamber devoid of any meaningful power. During the Cold War the floor of the General Assembly often became a platform for nations to denounce one or other of the superpowers — the Soviet Union and the United States. It did not, however, stop either superpower from invading or militarily intervening in other countries (Grenada, Vietnam, Czechoslovakia, Hungary and Afghanistan being cases in point) when they felt it necessary. Moreover, because of their veto rights on the Security Council, the only UN body with real power to stop these military incursions was rendered ineffective. As a result, the UN served as little more than an impotent spectator as the United States and the Soviet Union waged proxy wars around the world in opposition to one another between 1950 and 1989.

While the end of the Cold War has led to an increase in the United States' ability, as the world's sole remaining superpower, to manipulate outcomes on the floor of the General Assembly and inside the Security Council, they have not had it all their own way. In particular, it is clear that the current Bush government is viewed as being dangerously unilateralist by important sections within the UN administration. UN bureaucrats pleaded for extended dialogue, petitioned for more time and UN weapons inspections, and argued for alternatives to war in the lead up to the US-led invasion of Iraq in March 2003. The UN Security Council refused to give the US and Britain the diplomatic cover for an invasion of Iraq that they desired. In doing so the United Nations (but especially France and Russia on the Security Council) was seeking to affirm its independence from Washington. Such an approach was met with outright anger and frustration by US President Bush, who claimed that the UN was in danger of sinking into irrelevancy just like the League of Nations. Bush's criticisms played well with the 'neo-conservatives' who dominate his administration. Many of these people see the United Nations as overly bureaucratic, dominated by small 'anti-American' nations and increasingly unnecessary in a world where the United States' power is so obviously, and unquestionably, dominant (these views are supported by some conservatives within the Australian Liberal government). After 9/11, influential members of Bush's government did not hide their desire to ignore the polite constraints of UN diplomacy and bypass the organisation entirely. The current poor state of the US occupation of Iraq has, however, led to a subtle retreat on this front.

The March 2003 US-led invasion of Iraq went ahead without the United Nations' blessing. The United Nations' refusal to endorse the invasion was also an unacknowledged attempt to address concerns that since the 1991 Gulf War the UN had been little more than an appendage of United States foreign policy. Such a view may be overly reductionist and simplistic, but no more so than that which continues to see the United Nations as an independent and equal community of nations. For example, despite the UN's opposition to the invasion of Iraq, in October 2003 the United Nations Security Council recognised the Iraqi Governing Council that US-forces had installed following their military overthrow of Saddam Hussein's regime. The haste was telling. The United Nations had allowed the genocidal Pol Pot regime in Cambodia to keep its seat in the United Nations for fourteen years after it was overthrown by the Communist government of Vietnam. The cynics pointed out, once again, that at the time Vietnam was an arch-enemy of the United States and that Pol Pot's regime had been supported by China, also a member of the Security Council.

Moreover, the western powers have shown themselves to be

willing to defy the United Nations when its resolutions do not suit their interests. Like Iraq under Saddam Hussein, the United States has seen it as its right to pick and choose which UN resolutions should be implemented and which should be ignored. No nation has used its veto on the United Nations Security Council more than the United States. For example, the US has invoked its veto rights no less than thirty times to protect Israel from enforcement of UN resolutions. And no nation on earth has provided more aid (military and non-military) to consistent UN Security Council resolution violators — like Israel, Turkey or Indonesia — than the United States.

Such behaviour, from the most powerful nation on earth, has compromised the United Nations' authority and weakened its ability to enforce international law. Other nations have followed the United States' lead. Australia, for example, is theoretically a staunch supporter of the UN system. It has signed all the major UN treaties and has participated in the organisation since its inception. Australia has also supported various UN peacekeeping operations and in the lead-up to the March 2003 invasion of Iraq, Prime Minister John Howard emphasised that Iraq's defiance of the UN provided justification for an invasion and 'regime change' in the country. Yet, Australia seems to view the UN's policies and resolutions to only be relevant to the extent that they can be used to point out the shortcomings of other countries. For example, Australia has recently been directly criticised by the UN Human Rights Committee in three major decisions around the issue of detaining refugees and asylum seekers. The Australian government has rejected the recommendations of the UN Human Rights Committee and continues to proclaim, incorrectly, that Australia's refugee policy is a purely domestic issue and not an obligation under international law.

Australian Attorney General Daryl Williams' response to the UN's criticism was to point out that, as compared to 'having your arms chopped off for belonging to the wrong political party,' Australia's alleged violations of UN standards and protocols regarding refugees were relatively minor. The argument of Devika Hovell, a lecturer in international law, is however interesting in this regard. Hovell comments that the effect of the Australian government's approach 'is to reduce human rights standards to the lowest common denominator.'[58] Despite the UN's ongoing claims that Australia is in violation of various international standards for the treatment of refugees (not least of all the 1951 UN Convention on Refugees), Australian policy remains unchanged.

Perhaps the final word on the issue of contemporary global politics and the United Nations can be left to John Bolton in a speech he gave in 1994, before he became US Undersecretary of State for Arms Control and International Security under President George W Bush. At a time when he was less concerned about diplomatic niceties, Bolton boldly proclaimed that, 'There is no such thing as the United Nations. There is an international community that can be led by the only real power left in the world, and that is the United States, when it suits our interests and when we can get others to go along.'[59] It was a sad but accurate insight into the state of the UN and the reality of contemporary international politics.

Epilogue:
Primo Levi's Ghost

As nightfall does not come at once, neither does oppression. In both instances, there is a twilight when everything remains seemingly unchanged. And it is in such twilight that we all must be most aware of change in the air, however slight, lest we become unwitting victims of the darkness.

US Supreme Court Justice William O Douglas

One afternoon after speaking at a public forum on the topic of the Iraq war on a university campus, I was asked by a woman who stayed around afterwards to chat, if I ever got depressed by the state of the world. She said she had trouble sleeping after watching television reports of the 'shock and awe' missile barrage of Iraqi cities that marked the beginning of the US-led invasion. She told me she kept thinking about the people on the receiving end of the cruise missiles, those families huddling in small houses near Iraqi ministries that were being pulverised, or those pictured on CNN mourning over the bodies of civilians who were accidentally killed ('collateral damage') during the bombing. I told her that while such things appalled me, they seldom affected my sleep. I certainly didn't allow them to depress me.

Afterwards I wondered about my response. Why wasn't I more depressed? The entire world appeared to be moving in a direction I was opposed to. First came 9/11 when religious extremists carried out the world's most dramatic, tragic and elaborate suicide bombing. Then an illegal invasion of a sovereign nation (Iraq) had taken place in which literally thousands of innocent Iraqi civilians had been killed. Violent tensions between the so-called 'Muslim world' and 'the West' were at a level not experienced possibly since the crusades of the eleventh century. Presidents and prime ministers were fabricating lies about the WMDs of former client dictators. Terrorists were planting bombs in tourist nightclubs in the hope of murdering western 'infidels'. Moreover, the invasion of Iraq had taken place against the objections of millions of people around the world who had marched and protested. And the United Nations had been unable to stop it. Millions of feet and voices of protest in hundreds of cities across the globe were unable to prevent the war.

In retrospect I realised that the reason I wasn't depressed was precisely because so many people, from such diverse backgrounds, had protested against the Iraq war.

I'm not depressed because although 9/11 and the war on terror have made our world a more dangerous place to live in, they have also got people thinking about politics, history and all the troubles of this small planet. Every cruise missile fired, every day another US soldier is killed during the occupation of Iraq, every Al-Qaida terrorist attack causes someone somewhere in the world to question why it is so, and whether there is an alternative.

Nor is our world entirely without justice. In my own lifetime I have seen popular revolutions sweep Stalinist dictators from power in Eastern Europe and overthrow General Suharto in Indonesia. Thanks to the magic of satellite television I watched Nelson Mandela walk from prison in February 1990. Five years later apartheid was dead and I was actually working in Soweto with former political prisoners who had fought the most powerful army on the African continent to a standstill with sticks, stones and the strength of superior political ideas. I got to work in East Timor as it was experiencing its transition to independence. On a personal level this has been both inspirational and exhilarating. It has taught me that people, history and ideas change.

On 3 October 2001, a few weeks after 9/11, I flew into Minnesota in the American mid-west, in the midst of that state's biggest ever public sector strike. According to the local paper, the *Star Tribune*, about 22,000 out of Minnesota's 27,000 state employees were on strike. Meanwhile the ex-professional wrestler turned state governor, Jesse Ventura, was in New York visiting the ruins of the World Trade Center. In other news, President Bush had, for the first time, called for the establishment of a Palestinian state, claiming it had 'always been part of a vision' for peace in the Middle East. It was strange how he only seemed to have remembered having this vision after September 11, but I guess visions can be funny that way. The editorial in that day's *Star Tribune* was dedicated to the issue of the state employees' strike and allegations that striking at that time, so soon after September 11, might be 'unpatriotic'. Later in the paper the relevant unions had placed a full-page advertisement:

> Many members of these great unions are veterans who served in the Gulf War, in Viet Nam, and in other conflicts. They remind us that the freedom to organise, and the right to withhold our labour when

necessary to secure a fair contract, are rights they fought for as part of the American Dream.

What I remember most about that day, however, was that on the drive out of Minneapolis the amazing bruised purple and orange colours of the fall leaves were intoxicating and evocative. On the one hand it was sad to think that it was once all Native American territory. I could vividly imagine them out there on the prairie or in the woods. I wondered what their descendants thought of the America that 'Team Bush' was constructing? But for some reason I also kept thinking of Emma Goldman, the deported Russian-American anarchist, labour organiser and feminist, who once wrote of America: 'And you, are you so forgetful of your past, is there no echo in your soul of your poets' songs, your dreamers' dreams, your rebels' calls?' As for me, I remained entranced by America and by our world in all its contradictions and delights. I know that the blood trails of our shared history are sometimes faint but you can always follow them if you try hard enough. The lessons learned are often important, but are seldom broadcast on CNN.

To lose hope is a sad and terrible thing. In his powerful book of Auschwitz reminiscences, *Moments of Reprieve*, Jewish-Italian writer Primo Levi reveals how a single moment of kindness or subtle resistance — the sharing of a piece of bread with a fellow prisoner, writing a clandestine letter home, forbidden laughter in the face of insufferable daily horrors — appeared like a brittle thaw in the moral winter of the Holocaust. These fragile moments could, under such extreme circumstances, sometimes accumulate into the most dangerous of commodities — hope. Hope that all people were not capable of the barbarism of gas chambers and mass crematoria, and that something essential to the human condition transcended selfishness and irrational hatred and bound human beings together in an elemental struggle for a better world. Levi, at several points of his book, hinted that such incidental but extraordinary 'moments of reprieve' made surviving Auschwitz possible.

Tragically, despite writing such an inspiring book of human tenderness and peculiar frailty in the face of cold malevolence, Levi himself never really regained his own hope. He suffered from the 'survivors' disease', guilty despair, and committed suicide in 1987. Yet, I would argue that Levi's writing teaches us, above all else, that loss of hope is a terminal condition. And to hold on to it in the face of inhumanity and injustice, even if the grip is momentary, weak and tenuous, is a powerful thing.

The corollary to all of this, as American historian Howard Zinn has written, is that 'in such a world of conflict, a world of victims and executioners, it is the job of thinking people' to make sure they are never 'on the side of the executioners.' Zinn, writing his magnificent *A People's History of the United States*, constructed his entire theory of history upon this premise. He also argued that this does not mean that historians should simply become woeful hand wringers, grieving for a past they cannot change. Such tears only 'deplete our moral energy for the present.' But neither should historians simply be scribes and 'collaborators in an endless cycle of defeat,' siding with the powerful, ignoring injustice, and avoiding the struggles of those who all too often seem neglected in history. Perhaps, Zinn writes, 'our future may be found in the past's fugitive moments of compassion.'[60]

In short, in these troubled times, history and politics should act as a moral compass — if we fail to learn from the past, fail to notice those who have been exiled to the blurred margins of public memory, we fail ourselves. You did not have to be an

American to be sickened by September 11, or to empathise with the firefighters, office workers, and those who died on the planes. In the same way, you should not have to be a Palestinian refugee, an Israeli refusenik, a North Korean child, or an Afghan peasant sheltering in the bombed-out rubble of your country, to be moved by their plight and to want a better world. Although injustice inculcates despair, hope can resuscitate and rekindle. But history teaches us that hope cannot be sustained by itself alone. Together — despite distance and divisions of class, culture and 'civilisation' — we can create our own moments of resistance and reprieve.

Notes

Introduction

1   Quotes and information in this introduction regarding the African Burial Ground are from 'Honouring the Slaves of New York,' *New York Times*, 4 October 2003 and *New York State Freedom Trail Commission Report*.

2   Quoted in Australian Academy of the Humanities, *The Humanities and Australia's National Research Priorities*, Commonwealth of Australia, Canberra, 2003, p. 5.

3   Quoted in D. Krieger, 'Remembering Hiroshima and Nagasaki,' *CounterPunch*, 6 August 2003. Available on the web at <www.counterpunch.org/krieger08062003.html>.

4   C. Johnson, *Blowback: The Costs and Consequences of American Empire*, Time Warner, London, 2002, p. 21.

5   ibid.

6   See Li Zhensheng, *Red-Color News Soldier*, Phaidon Press, 2003; J. Gittings, 'Blood-red Lens,' *Guardian Weekly*, 2–8 October 2003. There is a wonderful online exhibition of Li Zhensheng's photography available at <http://red-colornewssoldier.com/index.html>.

1. The War on Terror

1   Bush quoted while discussing post-9/11 strategies with the Japanese Prime Minister, see B. Woodward, *Bush at War*, Simon & Schuster, Sydney, 2002, p. 138.

2   A report on Bush's speech was published as 'Get Ready for War, Bush Tells America,' *Observer*, 16 September 2001. It is available on the internet at the *Guardian Unlimited* website, <www.guardian.co.uk/wtccrash/story/0,1300,552788,00.html>.

3   US defence budget details from *Guardian Weekly*, 17–23 January 2002; *Guardian Weekly*, 7–13 February 2002; *New York Times*, 2 February 2002.

4   *Guardian Weekly*, 11–17 September 2003.

5   The interview was republished in English in *Guardian Weekly*, 11–17 September 2003.

6   ibid.

7   *New York Times*, 29 September 2003.

8   ibid., 12 September 2003.

9   N. Solomon, 'The Political Capital of 9/11,' accessed at *Z-Net Magazine*, <www.zmag.org>, 12 September 2003. Also 'Bush Clears Saddam on 9/11,' *Australian*, 19 September 2003; 'How 9/11 anniversary has become the victim of spin,' *Guardian Weekly*, 18–24 September 2003.

10 *Guardian Weekly*, 9–15 October 2003.

11 *New York Times*, 14 September 2003.

12 ibid., 15 September 2003.

13 ibid., 2 November 2003.

14 ibid.

15 *Los Angeles Times*, 9 September 2003.

16 *New York Times*, 22 September 2003.

17 *Guardian Weekly*, 11–17 September 2003.

18 *New York Times*, 25 September 2003.

19 ibid., 27 September 2003, 2 November 2003.

20 For quotes see, for instance, B. Woodward, *Bush at War*, Simon & Schuster, Sydney, 2002; 'Bush's Messiah Complex,' *The Progressive*, February 2003; P. Kengor, 'God & W at 1600 Penn,' *National Review Online*, 5 March 2003, <www.nationalreview.com>.

21 *Guardian Weekly*, 23–29 October 2003; B. Graham, 'General Rebuked for Talk of God,' *Washington Post*, 17 October 2003.

22 B. Woodward, *Bush at War*, Simon & Schuster, Sydney, 2002, p. 94.

23 On the Crusades see T. Jones & A. Ereira, *The Crusades*, Penguin, New York, 1996, pp. 49–54; T. Ali, *The Clash of Fundamentalisms: Crusades, Jihads and Modernity*, Verso, London, 2002, pp. 32, 39–43; J. J. Spielvogel, *Western Civilization*, Thomson, Melbourne, 2003, pp. 264–71.

24 Fulcher's writings are reproduced in J. J. Spielvogel, *Western Civilization*, 2003, p. 267.

25 *New York Times*, 1 December 2001.

26 Quoted in B. Woodward, *Bush at War*, 2002, p. 103.

27 J. F. Burns, 'New Afghan Force Takes Hold, Turning to Peace,' *New York Times*, 16 February 1995. See also J. C. Griffiths, *Afghanistan: A History of Conflict*, Timat, London, 2001, p. 236; W Maley, 'Interpreting the Taliban,' in W. Maley (ed.), *Fundamentalism Reborn*, Hurst, London, 2001, p. 2.

28 For more see R. Mackenzie, 'The United States and the Taliban,' in W Maley (ed.), *Fundamentalism Reborn*, 2001, pp. 90–103. P. E. Tyler, 'Officers Say US Aided Iraq in War Despite Use of Gas,' *New York Times*, 18 August 2002.

29 A. Rashid, *Taliban*, Pan Books, London, 2001, pp. 49–50.

30 These figures are based on various estimates. They are conservative, not taking into account, for instance, that in one year the Soviets lost $2.5 billion worth of aircraft alone in Afghanistan. See, for instance, J. C. Griffiths, *Afghanistan*, 2001, pp. 182–84. L. P. Goodson, *Afghanistan's Endless War: State Failure, Regional Politics and the Rise of the Taliban*, UWP, London, 2001, pp. 145–47.

31 Figure from the International Committee of the Red Cross in 1998 quoted in A. Rashid, *Taliban*, 2001, p. 207. Also, J. C. Griffiths, *Afghanistan*, p. 227.

32 See A. Rashid, *Taliban*, 2001, pp. 217–19.

33 ibid., pp. 6, 32. On the 'social and doctrinal roots of the Taliban,' see also, W. Maley, 'Interpreting the Taliban,' in W. Maley (ed.), *Fundamentalism Reborn*, 2001, pp. 14–23.

34 Decree from November 1996 is quoted in full in A. Rashid, *Taliban*, 2001, pp. 217–18. See also pp. 104–06. For more see, N. H. Dupree, 'Afghan Women under the Taliban,' in W. Maley (ed.), *Fundamentalism*, 2001, pp. 145–66.

35 Ironically, the Taliban's obsession with the violent suppression of homosexuality seemed to sit in opposition to traditional Pastun practices. See for instance M. Reynolds, 'Kandahar's Lightly Veiled Homosexual Habits,' *Los Angeles Times*, 3 April 2002. Also A. Rashid, *Taliban*, 2001, p. 115; J. C. Griffiths, *Afghanistan*, 2001, p. 91; T. Ali, *Clash of Fundamentalisms*, 2002, p. 211.

36 For more on the foundation of the Taliban, see A. Rashid, *Taliban*, 2001, pp. 25–29, 32; J. C. Griffiths, *Afghanistan*, 2001, pp. 226–48.

37   A. Rashid, *Taliban*, 2001, pp. 7–9, 19–20, 37, 57, 68. J. C. Griffiths, *Afghanistan*, 2001, pp. 17–24, 248.

38   B. R. Rubin, *The Fragmentation of Afghanistan*, Yale University Press, 2002. A. Rashid, *Taliban*, 2001, pp. 37, 68, 82–83. J. C. Griffiths, *Afghanistan*, 2001, pp. 103–06.

39   A. Rashid, *Taliban*, 2001, pp. 37–38.

40   For more on Britain and Russia in Afghanistan during the nineteenth century's 'Great Game' see J. C. Griffiths, *Afghanistan*, 2001, pp. 28–51. B. R. Rubin, *The Fragmentation of Afghanistan*, 2002, pp. 45–54.

41   On the Soviet Union's long entanglement in Afghanistan, see J. C. Griffiths, *Afghanistan*, 2001, pp. 128–44, 158–60, 164–91. T. Ali, *The Clash of Fundamentalisms*, 2002, pp. 204–8. B. R. Rubin, *The Fragmentation of Afghanistan*, 2002.; L. P. Goodson, *Afghanistan's Endless War*, 2001.

42   Bush quoted in *New York Times*, 28 October 2003.

43   *Australian*, 20 September 2001. See also, S. Jackson, 'Eye on the Inferno,' Media Magazine, *Australian*, 20–26 September 2001, pp. 6–7.

44   S. Danielsen, 'Images of Terror,' Media Magazine, *Australian*, 20–26 September 2001, p. 7.

45   E. Charles, 'Bad News Is Good for Some,' Media Magazine, *Australian*, 1–7 November 2001; S. Danielsen, 'Images of Terror,' Media Magazine, *Australian*, 20–26 September 2001, p. 7; J. Baxter & M. Downing, *The Day That Shook the World: Understanding September 11*, ABC Books, Sydney, 2001, pp. 13, 30, 199. Rupert Murdoch's News Corporation claimed it lost $100 million in advertising due to September 11.

46   Quoted in J. Este, 'Under Cover of Darkness,' Media Magazine, *Australian*, 25–31 October 2001, p. 8.

47   S. Jackson, 'Eye on the Inferno,' Media Magazine, *Australian*, 20–26 September 2001, p. 6.

48   D. Guthrie, 'Dogwatch,' *Grants Pass Daily Courier*, 15 September 2001; *Texas City Sun*, 23 September 2001; S. Jackson, 'Journalists Fight for Information,' Media Magazine, *Australian*, 11–17 October 2001, p. 13.

49   S. Danielsen, 'No Laughing Matter,' Media Magazine, *Australian*, 11–17 October 2001, p. 9.

50   A. Coulter, 'This Is War,' *National Review Online*, accessed at <www.nationalreview.com/coulter/coulter091301.shtml>.

51 See, A. Coulter, 'Where's Janet Reno When We Need Her,' and 'Future Widows of America: Write Your Congressman.' Both columns can be accessed from the columnists' archive at <www.townhall.com>. Also D. Horowitz, 'Introducing Ann Coulter,' accessed at <www.frontpagemag.com/horowitzsnotepad/2001/hn10-03-01p.htm>. H. Kurtz, 'National Review Cans Columnist Ann Coulter,' *Washington Post*, 2 October 2001. For attacks on Arab-Americans, see *ADC Fact Sheet: The Condition of Arab Americans Post 9/11*, 20 November 2001.

52 Quoted in J. Rutenberg & B. Carter, 'Network Coverage a Target of Fire from Conservatives,' *New York Times*, 7 November 2001.

53 ibid. Also B. Kovach & T. Rosentiel, 'In Wartime, the People Want the Facts,' *New York Times*, 29 January 2002.

54 S. Jackson, 'Journalists Fight for Information,' Media Magazine, *Australian*, 11–17 October 2001, pp. 12–13.

55 C. Taylor, '"Arab CNN" Rides the World's Airwaves,' Media Magazine, *Australian*, 18–24 October 2001, p. 13.

56 ibid.

57 H. Ibish & A. Abunimah, 'The CNN of the Arab World Deserves Our Respect,' *Los Angeles Times*, 22 October 2001.

58 Interestingly, the first two presenters to appear on Afghan television after the fall of the Taliban were both women. It was the first television broadcast in Afghanistan in five years.

59 E. Said, 'Thoughts about America,' *Al-Ahram Weekly*, 2 March 2002. See also, G. Monbiot, 'Both Saviour and Victim,' *Guardian*, 29 January 2002.

60 E. Said, 'Thoughts about America,' *Al-Ahram Weekly*, 2 March 2002. For an example of Bush's ideas regarding good and evil, and the clash of civilisations post-September 11, see 'Bush Marks Pearl Harbor Anniversary,' *New York Times*, 8 December 2001.

61 See H. Zinn, 'The Others,' *Nation*, 11 February 2002; G. Alcorn, 'Civilian Deaths No Cause for Concern,' *Sydney Morning Herald*, 12 January 2002; J. Treanor, 'US Raids "Killed 800 Afghan Civilians",' *Guardian Weekly*, 25–31 July 2002.

62 H. Zinn, 'The Others,' *Nation*, 11 February 2002.

63 See FAIR (Fairness & Accuracy in Reporting), *Action Alert — Fox: Civilian Casualties Not News*, 8 November 2001.

64 Quote from S. R. Shalom, 'Confronting Terrorism and War,' *New Politics*, No. 32, Winter 2002. Also, FAIR (Fairness & Accuracy in Reporting), *Action Alert — Fox: Civilian Casualties Not News*, 8

November 2001; G. Alcorn, 'Civilian Deaths No Cause for Concern,' *Sydney Morning Herald*, 12 January 2002.

65   On this issue see, for example, T. J. Nagy, 'The Secret behind the Sanctions,' *Progressive*, August 2001, accessed at <www.progressive.org>. T. Ali, *The Clash of Fundamentalisms: Crusades, Jihads and Modernity*, Verso, London, 2002, pp. 144–47. Also, H. Von Sponeck, 'There Are Alternatives to a Military Option,' *Counterpunch*, 10 January 2002. Sponeck is a former UN Humanitarian Coordinator for Iraq. He and Dennis Halliday, the UN Humanitarian Coordinator for Iraq, both resigned in protest against the sanctions.

66   T. J. Nagy, 'The Secret behind the Sanctions,' *Progressive*, August 2001, accessed at <www.progressive.org>; H. Von Sponeck, 'There Are Alternatives to a Military Option,' *Counterpunch*, 10 January 2002. One of the very few journalists to regularly report on this subject was Australian John Pilger. See, J. Pilger, *New Rulers of the World*, 2002, pp. 45–97. Also T. Ali, *The Clash of Fundamentalisms*, 2002, pp. 145–46.

67   See, M. Dowd, 'Office of Strategic Mendacity,' *New York Times*, 20 February 2002. Also, E. Schmitt, 'Pentagon and Bogus News: All Is Denied,' *New York Times*, 5 December 2003.

68   See, FAIR (Fairness and Accuracy in Reporting), *Pentagon Propaganda Plan Is Undemocratic, Possibly Illegal* (Media Release), 19 February 2002.

69   J. Borger, 'Information Is Now a Casualty of War,' *Guardian Weekly*, 7–13 March 2002.

70   See, FAIR (Fairness and Accuracy in Reporting), *Pentagon Propaganda Plan Is Undemocratic, Possibly Illegal* (Media Release), 19 February 2002; F. Rich, 'Freedom from the Press,' *New York Times*, 2 March 2002.

71   R. Lusetich, 'Sunset on Hollywood Boulevard,' *Australian*, 18 October 2001; 'Hollywood's War Effort,' Media Magazine, *Australian*, 22–28 November 2001.

72   Quoted in R. Lusetich, 'Sunset on Hollywood Boulevard,' *Australian*, 18 October 2001.

73   R. Brown, 'Making Sense of It,' *Hard News*, 14 September 2001, transcript available at <www.scoop.co.nz/mason/archive/scoop>.

74   S. Burchill, 'Asking Why Is Not to Excuse the Terrorists' Actions,' *Sydney Morning Herald*, 4 October 2001.

75   'Woman Who Joined the Band of Martyrs,' *Guardian Weekly*, 7–13 February 2002; 'Hatred Sown in a Carer's Heart,' *Observer*, 3 February 2002.

76 *Guardian Weekly*, 7–13 March 2002; *New York Times*, 28 February 2002; *New York Times*, 5 March 2002, 12 March 2002.

77 *New York Times*, 28 February 2002. Also Y. Arafat, 'The Palestinian Vision of Peace,' *New York Times*, 3 February 2002.

78 For those seeking a fair and detailed assessment of the history of Israel/Palestine, a good source of general information is I. J. Bickerton & M. N. Pearson, *The Arab–Israeli Conflict: A History*, Longman Cheshire, 1990.

79 ibid., pp. 38–44.

80 Herzl quoted in J. Rose, *Israel: The Hijack State*, SWP, London, 1988, p. 30.

81 This quote has become a favourite of those opposed to Western intervention in the Middle East. See, for example, the website of the pro-Palestinian 'Islamic Network,' <www.islaam.net/main/display.php?part=1&category=20&id=567>.

82 E. Said, 'A People in Need of Leadership,' *New Left Review*, No. 11, September–October 2001, p. 28; World Bank, *Two Years of Intifada, Closures and Palestinian Economic Crisis: An Assessment*, 5 March 2003; C. McGreal, 'Dying for a Drink in the Middle East,' *Guardian Weekly*, 22–28 January 2004.

83 *New York Times*, 5 March 2002, 31 January 2002; *Guardian Weekly*, 31 January–6 February 2002.

84 Annan quoted in *New York Times*, 12 March 2002. See also *New York Times*, 15 March 2002, 31 March 2002, 2 April 2002.

85 Figures from *New York Times*, 12 March 2002.

86 *Guardian Weekly*, 18–24 April 2002. See also, C. McGreal & B. Whitaker, 'Israel Accused over Jenin Assault,' *Guardian* (UK), 23 April 2002.

87 UN envoy Terje Roed-Larsen quoted in 'Jenin Camp "Horrific beyond Belief",' *BBC News Online*, 18 April 2002. Accessed at <http://news.bbc.co.uk>. On the Israeli opinion polls, see S. Goldenberg, 'Likud Rejects Statehood for Palestinians,' *Guardian Weekly*, 16–22 May 2002.

88 *Guardian Weekly*, 14–20 February 2002; *New York Times*, 1 February 2002, 2 February 2002. On the refusenik issue more broadly, see also C. Dupeyron, 'Israeli Patriots Who Refuse to Join a "Racist" army,' *Guardian Weekly*, 3–9 January 2002; J. Steele, 'Soldier Battling for His People's Soul,' *Guardian Weekly*, 31 October–6 November 2002. There were some slightly different translations of the petition's text. See also

the refuseniks website at <www.seruv.org.il/defaulteng.asp>.

89 A. Oron, 'Personal Testimony of an Israeli Refusenik,' *Jewish Peace News*, 24 February 2002.

90 *Washington Post*, 5 June 2003.

91 J. Irwin, email to S. Adams, 12 November 2002. See also L. Yaxley, 'PM — Israel Motion Divides Parliament, ALP,' 11 November 2001. Archived at *ABC Online*, <www.abc.net.au/pm/s724218.htm>.

92 *New York Times*, 25 September 2003; *Jerusalem Post*, 28 September 2003, 29 September 2003; L. El-Haddad, 'Israeli Refuseniks Reap Leaders' Abuse,' 12 October 2003, available at Al-Jazeera's website, <http://english.aljazeera.net>.

93 *New York Times*, 25 September 2003; *Jerusalem Post*, 28 September 2003, 29 September 2003; L. El-Haddad, 'Israeli Refuseniks,' 2003.

94 *New York Times*, 25 September 2003; *Jerusalem Post*, 28 September 2003, 29 September 2003; L. El-Haddad, 'Israeli Refuseniks,' 2003.

95 A shorter version of this essay was originally published as S. Adams, 'Don't Mention the Arms,' *West Australian*, 10 April 2003.

96 Protest figures from T. Ali, *Bush in Babylon*, Verso, London, p. 144.

97 See, *Biographical Sketch of Saddam Hussein by British Embassy Baghdad*, 15 November 1969, and *Telegram from British Embassy Baghdad to Foreign and Commonwealth Office*, 20 December 1969, both of which are available in PDF format from the National Security Archive online at <www.gwu.edu/~nsarchiv/>.

98 *Secretary's Principals and Regionals Staff Meeting, 28 April 1975 (Excerpt)*, available in PDF format from the National Security Archive online at <www.gwu.edu/~nsarchiv/>.

99 W Choong, 'Lessons from Iraq's History,' *Straits Times*, 20 March 2003; J. Glancey, 'Our last occupation: Gas, chemicals, bombs', *Guardian*, 19 April 2003.

100 State Department Cable to Embassy Amman and US Interests Section Baghdad, 'Kittani Call on Under Secretary Eagleburger,' 18 March 1984. Also, Cable from US Interests Section Baghdad to State Department, 'Ismet Kittani's Reaction to US Chemical Weapons Statement and Next Steps in US–Iraq Relations,' 7 March 1984. Both documents available in PDF format from the National Security Archive online at <www.gwu.edu/~nsarchiv/>.

101 For more on this issue, see P. E. Tyler, 'Officers Say U. S. Aided Iraq in War Despite Use of Gas,' *New York Times*, 18 August 2002; M. Dobbs, 'US Had Key Role in Iraq Build-up,' *Washington Post*, 30

December 2002; D. Hiro, 'Iraq and Poison Gas,' *Nation*, posted online 28 August 2002 at <www.thenation.com>. Stockholm International Peace Research Institute, *SIPRI Fact Sheet: Chemical Warfare in the Iraq–Iran War*, May 1984. The report is available at SIPRI's webpage, <www.sipri.se>. For UN Security Council Resolutions, see the Council's internet archive at <www.un.org/Docs/sc/>.

102 On US companies exporting chemicals to Iraq, see M. Dobbs, 'US Had Key Role in Iraq Build-up,' *Washington Post*, 30 December 2002; W. Blum, 'Anthrax for Export: US Companies Sold Iraq the Ingredients for a Witch's Brew,' *Progressive*, April 1998.

103 On US chemical and biological weapons programs and the 1969 decision to stop producing them for 'offensive use,' there are more than 25 previously classified US government documents now available in PDF format at the National Security Archive, online at <www.gwu.edu/~nsarchiv/>.

104 *Memorandum, Presidential Science Advisor Lee A. DuBridge to National Security Advisor Henry Kissinger, 22 October 1969.* This previously top secret US government document is now available in PDF format at the National Security Archive, online at <www.gwu.edu/~nsarchiv/>.

105 This essay is based on a speech originally given at a public forum on 'Invading Iraq — A World in Conflict,' Murdoch University, 16 April 2003.

106 For more regarding Omar and civilian casualties of the US-led war in Iraq, see R. Ourdan, 'Paying the Price for Pointless Violence,' *Guardian Weekly*, 27 November–3 December 2003.

107 Garner was soon replaced by Paul Bremer.

108 *New York Times*, 13 April 2003.

109 Data presented in C. Johnson, 'America's Empire of Bases,' 15 January 2004, accessed at <www.zmag.org>.

110 Bush quotes from 'Editorial,' *Texas Observer*, 28 September 2001; *Remarks by the President at 2002 Graduation Exercise of the US Military Academy, West Point*, 1 June 2002, full transcript available at <www.whitehouse.gov>.

111 C. Johnson, *Blowback*, 2002, p. 20.

112 A shorter version of this essay was originally published in the *West Australian* on 27 August 2003 as 'Ghosts of Vietnam Stalk the US in Iraq.'

113 *New York Times*, 25 August 2003.

114 The *Newsweek* poll mentioned here involved interviews with 1011 Americans and was conducted on 21–22 August 2003. See J. Barrett,

'When Is Enough Enough,' *Newsweek*, 24 August 2003.

115 *New York Times*, 19 August 2003.

116 'The Worst Month Yet,' *Guardian*, 1 May 2004; M. Dowd, 'Wolfie's Fuzzy Math,' *New York Times*, 2 May 2004.

117 N. Klein, 'Mutiny in Iraq,' *Nation*, 17 May 2004; 'The Worst Month Yet,' *Guardian*, 1 May 2004; P. Cockburn, '"Even the Dogs Were Hunting Us": Change of Hands in Fallujah,' available at *CounterPunch* on the net, <www.counterpunch.org/>.

118 N. Klein, 'Mutiny in Iraq,' 2004; 'The Worst Month Yet,' *Guardian*, 1 May 2004; '"Even the Dogs Were Hunting Us."'

119 'Support for War Is Down Sharply, Poll Concludes,' *New York Times*, 29 April 2004.

120 *New York Times*, 19 September 2001.

121 J. D. Farley, 'Where Next — Alabama?' *Guardian*, 17 November 2001.

122 D. M. Halbfinger & S. A. Holmes, 'Military Mirrors Working Class America,' *New York Times*, 30 March 2003.

123 ibid.; L. Clemetson, 'Diversity Starting to Rise through Navy Carrier's Ranks,' *New York Times*, 30 March 2003.

124 T. Harper, 'Pentagon Keeps Dead out of Sight,' *Toronto Star*, 5 November 2003; 'Army Denied Special Treatment for Jessica Lynch,' *CNN Online*, at <www.cnn.com>; L. Hockstader, 'Ex-POW's Family Accuses Army of Double Standard on Benefit,' *Washington Post*, 24 October 2003. Interestingly, Lynch later criticised the US government's use of her rescue as a propaganda device. She also appeared in public with Shoshana Johnson. See *Sydney Morning Herald*, 12 November 2003.

125 D. M. Halbfinger & S. A. Holmes, 'Military Mirrors,' 2003.

126 J. Meek, 'Marines Losing the Battle for Hearts and Minds,' *Guardian*, 25 March 2003. W. Broyles, 'A war for Us, fought by Them,' *New York Times*, 4 May 2004.

127 D. M. Halbfinger & S. A. Holmes, 'Military Mirrors,' 2003.

128 ibid.

129 US Department of Justice, *Bureau of Justice Statistics*, 2003; The *Post and Courier* (Charleston), 1 June 2003.

130 *New York Times*, 7 April 2003; US Department of Justice, *Bureau of Justice Statistics*, 2003.

131 American Civil Liberties Union, *How Ex-Felons Can Regain the Right to Vote in Washington*, (ACLU leaflet), November 2002; J. Cartagena, J. Nelson & J. Gibbs, 'Felons and the Right to Vote,' *Gotham Gazette*, 2 February 2003.

132 *New York Times*, 2 November 2003.

133 ibid., 27 September 2003, 2 November 2003.

134 D. Zirin, 'Interviewing John Carlos,' *Prince George's Post*, 29 October 2003. Also posted on the web at *Z-Net*, <www.zmag.com>. See also John Carlos' website at <www.johncarlos.com>.

135 Peter Norman, the Australian medallist, wore an OPHR badge on the podium in solidarity with the two black athletes.

2. 'Our Backyard'

1   A transcript of this speech, and all others quoted in this essay, is available from the prime minister's website at <www.pm.gov.au>.

2   For more on Australia's military history, see G. Odgers, *100 Years of Australians at War*, Ken Fin, Collingwood, 2000; J. Grey, *A Military History of Australia*, CUP, Melbourne, 1999.

3   P. Mares, 'Asylum Seekers: Australia's Sledgehammer,' available on the internet at *Australian Policy Online*, <www.apo.org.au>.

4   D. Day, *Claiming a Continent: A New History of Australia*, Harper Collins, Sydney, 2001, pp. 42–43.

5   A. Curthoys, 'Liberalism and Exclusionism: A Prehistory of the White Australia Policy,' in L. Jayasuriya et al. (eds), *Legacies of White Australia*, UWA Press, Crawley, 2003, p. 9.

6   D. Day, *Claiming a Continent*, 2001, pp. 198–99.

7   J. Grey, *Military History of Australia*, 1999, p. 25.

8   ibid., p. 26.

9   L. Carlyon, *Gallipoli*, Macmillan, Sydney, 2002, pp. 267–68.

10   Quoted in ibid., p. 270.

11   *Sydney Morning Herald*, 21 January 2003; *Age*, 18 January 2003.

12   'Securing Votes As the War Fades,' *Sydney Morning Herald*, 23 May 2003.

13   'Bush's "Sheriff" Comment Causes a Stir,' *Age*, 17 October 2003.

14   D. Day, *Claiming a Continent*, 2001, pp. 214, 223.

15   B. Nicolson, 'Burnet's solution: The Plan to Poison S-E Asia,' *Age*, 10 March 2002.

16   ibid.

17   M. Sexton, *War for the Asking: Australia's Vietnam Secrets*, Penguin, Melbourne, 1981, p. 2.

18   Quoted in D. Day, *Claiming a Continent*, 2001, p. 282.

19   M. Sexton, *War for the Asking*, 1981, p. 94.

20 The issue of how many people were killed in Indonesia in the massacres of 1965–66 is debateable. I have opted for a reasonably conservative figure — for varying political motives some historians have put the figure as low as 250,000, while some have said it is as high as one million. See, H. Crouch, *The Army and Politics in Indonesia*, Cornell University Press, London, 1988, p. 155.

21 For more on the PKI see C. Bowen, *From the Ashes — The Rise and Fall of the PKI*, Sydney, 1990.

22 Quoted in G. Kolko, *Confronting the Third World: United States Foreign Policy, 1945–1980*, Pantheon, New York, 1988, p. 174.

23 On Suharto's military background, see H. McDonald, *Suharto's Indonesia*, Fontana, Blackburn, 1980, pp. 13–19.

24 Quoted in G. Kolko, *Confronting the Third World*, 1988, p. 180. A very good overview of the violence of 1965–66 and Suharto's rise to power can be found in H. McDonald, *Suharto's Indonesia*, 1980, pp. 49–67.

25 See, for instance, H. Crouch, *Army and Politics in Indonesia*, 1988, pp. 142–43, 151–53.

26 G. Kolko, *Confronting the Third World*, 1988, p. 180. In some provinces other religious extremists, including young Catholics, were also used to lead anti-PKI massacres. See for instance, H. McDonald, *Suharto's Indonesia*, 1980, pp. 101–02; 'Hidden Holocaust of 1965,' *Sydney Morning Herald*, 10 July 1999.

27 A. Schwarz, *A Nation in Waiting: Indonesia in the 1990s*, Allen & Unwin, Sydney, 1994, pp. 20–21. See also, H. McDonald, *Suharto's Indonesia*, 1980, pp. 39, 64, 88; H. Crouch, *Army and Politics in Indonesia*, 1988, pp. 146–47; 'Hidden Holocaust of 1965,' *Sydney Morning Herald*, 10 July 1999.

28 *Time*, 15 July 1966. Also quoted in J. Pilger, *The New Rulers of the World*, Verso, London, 2002, p. 33.

29 G. Kolko, *Confronting the Third World*, 1988, pp. 181, 184–85.

30 Army figure quoted in H. McDonald, *Suharto's Indonesia*, 1980, p. 53.

31 G. Kolko, *Confronting the Third World*, 1988; W. Blum, *The CIA: A Forgotten History*, London, Zed Books, 1986, pp. 108–13, 217–22; P. D. Scott, 'The United States and the Overthrow of Sukarno, 1965–1967,' *Pacific Affairs*, 58, Summer 1985, pp. 239–64; 'Hidden Holocaust of 1965,' *Sydney Morning Herald*, 10 July 1999; H. McDonald, *Suharto's Indonesia*, 1980., p. 27.

32 W. Blum, *The CIA*, 1986, pp. 109, 111.

33 Quoted in J. M. Tesoro/Blitar, '"Sukarnoism" Again,' *Asia Week*, 2 July

1999, available online at <www.asiaweek.com>.

34 G. Kolko, *Confronting the Third World*, 1988, pp. 180–81.

35 From Kadane report as published in *San Francisco Examiner*, 20 May 1990.

36 ibid. Some PKI leaders were kept, tried and later executed by the Suharto regime. See for instance, H. McDonald, *Suharto's Indonesia*, 1980, p. 217.

37 Central Intelligence Agency Directorate of Intelligence, *Indonesia 1965 — the Coup That Backfired*, Langley, 1968; G. Kolko, *Confronting the Third World*, 1988, pp. 178–85; B. Anderson & R. McVey, 'What Happened in Indonesia?,' *New York Review of Books*, 1 June 1978.

38 On the secret documents, see '1975 East Timor Invasion Got US Go-Ahead,' *Washington Post*, 7 December 2001; 'US supported Indonesia in Timor Invasion,' *Weekend Australian*, 8–9 December 2001. All the relevant documents are available on the internet at the National Security Archive at <www.gwu.edu/percent7Ensarchiv/NSAEBB/NSAEBB62/index.html>.

39 J. G. Taylor, *East Timor: The Price of Freedom*, Zed, London, 1999, p. 169.

40 Quoted in A. Schwarz, *Nation in Waiting*, 1994, p. 171.

41 A. Schwarz, *Nation in Waiting*, 1994, pp. 172–73.

42 'Stanley,' 'Opening that dark page,' *Inside Indonesia*, No. 63, July–September 2000; G. Barton, 'Islam and Politics in the New Indonesia,' in J. F. Issacson & C. Rubenstein (eds), *Islam in Asia: Changing Political Realities*, Transaction Press, 2001.

43 B. Woodward, *Bush at War*, Simon & Schuster, Sydney, 2002, p. 149.

44 Megawati quoted in *Asia Times*, 20 October 2001.

45 Quoted in ibid.

46 *Sydney Morning Herald*, 11 September 2003.

47 *Age*, 10 February 2003; P. Lloyd, 'AM — Imam Samudra to Face the Death Penalty,' 10 September 2003, available on the internet at *ABC Online*, <www.abc.net.au/am/content/2003/s942690.htm>.

48 Quoted in 'Helen Todd, v. Sintong Panjaitan: Plaintiff's Memorandum of Law in Support of Motion for Default Judgement,' p. 18, accessed at <www.tan.org/news/2000a/suit/memo-law.htm>. Also, H. Todd, 'Death in East Timor,' *Asian Wall Street Journal*, 25 November 1991.

49 The relevant American laws were the *Alien Tort Claims Act* and the *Torture Victim Protection Act*. Some of the documentation and evidence from the court case can be viewed on the internet at <www.etan.org/news/2000a/suit/memo-law.htm>.

50 'Helen Todd, v. Sintong Panjaitan: Plaintiff's Memorandum of Law in Support of Motion for Default Judgement,' <www.tan.org/news/2000a/suit/memo-law.htm>.

51 ibid., p. 9.

52 Evans quoted in M. Aarons & R. Domm, *East Timor: A Western Made Tragedy*, Left Book Club, Sydney, 1992, p. 66. See also, *Age*, 16 July 1994.

53 R. Anderson, 'The Massacre of 12 November 1991,' in J. Aubrey (ed.), *Free East Timor: Australia's Culpability in East Timor's Genocide*, Vintage, Sydney, 1998, p. 149.

54 Quoted in M. Einfeld, 'Until Justice Is Theirs,' in ibid., p. 270.

55 For more on the Chinese in East Timor, see J. Dunn, *Timor: A People Betrayed*, ABC Books, Sydney, 1996, pp. 8–10; J. G. Taylor, *East Timor*, 1999, p. 1.

56 E. Wolf, *Europe and the People Without History*, UC Press, London, 1982, pp. 235–36; J. G. Taylor, *East Timor*, 1999, p. 3.

57 J. Dunn, *Timor: A People Betrayed*, 1996, pp. 3, 13–15, 18; J. Ramos Horta, *Funu: The Unfinished Saga of East Timor*, Red Sea Press, Lawrenceville, 1987, p. 21.

58 On this often unrecognised point, see J. G. Taylor, *East Timor*, 1999, pp. 4–5, 8–10.

59 Quoted in A. Schwarz, *Nation in Waiting*, 1994, pp. 198–99; J. G. Taylor, *East Timor*, 1999, p. 10.

60 See J. Dunn, *Timor: A People Betrayed*, 1996, pp. 4–5, 17; G. J. Aditjondro, *In the Shadow of Mount Ramelau: The Impact of the Occupation of East Timor*, Indonesian Documentation and Information Centre, Leiden, 1994, p. 7.

61 Some historians claim that Dominicans first landed on Timor in 1515, but this is disputed. For various perspectives on the Catholic Church's role in East Timor, see Bishop H. Deakin, 'East Timor and the Catholic Church,' in J. Aubrey (ed.), *Free East Timor*, 1998, p. 221–35; R. Archer, 'The Catholic Church in East Timor,' in P. Carey & G. C. Bentley (eds), *East Timor at the Crossroads: The Forging of a Nation*, University of Hawaii Press, Honolulu, 1995, pp. 120–33; A. S. Kohen, 'The Catholic Church and the Independence of East Timor,' in R. Tanter, M. Selden & S. R. Shalom (eds), *Bitter Flowers, Sweet Flowers: East Timor, Indonesia, and the World Community*, Rowman & Littlefield, New York, 2001, pp. 43–51. During the early colonial period missionaries sometimes openly sympathised with local rebellions

against the Portuguese colonial authorities. In 1834 Dominican missionaries had actually been expelled from East Timor by the Portuguese. See, J. Dunn, *Timor: A People Betrayed*, 1996, pp. 44–45.

62 J. G. Taylor, *East Timor*, 1999, pp. 13, 17; A. Schwarz, *Nation in Waiting*, 1994, p. 199.

63 There were debates inside East Timor about whether the Pope should visit — it was feared his visit might be seen as legitimising the Indonesian occupation. See J. G. Taylor, *East Timor*, 1999, pp. 155–56. Also G. J. Aditjondro, *Shadow of Mount Ramelau*, 1994, p. 10.

64 C. Pinto, 'The Student Movement and the Independence Struggle in East Timor: An Interview,' in R. Tanter, M. Selden & S. R. Shalom (eds), *Bitter Flowers, Sweet Flowers*, 2001, pp. 33–34, 40.

65 Quoted in A. Schwarz, *Nation in Waiting*, 1994, p. 210; J. G. Taylor, *East Timor*, 1999, p. 197.

66 'Helen Todd, v. Sintong Panjaitan: Plaintiff's Memorandum of Law in Support of Motion for Default Judgement,' p. 6, accessed at <www.etan.org/news/2000a/suit/memo-law.htm>.

67 Kamal's diary quoted in H. Todd, 'Death in East Timor,' *Asian Wall Street Journal*, 25 November 1991.

68 Kamal's diary as quoted in 'Helen Todd, v. Sintong Panjaitan: Plaintiff's Memorandum of Law in Support of Motion for Default Judgement,' p. 6, accessed at <www.etan.org/news/2000a/suit/memo-law.htm>. Also H. Todd, 'Death in East Timor,' 1991.

69 For an inside perspective on the student movement, see C. Pinto, 'Student Movement and Independence Struggle,' 2001, pp. 31–41. Also, eyewitness account of the Dili massacre from Amy Goodman, 'New Exception to the Rulers, Part 2,' Z-Media Institute talk, transcript accessed via *Z-Net* site at <znet/zmag/zarticle>.

70 Kamal's diary as quoted in S. Gan, 'The Untimely Death of Kamal Bamadhaj,' *Nation*, 12 November 1997.

71 The most detailed account of Kamal's death is provided in 'Helen Todd v. Sintong Panjaitan: Plaintiff's Memorandum of Law in Support of Motion for Default Judgement,' p. 7, accessed at <www.etan.org/news/2000a/suit/memo-law.htm>.

72 For the student statements see G. J. Aditjondro, *Shadow of Mount Ramelau*, 1994, p. 83. Chomsky's speech is reproduced at N. Chomsky, 'The Case of East Timor,' in J. Aubrey (ed.), *Free East Timor*, 1998, p. 189–210.

73 See, C. Fermont, 'Indonesia: the Inferno of Revolution,' *International*

Socialism, No. 80, September 1998.

74 'After Suharto Resignation, Students Rejoice,' *CNN Online*, 21 May 1998, available on the web at <cnn.com>.

75 For a more developed appraisal of the application of international law to the situation in East Timor, see A. Devereux, 'Accountability for Human Rights Abuses in East Timor,' in D. Kingsbury (ed.), *Guns and Ballot Boxes: East Timor's Vote for Independence*, Monash Asia Institute, Clayton, 2000, pp. 135–55. On the issue of human rights violations and the few trials that have taken place, see 'Getting Away with Murder: Why the Guilty Will Get Off Scot-Free,' *Sydney Morning Herald*, 20 May 2002.

76 On the Indonesian student movement and the fall of Suharto, see for instance, D. McRae, 'Mobilise or Perish,' *Inside Indonesia*, No. 59, July–September 1999; C. Brown, 'Blood in the Streets,' *Inside Indonesia*, No. 58, April–June 1999; A. Ride, 'Indonesia: Power of Protest,' *New Internationalist*, No. 318, November 1999.

77 On this point, see for instance, J. Dunn, *Timor: A People Betrayed*, 1996, p. 19.

78 Quoted in J. Aubrey (ed.), *Free East Timor*, 1998, p. xiii–xiv. For more on the situation in Timor during the Second World War, see J. Dunn, *Timor: A People Betrayed*, 1996, pp. 19–23.

79 Kennealy from transcript of N. Franklin, 'Living in Limbo,' Radio National, 26 August 2001, transcript accessible on the web at <www.abc.net.au/rn/relig/enc/stories/s353423.htm>.

80 Quoted in J. Pilger, *Hidden Agendas*, 1998, p. 251. Also 'Personal Testimony 1: Lance Bomford, 2/40th Battalion,' published on Anzac Day Commemoration Committee website, accessed at <anzacday.org.au>.

81 Quoted in Hobart East Timor Committee, 'World War II and East Timor,' in J. Aubrey (ed.), *Free East Timor*, 1998, p. 20, footnote 6.

82 E. Hobsbawm, *Age of Extremes: The Short Twentieth Century, 1914–1991*, Abacus, London, 1994, p. 117.

83 R. East, 'East Timor's Border War' in J. Aubrey (ed.), *Free East Timor*, 1998, p. 29.

84 J. Aubrey, 'Complicity in Genocide,' in J. Aubrey (ed.), *Free East Timor*, 1998, p. 283–84. Also, J. Ramos Horta, *Funu*, 1987, p. 78. For Woolcott's extended rationalisation of his handling of the East Timor issue as Australian Ambassador see R. Woolcott, *The Hot Seat*, Harper Collins, Sydney, 2003.

85   For more on Roger East, see J. Dunn, *Timor: A People Betrayed*, 1996, pp. 254–56; J. Ramos Horta, *Funu*, 1987, pp. 100–2.

86   This previously secret diplomatic 'inward cablegram' was reproduced by Richard Woolcott in his book. See R. Woolcott, *Hot Seat*, 2003, pp. 306–17. See also B. Juddery, 'My Timor Story,' in J. Aubrey (ed.), *Free East Timor*, 1998, p. 82.

87   A very good and detailed overview of the various phases of East Timorese resistance to Indonesian occupation appears in J. G. Taylor, *East Timor*, 1999.

88   X. Gusmao, *To Resist Is to Win!*, Aurora Books, Richmond, 2000, p. 183.

89   J. Martinkus, *A Dirty Little War*, Random House, Sydney, 2001, pp. 13–21.

90   For more on Whitlam and Timor the work of James Dunn, a former Australian diplomat, gives the best overview of the period. J. Dunn, *Timor: A People Betrayed*, 1996, pp. 118–44. Also J. Birmingham, 'Appeasing Jakarta: Australia's Complicity in the East Timor Tragedy,' *Quarterly Essay*, No. 2, 2001, pp. 43–52; D. Greenlees & R. Garran, *Deliverance: The Inside Story of East Timor's Fight For Freedom*, Allen & Unwin, Crows Nest, 2002, pp. 6–7. On West Papua, see for instance, J. Martinkus, 'Paradise Betrayed: West Papua's Struggle for Independence,' *Quarterly Essay*, No. 7, 2002, pp. 1–83.

91   J. Dunn, *Timor: A People Betrayed*, 1996, pp. 117, 132.

92   Whitlam quoted in J. Birmingham, 'Appeasing Jakarta,' 2001, pp. 50–51. For a deeper analysis of the April 1975 meeting, see J. Dunn, *Timor: A People Betrayed*, 1996, pp. 132–34, 138–39. For more on the advance notice the Australians had regarding the intentions of the Indonesians with regard to East Timor (i.e. their plan to invade), see D. Greenlees & R. Garran, *Deliverance*, 2002, pp. 1–2, 6–7.

93   The Fraser period has largely been neglected in most critiques of Australia's diplomatic history regarding East Timor. For more on this question, see M. Aarons, 'Correspondence,' *Quarterly Essay*, No. 3, 2001, pp. 66–71; J. Birmingham, 'Appeasing Jakarta,' 2001, J. Dunn, *Timor: A People Betrayed*, 1996, pp. 342–46. It should be noted that Fraser's government voted for the initial UN resolution condemning the Indonesian invasion.

94   G. J. Aditjondro, *Shadow of Mount Ramelau*, 1994, pp. 39, 44, 45.

95   See 'Blue Book of Horrors Makes a Diplomatic Time Bomb,' *Sydney Morning Herald*, 15 February 2002.

96   S. Burchill, 'East Timor, Australia and Indonesia,' in D. Kingsbury (ed.), *Guns and Ballot Boxes*, 2000, pp. 169–184; N. Chomsky, *Year 501: The Conquest Continues*, London, 1993, p. 135.

97   Howard quoted in the *Age*, 16 July 1996. For more, see also, R. W. Smith, 'Radio Maubere and links to East Timor,' in J. Aubrey (ed.), *Free East Timor*, 1998, pp. 92–93; J. Pilger, *Hidden Agendas*, Verso, Sydney, 1998, p. 277.

98   Evans quoted in N. Chomsky, *Year 501*, 1993, p. 135. See also, G. Evans, 'Indonesia's Military Culture Has to Be Reformed,' *International Herald Tribune*, 24 July 2001.

99   Xanana quoted in R. Domm, 'East Timor: "To Resist Is To Win",' in J. Aubrey (ed.), *Free East Timor*, 1998, p. 141.

100 J. Birmingham, 'Appeasing Jakarta,' 2001, pp. 55–56.

101 Details on this issue from D. Fickling, 'Timorese Furious at Australian "Oil and Gas Grab",' *Guardian Weekly*, 22–28 April 2004; M. Lane, 'East Timor: Australia's Double Betrayal,' *Green Left Weekly*, 24 March 2004.

102 D. Fickling, 'Timorese Furious,' 2004.

103 Report quoted in J. Aubrey (ed.), *Free East Timor*, 1998, p. 295. For the powerful testimony of Greg's wife Shirley, see also S. Shackleton, 'Planting a Tree in Balibo: A Journey to East Timor,' in P. Carey & G. C. Bentley (eds), *East Timor at the Crossroads: The Forging of a Nation*, University of Hawaii Press, Honolulu, 1995. For more on the Balibo murders, see D. Greenlees & R. Garran, *Deliverance*, 2002, pp. 11–12.

104 J. Pilger, *Hidden Agendas*, Verso, Sydney, 1998, p. 262.

105 'Interview with Xanana Gusmao,' *Background Briefing*, Radio National, 19 November 2000, transcript in author's possession.

106 Domm in ibid.

107 See A Goodman, 'Democracy Now: Exception to the Rulers, III,' Z-Media Institute Talk, June 1997; A Goodman, 'Freeing the Media: The Exception to the Rulers,' Z-Media Institute Talk; A Goodman, 'New Exception to the Rulers, II,' Z-Media Institute Talk; transcripts accessed via *Z-Net* site at <znet/zmag/zarticle>.

108 ibid.; D. Edwards & D. Cromwell, 'The British Press Bury Western Complicity in East Timor Genocide,' *Media Lens*, 31 May 2002.

109 See A Goodman, 'Democracy Now: Exception to the Rulers, III,' Z-Media Institute Talk, June 1997; A Goodman, 'Freeing the Media: The Exception to the Rulers,' Z-Media Institute Talk; A Goodman, 'New Exception to the Rulers, II,' Z-Media Institute Talk; transcripts accessed via *Z-Net* site at <znet/zmag/zarticle>.

110 'José Ramos Horta, 31 May 1984, National Press Club Speech,' in J. Aubrey (ed.), *Free East Timor*, 1998, p. 82.

111 For Ramos Horta's account of this, see J. Ramos Horta, *Funu*, 1987, pp. 41–44.

112 A. Schwarz, *Nation in Waiting*, 1994, pp. 201, 202; D. Greenlees & R. Garran, *Deliverance*, 2002, p. 6. The best accounts of the emergence of political parties in East Timor during the 1970s and the formation of Fretilin, are J. Dunn, *Timor: A People Betrayed*, 1996, pp. 56–62, 96; J. Ramos Horta, *Funu*, 1987, pp. 29–39.

113 A. Schwarz, *Nation in Waiting*, 1994, p. 205; H. McDonald, *Suharto's Indonesia*, 1980, p. 214.

114 Ramos Horta quoted in 'Dimensions of Domination: An East Timor Colloquy, Washington DC, 25–26 April 1991,' in G. C. Bentley & P. Carey (eds), *East Timor at the Crossroads*, 1995, pp. 177–78. Ramos Horta later wrote about the discovery of his sister's grave and her reburial after East Timor's liberation. See J. Ramos Horta, 'War for Peace? It Worked in My Country,' *New York Times*, 25 February 2003.

115 C. Pinto, 'Student Movement and Independence Struggle,' 2001, p. 35.

116 M. Jardine, 'APEC, the US and East Timor,' *Z-Magazine*, January 1994, available on the web at <www.zmag.org/zmag/articles/jan94jardine.htm>.

117 J. Martinkus, *A Dirty Little War*, Random House, Sydney, 2001, pp. xv, 61, 96.

118 Eurico Guterres actually faxed a death threat to Australian journalists in Jakarta on 20 February 1999. On 30 May he repeated a specific death threat directed at Australian reporters. On the death of Theones, see D. Greenlees & R. Garran, *Deliverance*, 2002, pp. 280–81.

119 *Timor Post*, 13 July 2001.

120 ibid.

121 Fischer in *Canberra Times*, 15 May 1996; S. Burchill, 'East Timor, Australia and Indonesia,' in D. Kingsbury, *Guns and Ballot Boxes*, 2000, p. 171. Fischer, after serving as part of an Australian government observer mission for the UN ballot in East Timor, later tried to distance himself from his earlier praise of Suharto. He admitted that in the past he had 'made the mistake of over-praising Soeharto's economic leadership' but defended the substance of his support for the regime. See T. Fischer, *Ballot and Bullets: Seven Days in East Timor*, Allen & Unwin, Sydney, 2000, pp. 64–65.

122 For the Department of Foreign Affairs and Trade's official version of the policy shift, see *East Timor in Transition 1998–2000: An Australian Policy Challenge*, DFAT, Canberra, 2001, pp. 29–40, 109–12, 180–84. For Habibie's thinking and an analysis of the Howard letter, see D. Greenlees & R. Garran, *Deliverance*, 2002, pp. xiii, 25–27, 74–75, 86–88, 338–39.

123 ibid., pp. xiii, 74–75, 86–88, 338–39.

124 J. Birmingham, 'Appeasing Jakarta,' 2001, p. 6.

125 For a chronological overview of some of Downer's more awful statements in this regard, see the press release of his Labor rival, 'East Timor: Selective and Partisan Publication of DFAT Records,' News Release from Office of L. Brereton MP, Shadow Minister for Foreign Affairs, 17 July 2001. The document is still accessible on the internet at <www.tip.net.au/~wildwood/01julselective.htm>. Also, D. Greenlees & R. Garran, *Deliverance*, 2002, pp. 166–67.

126 Quoted in *Time* (Australia), 19 June 2000. For the Australian Department of Foreign Affairs and Trade's version of Australia's involvement in Interfet and UNTAET, see *East Timor in Transition 1998–2000: An Australian Policy Challenge*, DFAT, Canberra, 2001, pp. 137–72.

127 J. Martinkus, *A Dirty Little War*, Random House, Sydney, 2001, pp. 1–2.

128 See D. Kingsbury, 'The TNI and the Militias,' in D. Kingsbury (ed.), *Guns and Ballot Boxes*, 2000.

129 G. Evans, 'Indonesia's Military Culture Has to Be Reformed,' *International Herald Tribune*, 24 July 2001. Also J. Pilger, *Hidden Agendas*, Verso, Sydney, 1998, pp. 266–67.

130 Details regarding Guterres in this section are from J. Martinkus, *A Dirty Little War*, Random House, Sydney, 2001, pp. 125–29, 167, 270; H. McDonald et al., *Masters of Terror: Indonesia's Military and Violence in East Timor in 1999*, ANU Strategic & Defence Studies Centre, Canberra, 2002. For more general background on the militias, see D. Greenlees & R. Garran, *Deliverance*, 2002, pp. 129–43.

131 J. Martinkus, *A Dirty Little War*, Random House, Sydney, 2001, p. 128.

132 ibid., p. 167.

133 General information in the section below regarding the militias in the Ermera district is drawn from A. Smith, 'The Popular Consultation in the Ermera District: Free, Fair and Secret?', in D. Kingsbury (ed.),

Guns and Ballot Boxes, 2000, pp. 29–41; H. van Klinken, 'Taking the Risk, Paying the Price: East Timorese Vote in Ermera District,' in R. Tanter, M. Selden & S. R. Shalom (eds), *Bitter Flowers, Sweet Flowers*, 2001, pp. 91–107; J. Martinkus, *A Dirty Little War*, Random House, Sydney, 2001, pp. 182–83, 199, 270; *Observer* (UK), 25 April 1999; *Washington Post*, 31 August 1999; *Age*, 27 April 1999; *Washington Post*, 1 September 1999.

134 H. van Klinken, 'East Timorese Vote in Ermera District,' 2001, pp. 93, 107; J. Martinkus, *A Dirty Little War*, Random House, Sydney, 2001, pp. 182–83.

135 Tim Fischer, former Australian deputy prime-minister, was part of an Australian government observer mission which witnessed some of the Gleno violence. See T. Fischer, *Ballot and Bullets,* 2000, pp. 42–44, 99–102. See also Department of Foreign Affairs and Trade, *East Timor in Transition 1998–2000: An Australian Policy Challenge*, DFAT, Canberra, 2001, pp. 122–24; D. Greenlees & R. Garran, *Deliverance*, 2002, pp. 190, 193.

136 Frei quoted in J. Birmingham, 'Appeasing Jakarta,' 2001, p. 10.

137 M. Dodd, 'A New, but Devastated Beginning,' *Age*, 11 December 1999. See also, A. Smith, 'The Popular Consultation in the Ermera District: Free, Fair and Secret?', in D. Kingsbury (ed.), *Guns and Ballot Boxes*, 2000, pp. 40–41.

138 'Ex-General to Make Run for President of Indonesia,' *New York Times*, 16 January 2004; 'Getting Away with Murder: Why the Guilty Will Get Off Scot-Free,' *Sydney Morning Herald*, 20 May 2002; *Australian*, 15 January 2002; 'Ex-Governor of East Timor Gets 3 Years in Army Killings,' *New York Times*, 14 August 2002; 'Indonesia Clears 6 of Rights Abuses in East Timor Killings,' *New York Times*, 15 August 2002; *Sydney Morning Herald*, 28 November 2002.

139 A. Schwarz, *Nation in Waiting*, 1994, p. 197.

140 A. Booth, 'Will Indonesia Break Up?', *Inside Indonesia*, No. 59, July–September 1999.

141 For a very good discussion of some of these issues, see G. van Klinken, 'Big States and Little Independence Movements,' in R. Tanter, M. Selden & S. R. Shalom (eds), *Bitter Flowers, Sweet Flowers*, 2001, pp. 209–25.

142 J. Martinkus, 'Paradise Betrayed: West Papua's Struggle for Independence,' *Quarterly Essay*, No. 7, 2002, pp. 43–45; H. McDonald, *Suharto's Indonesia*, 1980, pp. 64–66, 81–82; 'West Papua:

The Facts,' *New Internationalist*, No. 344, April 2002.

143 S. Lekic, 'Historic Vote Was Sham, Ex-UN Chiefs Admit,' *Sydney Morning Herald*, 23 November 2001; J. Martinkus, 'Paradise Betrayed: West Papua's Struggle for Independence,' *Quarterly Essay*, No. 7, 2002, p. 21. See also, H. McDonald, *Suharto's Indonesia*, 1980, pp. 64–66, 81–82; 'West Papua — a history of betrayal,' *New Internationalist*, No. 344, April 2002.

144 *Liberation Army of the Free Papua Movement Homepage*, accessed at <www.eco-action.org/opm/>.

145 ibid.

146 On Suharto's role in West Papua, see H. McDonald, *Suharto's Indonesia*, 1980, pp. 35–36; H. Crouch, *Army and Politics in Indonesia*, 1988, p. 47.

147 On Eluay's death and its aftermath, see C. Richards, 'West Papua Rising,' *New Internationalist*, No. 344, April 2002 or J. Martinkus, 'Paradise Betrayed: West Papua's Struggle for Independence,' *Quarterly Essay*, No. 7, 2002, pp. 25–28. Also, *Australian*, 12 November 2001; *West Australian*, 12 November 2001; *Asia Times*, 16 November 2001; P. Jain & J. Bruni, 'Indonesia–Australia: Shaking Hands with Clenched Fists,' *Asia Times*, 12 February 2002.

148 J. Martinkus, 'Paradise Betrayed: West Papua's Struggle for Independence,' *Quarterly Essay*, No. 7, 2002, pp. 44–45, 73–74.

3. The 'Axis of Evil'

1 C. Johnson, *Blowback*, 2002, p. 89.

2 G. Monbiot, 'Tony Blair's New Friend,' *Guardian*, 28 October 2003. Also published in *Guardian Weekly*, 6–12 November 2003, or available with footnotes at *Z-Net Online*, <www.zmag.org>. For a detailed account of human rights abuses in Uzbekistan, see Human Rights Watch's 2004 report, *Creating Enemies of the State: Religious Persecution in Uzbekistan*, available in PDF format on the web at <www.hrw.org/reports/2004/uzbekistan0304/>.

3 Transcript of President Bush's News Conference, 11 October 2001, available on the internet at <www.pbs.org/newshour/terrorism/combating/bush_10-11d.html>.

4 *New York Times*, 5 February 2004.

5 Quoted in J. Feffer, *North Korea, South Korea*, 2003, p. 14.

6   P. Carlson, 'Sins of the Son,' *Washington Post*, 11 May 2002.

7   B. Woodward, *Bush at War*, 2002, p. 340.

8   Ms Rice's first name is often misspelled in the press and in books. 'Condoleezza' is the proper spelling of her name as presented on the US Government's website and in her official biography online.

9   'Bush's "Evil Axis" Comment Stirs Critics,' *BBC News Online*, 2 February 2002. 'Bush Calls North Korea "Evil" Again,' *USA Today*, 20 February 2002; 'Bush Peers into "Evil" North Korea,' accessed at <cnn.com>, 20 February 2002.

10   'Bush Calls North Korea "Evil" Again,' *USA Today*, 20 February 2002; 'Bush Peers into "Evil" North Korea,' accessed at <cnn.com>, 20 February 2002.

11   'Bush's "Evil Axis" Comment Stirs Critics,' *BBC News Online*, 2 February 2002.

12   P. Carlson, 'Sins of the Son,' 2002.

13   J. Feffer, *North Korea, South Korea*, 2003, p. 23.

14   G. McCormack, 'North Korea in the Vice,' *New Left Review*, No. 18, November–December 2002, p. 5; North Korea Advisory Group, *Report to The Speaker US House of Representatives*, November 1999; J. Feffer, *North Korea, South Korea*, 2003, p. 61.

15   Amnesty International's annual report regarding North Korea is available on the web at <http://web.amnesty.org/report2003/prk-summary-eng>.

16   ibid.; Also G. McCormack, 'North Korea in the Vice,' 2002, p. 15; North Korea Advisory Group, *Report to The Speaker US House of Representatives*, November 1999; *Guardian Weekly*, 27 November–3 December 2003; J. Feffer, *North Korea, South Korea*, 2003, pp. 72–74.

17   P. Carlson, 'Sins of the Son,' 2002; J. Cho & D. Struck, '"Dear Leader" Feted in N. Korea,' *Washington Post*, 17 February 2003; J. Feffer, *North Korea, South Korea*, 2003, p. 14.

18   G. McCormack, 'North Korea in the Vice,' 2002, p. 15.

19   J. Feffer, *North Korea, South Korea*, 2003, p. 33.

20   D. Anderson, 'Crisis in North Korea,' *Text of Speech Given at Croft Institute of International Studies*, 20 March 2003. Anderson worked for 35 years for the US State Department on 'Asian issues'. Also G. McCormack, 'North Korea in the Vice,' 2002, p. 17.

21   G. McCormack, 'North Korea in the Vice,' 2002, p. 18. See also, W. J. Perry (Special Adviser to the President), *Review of United States Policy toward North Korea: Findings and Recommendations*, 12 October 1999,

report available online at *National Security Archive*,
<www.gwu.edu/~nsarchiv/>.

22   For more on this, see 'Pakistan Bars Its Nuclear Scientists from Traveling Abroad,' *New York Times*, 21 January 2004; J. Feffer, *North Korea, South Korea*, 2003, p. 11. Also L. A. Miksch, *Issue Brief for Congress: North Korea's Nuclear Weapons Program*, 17 March 2003, report available online at *National Security Archive*, <www.gwu.edu/~nsarchiv/>.

23   *Age*, 15 July 2003; J. Feffer, *North Korea, South Korea*, 2003, p. 115.

24   J. Feffer, *North Korea, South Korea*, 2003, pp. 66–67.

25   ibid., p. 86.

26   For more on the issue of US support for General Chun's repression and the investigation into the Kwangju massacre, see C. Johnson, *Blowback*, 2002, pp. 113–22.

27   J. Feffer, *North Korea, South Korea*, 2003, p. 12.

28   'U. S. Policy toward Iran,' *Draft National Security Decision Directive*, 17 June 1985, available in PDF format online at *National Security Archive* at <www.gwu.edu/~nsarchiv/>.

29   US Department of State, *Background Note: Iran*, June 2003, available on the internet at the US State Department's website, <www.state.gov/p/nea/ci/c2404.htm>.

30   Secretary of State M. Albright, *Remarks before the American–Iranian Council*, 17 March 2000, US State Department Official Transcript.

31   J. Risen, 'ABC of Coups,' *New York Times*, 18 June 2000. The *New York Times* has now made Risen's articles, and documents from the CIA's secret history, available on the internet at <www.nytimes.com/library/world/mideast/041600iran-cia-intro.html>. All quotes in this section are from these sources.

32   W. Blum, *Rogue State*, Zed Books, London, 2002, p. 51.

33   From a 17 June 2003 public speech by John Gerassi, transcript available on the internet at <www.globalpolicy.org/security/issues/iraq/attack/2003/0617time.htm>.

34   A. J. Langguth, 'Torture's Teachers,' *New York Times*, 11 June 1979. Also S. Hersh, 'Ex-Analyst Says CIA Rejected Warning on Shah,' *New York Times*, 7 January 1979.

35   Quoted in W. Blum, *The CIA*, 1986, p. 76.

36   'The Speeches of Ayatollah Khomeini', available at BBC Online, <www.bbc.co.uk/Persian/revolution/khomeini/shtm>

37   C. Johnson, *Blowback*, 2002, pp. xii–xiii.

38   B. Lewis, *The Middle East*, Phoenix, London, 2003, p. 368.

39   C. Johnson, *Blowback*, 2002, p. 134.

40   'Iran's Hardliners Refuse to Back Down,' *Guardian Weekly*, 22–28 January 2004. Also *New York Times*, 2 February 2004.

41   'Iran's Hardliners Refuse to Back Down,' *Guardian Weekly*, 22–28 January 2004.

42   J. R. Bolton, *Beyond the Axis of Evil: Additional Threats from Weapons of Mass Destruction*, 6 May 2002, complete transcript available at US Department of State website at <www.state.gov>.

43   'Why Carter Is Smarter,' *Guardian* (UK), 15 May 2002; M. Colby, 'Bush's Cuba Blunder,' *Counterpunch*, 14 May 2002.

44   M. Colby, ibid.

45   M. Moore & K. Glynn, *Adventures in a TV Nation*, HarperPerennial, New York, 1998, pp. 162.

46   This, as far as I know, is still true. I last checked with the US State Department about this in December 2003. It was still legal for US citizens to travel to North Korea at that time although the State Department did offer safety warnings. See also US Department of State, *Background Notes: North Korea*, June 1996, available at State Department website at <www.state.gov>.

47   *Guardian Weekly*, 16–22 October 2003; *New York Times*, 11 October 2003; M. Morley & C. McGillion, *Unfinished Business: America and Cuba after the Cold War, 1989–2001*, CUP, Melbourne, 2002, p. 33.

48   *Guardian Weekly*, 16–22 October 2003; New York Times, 11 October 2003.

49   Quoted in H. Zinn, *A People's History of the United States*, Harper Collins, New York, 1999, p. 299.

50   ibid., p. 439.

51   R. Blackburn, 'Putting the Hammer Down on Cuba,' *New Left Review*, No. 4, July–August 2000, p. 20.

52   Taken from an official transcript of the speech, see 'Thirty Years of the Cuban Revolution,' in F. Castro, *In Defence of Socialism*, Pathfinder Press, New York, 1990.

53   Taken from an official transcript of the speech, see 'The Young Generation Must Improve and Defend Socialism,' in ibid.

54   R. Blackburn, 'Putting the Hammer Down on Cuba,' 2000, pp. 15–16; M. Morley & C. McGillion, *Unfinished Business*, 2002, pp. 61, 137.

55 M. Morley & C. McGillion, *Unfinished Business*, 2002, p. 65.

56 R. Benedetto, 'Bush: Cuba Must Change or Embargo Stays,' *USA Today*, 21 May 2002; R. Blackburn, 'Putting the Hammer Down on Cuba,' 2000, p. 12; M. Morley & C. McGillion, *Unfinished Business*, 2002, p. 15.

57 D. Campbell, 'The Bush Dynasty and the Cuban Criminals,' *Guardian* (UK), 2 December 2002; M. Morley & C. McGillion, *Unfinished Business*, 2002, p. 14.

58 D. Campbell, 'The Bush Dynasty and the Cuban Criminals,' *Guardian* (UK), 2 December 2002; M. Morley & C. McGillion, *Unfinished Business*, 2002, pp. 35–36. On US-supported terrorism against Cuba more generally, see W. Blum, *Killing Hope*, CC Press, Monroe, 1995, pp. 184–93.

59 D. Campbell, 'The Bush Dynasty and the Cuban Criminals,' *Guardian* (UK), 2 December 2002.

60 M. Morley & C. McGillion, *Unfinished Business*, 2002, p. 116.

61 S. Milne, 'Why the US Fears Cuba,' *Guardian* (UK), 8 September 2003.

62 A. Rashid, *Taliban*, 2001, pp. 129–30.

63 B. Woodward, *Veil: The Secret Wars of the CIA*, 1988, p. 79. Also, T. Ali, 'Former US Policies Allowed Taliban to Thrive,' *Australian*, 24 September 2001.

64 Z. Brzezinski, *The Grand Chessboard: American Primacy and Its Geostrategic Imperatives*, Harper Collins, New York, 1997, p. 73. 'Former US Policies Allowed Taliban to Thrive,' *Australian*, 24 September 2001.

65 On Osama bin Laden, the CIA and the Khost tunnel system, see T. Weiner, 'Afghan Taliban Camps Were Built by NATO,' *New York Times*, 24 August 1998; J. Steele, 'bin Laden May Flee in Tunnels,' *Guardian*, 18 September 2001; A. Rashid, *Taliban*, 2001, pp. 132, 134.

66 Alongside captured Soviet tanks, Saudi-supplied pick-up trucks were the main form of Taliban military transportation. A. Rashid, *Taliban*, 2001, p. 72.

67 A. Rashid, *Taliban*, 2001, pp. 183–84, 186, 192–94.

68 Amnesty International's annual report regarding Pakistan is available on the web at <http://web.amnesty.org/report2003/Pak-summary-eng>.

69 In response to Bush's 'Axis of Evil' speech the Russian defence minister, Sergei Ivanov, named Saudi Arabia — which Russia accused of funding

Islamic Chechen separatists — as a 'rogue state' and denied that Iran supported terrorism. *Guardian Weekly*, 7–13 February 2002.

70   *Guardian Weekly*, 7–13 February 2002.

71   The Filipinos, who were mainly low-paid 'guest workers', had been caught praying by the Saudi government's fanatical religious police, the Muttawa'in. *Guardian Weekly*, 7–13 March 2002; Human Rights Watch, *World Report 2001*, accessed at <www.hrw.org>.

72   Amnesty International's annual report regarding Saudi Arabia is available on the web at <http://web.amnesty.org/report2003/Sau-summary-eng>. On the beheading of the three gay men, see 'Saudis and Human Rights,' *San Francisco Chronicle*, 7 January 2002.

73   *Guardian Weekly*, 11–17 September 2003.

74   A. Rashid, *Taliban*, 2001, pp. 197–98.

75   *New York Times*, 17 September 2003.

76   S. R. Shalom, 'Confronting Terrorism and War,' *New Politics*, No. 32, Winter 2002; Human Rights Watch, *Backgrounder: United Front/Northern Alliance Poor Rights Record of Opposition Commanders*, 6 October 2001.

77   A. Rashid, *Taliban*, 2001, p. 56. For more on Dostum, see M. Ivins, 'How We Could Still Lose in Afghanistan,' *Boston Globe*, 28 December 2001; P. Cockburn, 'Rashid Dostum: The Treacherous General,' *Independent* (UK), 1 December 2001.

78   M. Ivins, 'How We Could Still Lose in Afghanistan,' 2001. Also B. Woodward, *Bush at War*, 2002, p. 290 and Amnesty International's 2003 annual report regarding Afghanistan, available at <http://web.amnesty.org/report2003/Afg-summary-eng>.

79   B. Woodward, *Bush at War*, 2002, pp. 143, 155.

4. Where the Past Is Not Dead

1   The reference to 1000 dead shopkeepers refers to those killed in riots caused by the economic crisis. Johnson does not suggest that the IMF was directly responsible for these deaths, but indirectly contributed to creating the political and economic climate that caused them. C. Johnson, *Blowback*, 2002, p. 220.

2   J. Faux, 'Debt: Just Forget It,' *Nation*, 22 November 1999. Also available on the internet at <www.thenation.com>.

3   ibid.

4   'Iraq debt deal sets African precedent, says World Bank head,' *Guardian Weekly*, 29 April–5 May 2004. See also the Quakers' American Friends Service Committee website for more information about African debt and the international campaign against it <www.afsc.org/africa-debt/congo.htm>.

5   'Casualties' refers to people killed and wounded. Figures from US State Department, *Patterns of Global Terrorism*, 2003. The report is available online in HTML and PDF format at the State Department's website <www.state.gov/s/ct/rls/pgtrpt/2003/>.

6   I am indebted to Val Noone for this piece of Irish wisdom.

7   L. de Paor, *Divided Ulster*, Penguin, Middlesex, 1970, p. 13.

8   Names changed.

9   Some of this essay was first published as S. Adams, 'Power-sharing Essential,' *Táin*, April 2000, p. 9, and in a guest editorial for the *Australian Irish Heritage Association Journal*, Vol. 8, No. 2, Winter 2000, pp. 7–9.

10 *Irish News*, 26 April 2001.

11 *Sydney Morning Herald*, 24 September 2001.

12 Quoted in J. Bardon, *A Shorter Illustrated History of Ulster*, Blackstaff Press, Belfast, 1996, pp. 84–86. The name of the town of Derry was changed to Londonderry by the conquering English early in the seventeenth century. Irish nationalists have always continued to refer to it as Derry.

13 Information here is mainly from personal interviews, plus *Belfast Telegraph*, 10 September 2003; *Observer*, 9 September 2001.

14 Ardoyne Commemoration Project, *Ardoyne: The Untold Truth*, Beyond the Pale Publications, Belfast, 2002, p. 507.

15 ibid., p. 508.

16 *Guardian Weekly*, 10–16 January 2002.

17 ibid.

18 Name changed.

19 There are numerous sources and several books on Ota Benga. This quote from the *Scientific American* comes from J. Bergman, 'Ota Benga: The Story of the Pygmy on Display in a Zoo,' available on the net at <www.rae.org/otabenga.html>.

20 Correspondence quoted in ibid.

21 For more on the Belgian conquest of the Congo, see T. Pakenham, *The Scramble for Africa*, Abacus, London, 1991.

22 Article available online at

<www.africaaction.org/docs96/zair9612.nzo.htm>. See also G. Monbiot, 'Rwanda: Victim's License,' *Guardian*, 13 April 2004.

23 S. R. Shalom, 'The Rwanda Genocide,' *Z-Magazine*, April 1996.

24 V. Brittain, *Hidden Lives, Hidden Deaths: South Africa's Crippling of a Continent*, Faber & Faber, London, 1988, pp. 65, 141–42.

25 S. R. Shalom, 'The Rwanda Genocide,' 1996.

26 ibid.

27 Lumumba quoted in L. De Witte, *The Assassination of Lumumba*, 2001, Verso, London, p. 2.

28 'Files Show UK Backed Murder Plot,' *Guardian* (UK), 28 June 2001.

29 *Guardian Weekly*, 5–11 February 2004.

30 *New York Times*, 21 October 2003.

31 S. Ebron, 'Of Oil, the Euro and Africa,' *Counterpunch*, 21 February 2003, available on the internet at <www.counterpunch.org/>; R. Goldstein, 'Africa, Oil & US Military,' *Asia Times Online*, 1 April 2004, available at <www.atimes.com/>.

32 'Oil firms financing crooked regimes,' *Guardian Weekly*, 1–7 April 2004; *New York Times*, 4 December 2003.

33 Lumumba quoted in L. De Witte, *The Assassination of Lumumba*, 2001, p. 185.

34 *Guardian Weekly*, 11–17 September 2003.

35 See, UNAIDS, AIDS Epidemic Update, December 2003, available online at the United Nations' AIDS Program's website, <www.unaids.org/en/default.asp>. Also *New York Times*, 22 September 2003, 1 October 2003, 27 November 2003; *Guardian Weekly*, 25 September–1 October 2003.

36 *Guardian Weekly*, 11–17 September 2003; E. Stillwaggon, 'AIDS and Poverty in Africa,' *Nation*, 21 May 2001.

37 *Guardian Weekly*, 25 September–1 October 2003.

38 *New York Times*, 9 July 2003, 28 March 2004, 26 April 2004.

39 *New York Times*, 1 October 2003, 11 October 2003, 27 November 2003; UNAIDS, AIDS Epidemic Update, December 2003, available online at the United Nations' AIDS Program's website, <www.unaids.org/en/default.asp>.

40 *New York Times*, 22 September 2003; *Guardian Weekly*, 25 September–1 October 2003.

41 *New York Times*, 1 October 2003.

42 ibid.

43 ibid., 15 October 2003.

44   ibid., 20 September 2003.

45   N. Ghouri, 'US Exports Anti-Abortion Policy,' BBC News, BBC Radio 5 transcript, accessed at <www.bbc.co.uk>, 1 October 2003.

46   B. Gellman, 'The Belated Global Response to AIDS in Africa,' *Washington Post*, 5 July 2000.

47   *Independent* (UK), 18 September 1995.

48   ibid., 7 August 1995. Also Quoted in L. German, 'The Balkan War: Can There Be Peace,' *International Socialism Journal*, No. 69, Winter 1995, p. 5.

49   'History in the Making,' BBC News, 25 March 1999, available on the internet at BBC News Online, <http://news.bbc.co.uk/1/hi/uk/303308.stm>.

50   From a speech by Churchill's representative to Tito during the war, Sir Fitzroy Maclean. See F. Maclean, 'People Have Been Rewriting History a Lot Lately…', Stratchur, Scotland, 28 May 1994, full transcript available on the net at <www.winstonchurchill.org/i4a/pages/index.cfm?pageid=623>.

51   L. German, 'The Balkan War: Can There Be Peace,' *International Socialism Journal*, No. 69, Winter 1995, pp. 4, 8–9, 13–14, 18–19. Tudjman died in December 1999.

52   Perry quoted in *New York Daily News*, 5 August 1995.

53   de Mello quoted in *Time* (Australia), 19 June 2000. For the Australian Department of Foreign Affairs and Trade's version of Australia's involvement in Interfet and UNTAET, see *East Timor in Transition 1998–2000: An Australian Policy Challenge*, DFAT, Canberra, 2001, pp. 137–72.

54   Quoted in J. Pilger, *Hidden Agendas*, 1998, pp. 300–01.

55   See J. Ramos Horta, *Funu*, 1987, 97–123. UN Security Resolution 384 was passed on 22 December 1975, and number 389 was passed on 22 April 1976. Both are available at the United Nations Security Council web archive at <www.un.org/Docs/sc/>.

56   S. Zunes, 'US Double Standards,' *Nation*, 28 October 2002.

57   Quoted in ibid.

58   See D. Hovell, 'The Sovereignty Stratagem: Australia's Response to UN Human Rights Treaty Bodies,' available in PDF format from *Australian Policy Online*, <www.apo.org.au>.

59   This Bolton quote and others attributed to him and similarly controversial were published and debated in the media when Bush first nominated Bolton as US Undersecretary of State. A collection of these

newspaper articles, including notorious Bolton quotes, have been archived on the web at <www.clw.org/bush/boltonnomination.html#1>.

Epilogue

1   H. Zinn, *A People's History of the United States*, 1999, pp. 10–11.

Select Bibliography

Aditjondro, G. J. *In the Shadow of Mount Ramelau: The Impact of the Occupation of East Timor*, Indonesian Documentation and Information Centre, Leiden, 1994.

Alcorn, G. 'Civilian Deaths No Cause for Concern,' *Sydney Morning Herald*, 12 January 2002.

Ali, T. *Bush in Babylon: The Recolonisation of Iraq*, Verso, London, 2003.

——. *The Clash of Fundamentalisms: Crusades, Jihads and Modernity*, Verso, London, 2002.

Aubrey, J. (ed.), *Free East Timor: Australia's Culpability in East Timor's Genocide*, Vintage, Sydney, 1998.

Bickerton, I. J. & M. N. Pearson, *The Arab–Israeli Conflict: A History*, Longman Cheshire, 1990.

Birmingham, J. 'Appeasing Jakarta: Australia's Complicity in the East Timor Tragedy,' *Quarterly Essay*, No. 2, 2001.

Blackburn, R. 'Putting the Hammer Down on Cuba,' *New Left Review*, No. 4, July–August 2000.

Blum, W. *Rogue State*, Zed Books, London, 2002.

——. *The CIA: A Forgotten History*, Zed Books, London, 1986.

Burchill, S. 'Asking Why Is Not to Excuse the Terrorists' Actions,' *Sydney Morning Herald*, 4 October 2001.

Carey, P. & G. C. Bentley (eds), *East Timor at the Crossroads: The Forging of a Nation*, University of Hawaii Press, Honolulu, 1995.

Carlson, P. 'Sins of the Son,' *Washington Post*, 11 May 2002.

Chomsky, N. *Year 501: The Conquest Continues*, London, 1993.

Cockburn, P. '"Even the Dogs Were Hunting Us": Change of Hands in Fallujah,' available at *CounterPunch* on the net, <www.counterpunch.org/>.

Crouch, H. *The Army and Politics in Indonesia*, Cornell University Press, London, 1988.

Day, D. *Claiming a Continent: A New History of Australia*, Harper Collins, Sydney, 2001.

De Witte, L. *The Assassination of Lumumba*, Verso, London, 2001.

Devereux, A. 'Accountability for Human Rights Abuses in East Timor,' in D. Kingsbury (ed.), *Guns and Ballot Boxes: East Timor's Vote for Independence*, Monash Asia Institute, Clayton, 2000.

Dunn, J. *Timor: A People Betrayed*, ABC Books, Sydney, 1996.

El-Haddad, L. 'Israeli Refuseniks Reap Leaders' Abuse,' 12 October 2003, available at Al-Jazeera's website, <http://english.aljazeera.net>.

FAIR (Fairness and Accuracy in Reporting), *Pentagon Propaganda Plan Is Undemocratic, Possibly Illegal* (Media Release), 19 February 2002.

Feffer, J. *North Korea, South Korea: U. S. Policy at a Time of Crisis*, Seven Stories Press, New York, 2003.

Fickling, D. 'Timorese Furious at Australian "Oil and Gas Grab",' *Guardian Weekly*, 22–28 April 2004.

Fischer, T. *Ballot and Bullets: Seven Days in East Timor*, Allen & Unwin, Sydney, 2000.

German, L. 'The Balkan War: Can There Be Peace,' *International Socialism Journal*, No. 69, Winter 1995.

Goodson, L. P. *Afghanistan's Endless War: State Failure, Regional Politics and the Rise of the Taliban*, UWP, London, 2001.

Greenlees, D. & R. Garran, *Deliverance: The Inside Story of East Timor's Fight For Freedom*, Allen & Unwin, Crows Nest, 2002.

Grey, J. *A Military History of Australia*, CUP, Melbourne, 1999.

Griffiths, J. C. *Afghanistan: A History of Conflict*, Timat, London, 2001.

Gusmao, X. *To Resist Is to Win!* Aurora Books, Richmond, 2000.

Halbfinger, D. M. & S. A. Holmes, 'Military Mirrors Working Class America,' *New York Times*, 30 March 2003.

Ivins, M. 'How We Could Still Lose in Afghanistan,' *Boston Globe*, 28 December 2001.

Johnson, C. 'America's Empire of Bases,' 15 January 2004, accessed at <www.zmag.org>.

———. *Blowback: The Costs and Consequences of American Empire*, TimeWarner, London, 2002.

Kingsbury, D. (ed.), *Guns and Ballot Boxes: East Timor's Vote for Independence*, Monash Asia Institute, Clayton, 2000.

Klein, N. 'Mutiny in Iraq,' *The Nation*, 17 May 2004.

Kolko, G. *Confronting the Third World: United States Foreign Policy, 1945–1980*, Pantheon, New York, 1988.

Maley, W. (ed.), *Fundamentalism Reborn: Afghanistan and the Taliban*, Hurst, London, 2001.

Martinkus, J. *A Dirty Little War*, Random House, Sydney, 2001.

McCormack, G. 'North Korea in the Vice,' *New Left Review*, No. 18, November–December 2002.

McDonald, H. *Suharto's Indonesia*, Fontana, Blackburn, 1980.

Morley, M. & C. McGillion, *Unfinished Business: America and Cuba after the Cold War, 1989–2001*, CUP, Melbourne, 2002.

Pilger, J. *The New Rulers of the World*, Verso, London, 2002.

———. *Hidden Agendas*, Verso, Sydney, 1998.

Pinto, C. 'The Student Movement and the Independence Struggle in East Timor: An Interview,' in R. Tanter, M. Selden & S. R. Shalom (eds), *Bitter Flowers, Sweet Flowers*, 2001.

Ramos Horta, J. *Funu: The Unfinished Saga of East Timor*, Red Sea Press, Lawrenceville, 1987.

Rashid, A. *Taliban: The Story of the Afghan Warlords*, Pan Books, London, 2001.

Rubin, B. R. *The Fragmentation of Afghanistan*, Yale University Press, 2002.

Said, E. 'Thoughts about America,' *Al-Ahram Weekly*, 2 March 2002.

Schwarz, A. *A Nation in Waiting: Indonesia in the 1990s*, Allen & Unwin, Sydney, 1994.

Sexton, M. *War for the Asking: Australia's Vietnam Secrets*, Penguin, Melbourne, 1981.

Shalom, S. R. 'Confronting Terrorism and War,' *New Politics*, No. 32, Winter 2002.

——. The Rwanda Genocide,' *Z-Magazine*, April 1996.

Spielvogel, J. J. *Western Civilization*, Thomson, Melbourne, 2003.

Tanter, R., M. Selden & S. R. Shalom (eds), *Bitter Flowers, Sweet Flowers: East Timor, Indonesia, and the World Community*, Rowman & Littlefield, New York, 2001.

Taylor, J. G. *East Timor: The Price of Freedom*, Zed, London, 1999.

Todd, H. 'Death in East Timor,' *Asian Wall Street Journal*, 25 November 1991.

van Klinken, H. 'Taking the Risk, Paying the Price: East Timorese Vote in Ermera District,' in R. Tanter, M. Selden & S. R. Shalom (eds), *Bitter Flowers, Sweet Flowers*, 2001.

Woodward, B. *Bush at War*, Simon & Schuster, Sydney, 2002.

——. *Veil: The Secret Wars of the CIA*, Headline, London, 1988.

Woolcott, R. *The Hot Seat*, Harper Collins, Sydney, 2003.

Zinn, H. *A People's History of the United States*, Harper Collins, New York, 1999.

Index

Hussein, Saddam, 21, 94–5
    Americans' perceptions of, 35
    as enemy of bin Laden, 35–6
    US support in Iran–Iraq war, 252,
        253
    as western ally, 23, 48, 94–6

Idrees, Wafa, 73–4
IMF *see* International Monetary Fund
imperialism, 102, 105–6, 354
Indonesia, 24, 149, 157, 161
    attitude to Australia post East
        Timor, 206
    communist purge, 148, 150–2,
        154–5
    currency crisis, 174–5, 288–9
    Dutch colonisation of, 167, 168
    East Timor annexation, 149, 155,
        182–3, 187–8, 198–9
    fragility of, 214, 217
    human rights abusers trials, 213
    IMF controls, 288–9
    Islamic movement, 159
    military aid to, 157, 196, 201
    Muslim extremists, 157–8, 159,
        160, 207
    student protests, 172–3, 174, 175,
        176–7
    Suharto regime, end of, 159, 174–5,
        176
    territorial integrity, 217
    US aid and investment, 152, 155
    West Papua annexation, 149,
        185–6, 215
    as western ally, 156–7, 176
Indonesian Communist Party (PKI),
    24, 149
    massacre of, 148, 150–2, 154–5
    US opposed to, 149, 154–5
Indonesian military
    atrocities in East Timor, 187–8
    attack at Santa Cruz cemetery, 173
    coup (1965), 23, 150
    East Timor as challenge, 213
    loyalties divided, 149–50
    militias, use of, 176, 203–4, 205–6,
        207–8
    weapons from US, 156
Indonesians
    perceptions of Australian
        involvement in Iraq, 140

    perceptions of US, 223
International Monetary Fund, 288–9
    and Third World debt, 289–91
Iran, 220, 240, 241–2
    airliner shot down by US, 238, 239,
        253
    Al-Qaida opposed by, 240
    arms trade, 249, 253
    democracy movement, 254–5
    as Islamic Republic, 250–1, 253–5
    Mossadeq government, 242–3
    Mossadeq overthrown, 243–6
    oil, 241, 242–3, 246
    relationships with US, 25, 238–40,
        242–4, 246, 248
    SAVAK secret police, 246–9
    Shah as dictator, 245–7, 249–50
    US secret trade with, 98
    youth culture, 254
Iran–Iraq war, 48, 94, 95–6, 252–3
    deaths in, 98
    use of gas, 96, 97
Iraq, 220
    impact of sanctions, 66–7
    infant mortality, 66–7
    invasion of Kuwait, 351
    UN resolutions ignored, 83, 352
    as US ally, 94, 95–9
    weaponry, 35, 139–40
    weapons, chemical, 96, 97
Iraq, 2003 invasion and occupation of,
    93–4
    Baghdad, fall of, 113–14
    deaths in, 32, 35, 36–7, 93, 101–2,
        112
    justification for, 34–6
    occupation, 33, 37, 103–4
    opposition to, 93, 110
    outcomes, 111
    resistance to, 108, 112–13
    Vietnam parallels, 36, 109–11
Iraqi National Museum, 104
Ireland
    Anglo–Irish War, 302
    as English colony, 299
    home rule for, 301–2
    partition of, 302
    see also Northern Ireland
Islam, 240–1
Islamic countries
    perceptions of Australian–US